MARATHON

MARATHON

*How One Battle Changed
Western Civilization*

RICHARD A. BILLOWS

OVERLOOK DUCKWORTH
New York • London

This edition first published in hardcover in the United States and the U.K. in 2010 by
Overlook Duckworth, Peter Mayer Publishers, Inc.

NEW YORK:
141 Wooster Street
New York, NY 10012
www.overlookpress.com
for bulk or special sales contact sales@overlookny.com

LONDON:
90-93 Cowcross Street
London EC1M 6BF
inquiries@duckworth-publishers.co.uk
www.ducknet.co.uk

PHOTO CREDITS: photos on pages 141, 149, 184, 185, 204, 211, 226, and 251 are by the author. All other illustrations are courtesy of Wikimedia Commons: bust of Homer p. 57 is at the British Museum; bust of Herodotos p. 69 is at the Stoa of Attalos in Athens; illustration of Chigi Vase p. 75 is from K.F. Johansen *Les Vases Sikyoniens* (Paris 1923); illustration of Greek phalanx p. 78 is courtesy Dept. of History, US Military Academy; photo of Cyrus Stele at Sydney p. 111 is by Siamax; illustration of Darius vase p. 121 is from A. Baumeister *Denkmaeler des klassischen Altertums* (1885) vol. I tafel VI; illustration of Darius's Bisutun monument p. 128 is from E. Pandin *Voyages en Perse* (Paris 1851); the Persian soldiers in glazed brick p. 132 are in the Dept. of Oriental Antiquities of the Louvre Museum, Paris; the illustration of beached triremes p. 191 is courtesy Dept. of History, US Military Academy; the helmet of Miltiades p. 223 is in the Olympia Museum, photo by Ken Russell Salvador; the bust of Perikles p. 246 is in the Altes Museum Berlin, photo by Gunnar Back Pedersen; the bust of Sokrates p. 253 is in the Vatican Museum, photo by Wilson Delgado.

Cataloging-in-Publication Data is available from the Library of Congress

Book design and typeformatting by Bernard Schleifer
Manufactured in the United States of America
FIRST EDITION
2 4 6 8 10 9 7 5 3 1
ISBN 978-1-59020-168-8 US
ISBN 978-0-71563-908-5 UK

For Madeline and Colette, who light up my life.

CONTENTS

MAPS

Scyths (Saka Paradraya)

Ister (Danube)

MACEDONIA
Skudra
THRACE
Y a u n a
Black Sea
Caucasus Mountains

PAPHLAGONIA

Thermopylae •
• Troy • Dascyleum
• Vani

LYDIA
• Gordium
Athens • • Marathon • Sardis
• Sparta
CARIA **PHRYGIA**
GALATIA
• Magnesia
• Miletus
Halys
ARMENIA
CAPPADOCIA
Lake Van

LYCIA **PAMPHYLIA**
• Cilician Gates
Tarsus •
ASSYRIA
AZERBAIJAN
• Carchemish
• Harran
• Nineveh
Lake Urmia
• Posideum • Aleppo
Salamis
Mediterranean Sea
Paphus • • Aradus
Thapsacus •
• Arbela
MEDIA
Curium Amathus
SYRIA
Tigris
Byblos •
Tyre •
• Damascus
Ashur •
Ecbatana (Hamadan) •
Sidon •
Alvar
Mounta

LIBYA
Hit •
LURISTAN
Baghdad •
• Opis
• Bisituı
Sippar •
Ascalon •
• Samaria
Borsippa •
• Kish
Naucratis • • Sais
• Jerusalem
Babylon •
• Nippur
ELAM
• Siwah Oasis
Gaza •
Pelusium
Memphis •
• Susa
Uruk (Erech) •
Ur •

E G Y P T
A R A B I A

Asyut • *Nile*
• Teima

Kharga Oasis •

First Cataract ┼ • Elephantine

Red Sea
Pers

400 miles

600 kilometres

ETHIOPIA

from *Thermopylae* by Paul Cartledge (Overlook, 2006)

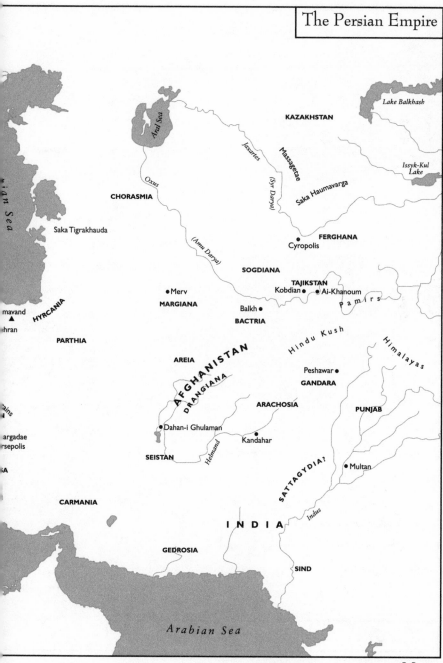

The Persian Empire

Lake Balkhash

KAZAKHSTAN

Aral Sea

Issyk-Kul Lake

Jaxartes

Massagetae

(Syr Darya)

Oxus

CHORASMIA

Saka Haumavarga

(Amu Darya)

FERGHANA

Cyropolis

Saka Tigrakhauda

ian Sea

SOGDIANA

TAJIKSTAN

Kobdian● ●Ai-Khanoum

●Merv

MARGIANA

Pamirs

mavand
▲

HYRCANIA

Balkh●

BACTRIA

hran

PARTHIA

Hindu Kush

Himalayas

AREIA

AFGHANISTAN

DRANGIANA

Peshawar●

GANDARA

ARACHOSIA

PUNJAB

ains
▲

●Dahan-i Ghulaman

Kandahar●

argadae
rsepolis

Helmand

SEISTAN

●Multan

SATTAGYDIA?

A

CARMANIA

Indus

INDIA

GEDROSIA

SIND

Arabian Sea

Map 1

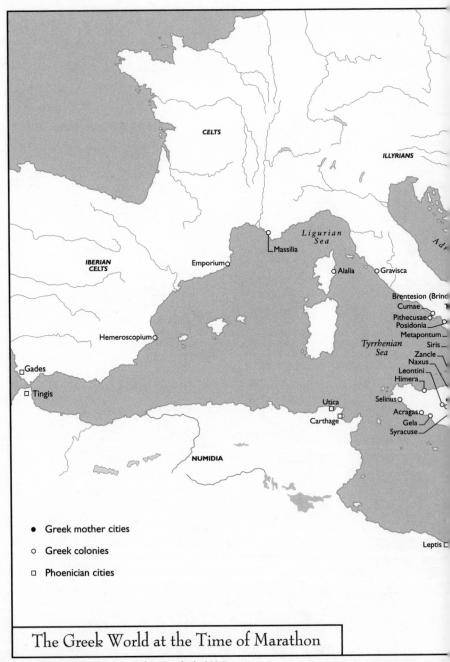

CELTS

ILLYRIANS

Ligurian Sea

○ Massilia

IBERIAN
CELTS

Emporium○

○ Alalia   ○ Gravisca

Ad

Brentesion (Brind
Cumae
Pithecusae○
Posidonia
Metapontum

Hemeroscopium○

Tyrrhenian Sea

Siris
Zancle
Naxus
Leontini
Himera

□ Gades

Selinus○

□ Tingis

Utica
□
Carthage □

Acragas○
Gela
Syracuse

NUMIDIA

● Greek mother cities

○ Greek colonies

Leptis □

□ Phoenician cities

The Greek World at the Time of Marathon

from *Thermopylae* by Paul Cartledge (Overlook, 2006)

SCYTHIANS

SARMATIANS

○Tanais

Olbia○

○Panticapaeum

Tyras○

Theodosia○

Istrus○

Black Sea

Phasis○

Callatis○

Odessus○

Mesembria○

Sinope○

○Trapezus

Apollonia○

○Amisus

THRACE

○Heraclea

Byzantium○ ○Chalcedon

Abdera

○

PERSIAN EMPIRE

MACEDONIA

Thasos○

○Abydus

CHALCIDICE

Sigeum

*Aegean
Sea*

●Corcyra

●Phocaea

Megara

●Chalcis

Corinth

●Eretria

●Athens

●Miletus

Phaselis

Achaea

○

*nian
Sea*

Sparta●

Paros●

·blaea

●Thera

□Citium

CYPRUS

Byblos□

Sidon□

Tyre□

e d i t e r r a n e a n   S e a

○Cyrene

○Euesperides

200 miles

400 kilometres

*Red
Sea*

Map 2

Greece and the Aegean with Persian Route to Marathon (broken line)

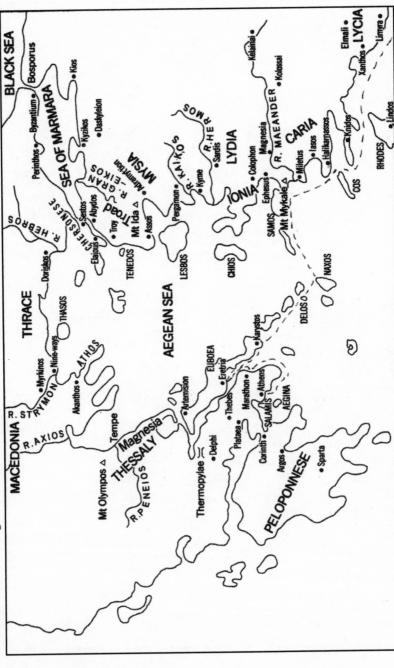

Drawn after J. M. Cook *The Persian Empire* (Schocken Books, 1985)

Map 3

Attica

Map 4

Drawn after Joint Association of Classical Teachers
The World of Athens (Cambridge UP, 1984)

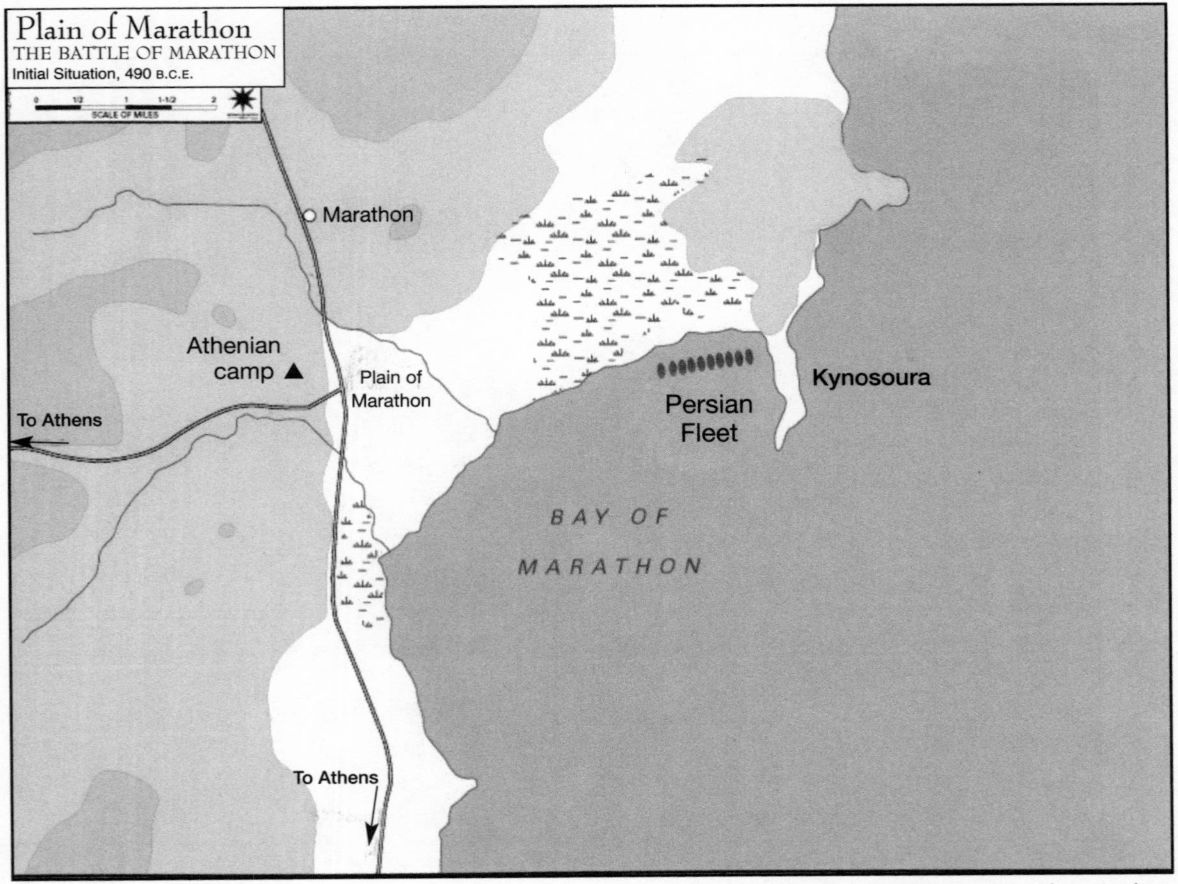

Plain of Marathon
THE BATTLE OF MARATHON
Initial Situation, 490 B.C.E.
0 1/2 1 1-1/2 2
SCALE OF MILES
Marathon
Athenian camp
Plain of Marathon
To Athens
To Athens
Persian Fleet
Kynosoura
BAY OF MARATHON

Map 5

Courtesy of Department of History, U.S. Military Academy

FAMILY TREES

Genealogies of the Agiad and Eurypontid Dynasties

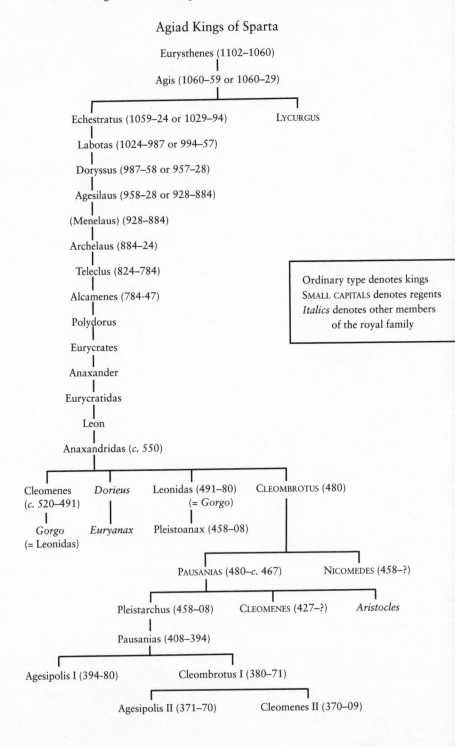

Eurypontid Kings of Sparta

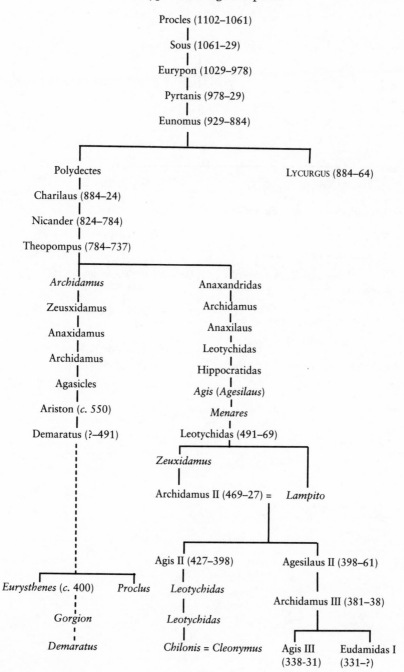

Procles (1102–1061)

Sous (1061–29)

Eurypon (1029–978)

Pyrtanis (978–29)

Eunomus (929–884)

Polydectes

LYCURGUS (884–64)

Charilaus (884–24)

Nicander (824–784)

Theopompus (784–737)

Archidamus

Zeusxidamus

Anaxidamus

Archidamus

Agasicles

Ariston (*c.* 550)

Demaratus (?–491)

Anaxandridas

Archidamus

Anaxilaus

Leotychidas

Hippocratidas

Agis (Agesilaus)

Menares

Leotychidas (491–69)

Zeuxidamus

Archidamus II (469–27) = *Lampito*

Agis II (427–398)

Agesilaus II (398–61)

Eurysthenes (*c.* 400)   *Proclus*   *Leotychidas*

Archidamus III (381–38)

Gorgion   *Leotychidas*

Demaratus   *Chilonis = Cleonymus*   Agis III (338–31)   Eudamidas I (331–?)

from HRM Jones 1964

19

The Achaimenids

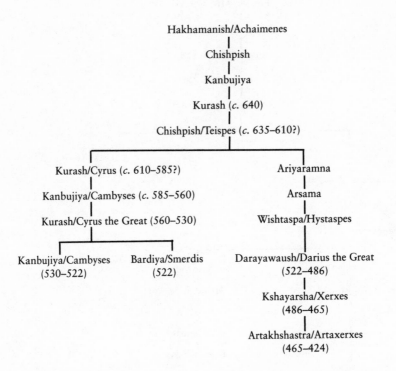

Hakhamanish/Achaimenes

Chishpish

Kanbujiya

Kurash (*c.* 640)

Chishpish/Teispes (*c.* 635–610?)

Kurash/Cyrus (*c.* 610–585?)

Kanbujiya/Cambyses (*c.* 585–560)

Kurash/Cyrus the Great (560–530)

Kanbujiya/Cambyses (530–522)

Bardiya/Smerdis (522)

Ariyaramna

Arsama

Wishtaspa/Hystaspes

Darayawaush/Darius the Great (522–486)

Kshayarsha/Xerxes (486–465)

Artakhshastra/Artaxerxes (465–424)

The Alkmaionidai

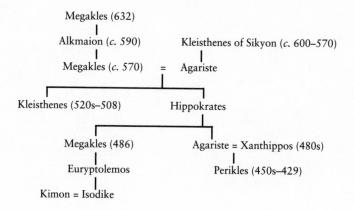

Megakles (632)
|
Alkmaion (*c.* 590)   Kleisthenes of Sikyon (*c.* 600–570)
| |
Megakles (*c.* 570)   =   Agariste

Kleisthenes (520s–508)   Hippokrates

Megakles (486)   Agariste = Xanthippos (480s)
| |
Euryptolemos   Perikles (450s–429)
|
Kimon = Isodike

The Family of Miliades (Philaidai)

Kypselos   =   x   =   Stesagoras
| |
Miltiades (*c.* 540)   Kimon (*c.* 530)   Oloros of Thrace

Stesagoras (*c.* 520)   Miltiades (490)   =   Hegesipyle
|
Kimon (470s–450s)

PREFACE

*T*HE WORD OR NAME *"MARATHON" IS A FAMILIAR ONE IN MODERN society, but it is associated in the public mind above all with an athletic competition, a race, rather than with an ancient battle. Some fans of the marathon race may be vaguely aware of the legendary "marathon run" of the ancient Athenian messenger sent from Marathon to Athens to announce victory in the great battle over the Persians; but very few, one suspects, realize that that run is indeed a legend, and a rather late legend at that, and that the historical reality is actually far more impressive than a single runner covering a twenty-six-mile distance.*

The aim of this book is to recover the historical reality of the battle fought in the plain of Marathon, two dozen miles from the city of Athens, between a small army of ancient Athenians and a much larger army of invading Persians; and of the amazing speed march accomplished by the entire Athenian army (about six thousand men as we'll see) from Marathon to Athens to prevent a force of Persians from capturing the city of Athens while its defenders were away—both the great battle and the speed march occurring on the same day: the battle in the morning, the march in the afternoon. These events, as interesting as they are in themselves, had an enormous importance for the future development of classical Greek, and so of Western, culture and society.

In the interest of producing a "clean" and readable text, I have

23

not cluttered the pages with source references or footnotes debating with other scholars. I provide at the end of the book an account of the sources and some discussion of useful further reading for each chapter.

Finally, a note on the spelling of Greek words and names. During the nineteenth and early twentieth centuries a customary spelling system arose in Britain and America that derived from Latin versions of Greek words and names, and further anglicized those Latin versions. For example, a famous Athenian statesman came to be known as "Pericles," though ancient Greek had no letter C and his name was properly spelled with a K. A great Greek historian was known as "Herodotus," though Greek masculine names tend to end with -os, not -us. I have preferred in most cases to use the original Greek spellings in this book—so Perikles and Herodotos, for example—because there is simply no good reason not to do so. However, a few names are so widely known in their anglicized forms that it seems excessively pedantic to change them: so the reader will find throughout the name Athens for the ancient Greek city properly called Athenai, and so on. In all cases, my aim has been to be as clear as possible, while sticking as closely as possible to the original Greek. I have applied that principle too, to my translations of Greek texts: all translations in this volume are my own, though I have often consulted other translations as a guide in deciding how to phrase my translations in English.

MARATHON

THE LEGEND OF
MARATHON

T WO THOUSAND FIVE HUNDRED YEARS AGO, IN EARLY AUGUST of the year 490 B.C.E., a smallish army of some ten thousand heavily armored Greek warriors—all but about six hundred of them Athenians—were encamped in the southern foothills overlooking the broad bay and coastal plain of Marathon in the northeast of Attica. The Athenians, and their six hundred or so Plataian allies, were there to defend their homeland of Attica against an invading Persian force. From their camp around a sanctuary of the hero Herakles they protected the roads from Marathon to Athens against a Persian advance and looked down on the Persian camp in the northern part of the coastal plain.

Between the two camps lay a broad marsh, making the route from either camp to the other narrow and difficult, and preventing any sudden or surprise attack. The two armies encamped thus, watching each other for a week. The Persians outnumbered the Athenians by perhaps as much as three to one, or even more, making the Athenians reluctant to advance from their secure defensive position to offer battle. For their part, the Persians did not wish to attempt an uphill attack against the strong Athenian position, especially given the Greeks' outstanding defensive armor.

Hence the long wait before the two sides came to blows. Yet at the end of a week of waiting, the Athenians did march down into the plain to initiate battle.

In the nineteenth century the Battle of Marathon came to be seen as a turning point in Greek and Western history. The British philosopher John Stuart Mill went so far as to claim that "the Battle of Marathon, even as an event in English history, is more important than the Battle of Hastings." Nowadays, the very notion of the "decisive battle" is not much accepted by many historians, and the idea underlying Mill's claim, that classical Greece was the cradle of Western civilization, and thus that a crucial event in Greek history could have affected all of Western history, is disputed by some historians. So, not surprisingly, to celebrate the Battle of Marathon as a true turning point in classical Greek history, and as a crucial event for all subsequent Western history, is controversial today. Even though as a rule history is shaped by longer term trends and developments—it is in fact possible for given events and decisions, on rare occasions, to have an enormous, far reaching, and even decisive impact—the Battle of Marathon was one of those rare events. For the stand made by those nine thousand plus Athenians and their six hundred or so Plataian allies in August of 490 B.C.E. made the classical Greek culture of the fifth and fourth centuries possible; a Persian victory in this campaign and battle would have led to a very different Greece and Greek culture. And a Persian victory was not only possible but, by most calculations, extremely likely.

Many historians point out that Marathon did not end the Persian threat to Greek freedom; that in fact the Persians invaded Greece again in much greater force in 480. How could Marathon then be the decisive battle it has been claimed to be? Simply put, if the Persians had won the battle and conquered Athens—as they were, by most observers and calculations, expected to do—Athenian democracy would have died in its infancy, a failed experiment after a mere fifteen or so years. The Athenians would have been deported to Iran, to be judged by King Darius, as happened to the Milesians in 494 and to the Eretrians in 490; there would have been no Athenian fleet of 200 warships to engage and defeat Persian naval power, as happened in 480; the tragic and comic drama, the philosophy and rhetoric, the historiography and political theory that were characteristic of fifth and fourth century democratic Athenian culture could not have come into being; and from a base (Athens) in the heart of central Greece, a full Persian conquest of Greece would have been an overwhelmingly likely outcome, so that even in the rest of Greece classical Greek culture as we know it could not have happened. All of this means that classical Greek history and culture truly hung in the balance on that August day in the plain of Marathon, and that the clash of those two armies that day was indeed one of those rare forks in the road of history, when the actions of a relative handful of people on a given day turned subsequent history away from one path of development and onto another.

All of this speaks to the importance of Marathon for classical Greek history, but what of the claim that Marathon was a turning point in Western history more generally, because classical Greek culture was the "cradle of Western civilization"? Some contemporary historians deride the idea of classical Greece as the cradle of Western civilization. They seem to me to be, quite simply, factually wrong; wrong not so much about classical Greece, as about the modern development of Western culture. However little many contemporary intellectuals may like European Renaissance and Enlightenment thought and culture, they and we are the intellectual descendants of Renaissance and Enlightenment—and for that matter nineteenth century—writers, artists, and thinkers who consciously sought in classical Greece, whether directly or via the Greeks' Roman pupils and imitators, their models and inspiration, making the likes of Euripides, Thucydides, Pheidias, Plato,

A romantic depiction of the Battle of Marathon

Aristotle, Demosthenes, and numerous others into something they might not otherwise have been: our intellectual and cultural forebears. Like it or not, modern Western culture and civilization have been deeply influenced by classical Greek models and ideas, and classical Greek civilization therefore really was, in a very important sense, the "cradle" of modern Western civilization—not because it was intrinsically destined to be that, but because the choices of European cultural leaders between the sixteenth and nineteenth centuries made it so.

Since a Persian victory at Marathon would have made Athenian democracy a failed experiment, would have prevented Athenian drama from coming into being, would have offered no scope or reason for the likes of Herodotos and Thucydides to write their great histories, would have offered no context for the likes of Plato and

Aristotle to philosophize, or the likes of Demosthenes to orate, such a Persian victory would have prevented the classical Greek culture from which our intellectual ancestors drew inspiration from coming about—at least in any form we know. A Persian victory would have, therefore, inevitably led to a fundamentally different modern Western culture. Different how, exactly, we cannot say.

Some might argue that modern Western culture might have been better: if one dislikes the ideas and influence of figures such as Thucydides, Plato, Aristotle, and the moderns who drew inspiration from them, one can argue that it would have been better had the Persians won. The point is, however, that it would have made a huge difference, not just to fifth century Greeks, but even to twenty-first century Europeans and Americans, if the outcome of the Battle of Marathon had been different. That is why that battle really can and should be seen as a decisive event in Western history generally. Mill may have exaggerated in his statement about Marathon and English history; but I believe the Battle of Marathon truly was a turning point event in the history of what we think of as "Western civilization." The lesson of that battle is that on some non-trivial level, humans can take charge of and affect their destinies: if ten thousand men had not made the stand they did on the plain of Marathon, history as we know it would not have come about.

Marathon became a legendary battle, then, both in ancient and in modern times, but in very different ways. The notion of the Battle of Marathon as a decisive "turning point" in Greek or "Western" history is a modern one. The battle had quite a different significance to the ancients, so one should better perhaps refer to the "legends" of Marathon: Marathon was a legendary battle to the ancient Athenians, and, after them, to the Greeks and the ancient world generally, as the ultimate expression of Athenian excellence. That Marathon could be viewed as a turning point in the history of the West was a notion that originated in the romantic philhellenic atmosphere of nineteenth century Europe. In England, that romantic philhellenism was stimulated above all by the sculptural decorations of the Parthenon brought to

England in 1806 and displayed in London—the so-called Elgin Marbles—and by the Greek uprising against Ottoman Turkish rule in 1821. The poet Lord Byron died from a fever contracted while aiding the Greeks in this uprising, further cementing the romance of the story. Between 1846 and 1856 interest in ancient Greece was further stimulated by the publication of George Grote's great twelve-volume *History of Greece*. The Battle of Marathon was treated at length in volume 4 of the history, published in 1848. Three years later another historical work, which became an instant classic, stimulated a passionate interest in the Battle of Marathon as such and spread the idea that this battle was a defining moment in Western history: Edward Creasy's *Fifteen Decisive Battles of the World*.

But there is yet a third element to the legend of Marathon: that of the twenty-six-mile run after the battle, with which the word "marathon" is generally connected in people's minds today. That legend became a part of Western culture with the founding of the modern Olympic games in 1896 by Baron Pierre de Coubertin. Each of these elements of the Marathon legend deserves to be considered in turn.

THE ATHENIAN LEGEND OF MARATHON

To the ancient Athenians, beginning only a few decades after the great battle, Marathon stood as the most glorious event in their history. In his biography of Themistokles, Plutarch tells us that already in the 480s that great Athenian general was kept awake at night by the thought of Miltiades' glory and his restless ambition to emulate him: Miltiades was the general who led the Athenians at Marathon. If that was true, the battle of Salamis in 480—at which the Athenian fleet, led by Themistokles, defeated the Persian fleet—certainly gave Themistokles his wish, and throughout subsequent Athenian history Marathon and Salamis were often cited together as the crowning achievements of Athenian martial prowess. At times, certainly, Salamis was named alone or given precedence because the Persian invasion under Xerxes was grander and more threatening, its defeat was the one that truly ended the Persian threat to Greece, and of course Salamis also represented the birth of Athenian naval power, the pride of the fifth and fourth century Athenians. Yet Marathon enjoyed, in Athenian public art and monuments, in plays, in public speeches of various sorts, and especially in the "funeral orations" composed to honor those who had died in battle during any given year of warfare, a unique position as the ultimate expression of Athenian *aristeia* or "bestness," that peculiarly Homeric virtue to which all Greeks aspired. The reason for this is found in the way the battle is characteristically referenced: it was the day the Athenians fought the might of Asia *alone*.

Further, although the Athenians were, after the Battle of Salamis, the acknowledged masters of naval warefare, they always faced an invidious comparison with the Spartans when it came to the art of hoplite battle on land. Yet, as Thucydides has Perikles boast in the funeral oration in book 2 of his history, whereas the Spartans trained their whole lives to be courageous on the field of battle, the Athenians lived their lives without such restrictions, enjoying life to the full, yet they were just as ready to face the same dangers as the Spartans. The Battle of Marathon was the proof of this boast, that the Athenians, for all their lifestyle of pleasure and freedom and culture, could and did, when the day of danger arrived, stand their ground just as nobly as any Spartans.

This glorification of Marathon can be said to have begun with the painting of the public building in the central square of Athens called the *stoa poikile* or "painted portico." This building was set up and decorated in the middle of the fifth century, within decades of the battle, and it featured prominently, in its decorative scheme, a mural painting of the Battle of Marathon, in which several gods and the hero Theseus were depicted fighting for the Athenians, and the general Miltiades was prominently shown fighting in the front ranks. Monuments were also set up at Marathon itself: the Athenian dead had been buried collectively there in a great funeral mound still visible in the plain today—the so-called

Soros—and this mound was monumentalized by the setting up of stone columns on the top with the names of those who had died in the battle and been buried there. Reputedly, the great poet Simonides, famed for his epigrams—a genre in which he was unsurpassed—was commissioned to write a verse epitaph to introduce the names of the heroic dead:

> The Athenians, front-fighters of the Greeks, at Marathon
> destroyed the power of the gold-bearing Medes.

We also hear of a memorial to Miltiades at Marathon, and of another at Delphi. In so far as we can rightly take these monuments to belong to the first half of the fifth century, they are likely to reflect the influence of Miltiades' son Kimon. Advertising his father's success at Marathon was an excellent way for Kimon to glorify himself too, without arousing the envy that was characteristic of Greek and Athenian life, as he certainly would have done by too obvious glorification of his own successes at Eion and Eurymedon, among other victories. But whether or not due to Kimon's personal influence, these kinds of monumental and artistic commemoration of Marathon are hardly surprising or unusual: it was normal for Greek states to mark their successes in this way.

Slightly more unusual is the way the great poet and dramatist Aischylos—the celebrated author of the still-performed masterworks *The Persian Women, Seven Against Thebes*, and *Agamemnon*, among other extant and lost plays—reacted to Marathon. He personally fought in the battle, and tradition has it that after all his brilliant career and successes and the fame he had achieved around the Greek world as a poet and tragic dramatist, when he was dying in Sicily in 456 he wrote for his tombstone an epitaph that commemorated not his fame as a poet and playwright, nor even his participation in the battle of Salamis, but the fact that he fought at Marathon:

This memorial covers Aischylos son of Euphorion
an Athenian, though he died at wheat-bearing Gela.
Of his glorious prowess the sacred land of Marathon can tell
and the long-haired Mede who knows it well.

For Aischylos, then, the Battle of Marathon was a special
and unique event, the high point of his life, the one thing of which
he was most proud. That might not mean very much if Aischylos's epitaph had been found on some tombstone by archaeologists, the tombstone of an Athenian Joe Average. But Aischylos
was a man whose cultural achievements were monumental. For
him to decide the Battle of Marathon was the one thing he
wanted in his epitaph indicates that Marathon was already seen,
towards the end of his life, as a defining event in Athenian history. That attitude to the Battle of Marathon is what we see fully
developed in the last quarter of the fifth century, in the comedies
of Aristophanes.

For Aristophanes, the *Marathonomachoi*, the men who
fought at Marathon, were the supreme expression of what Athenian citizens could be, and had been, at their best. The Battle of
Marathon and the men who fought there crop up over and over in
his plays. In his earliest surviving play, *The Acharnians*, the maver-
ick Athenian Dikaiopolis (the name means "Just City," a swipe at
the Athens of Aristophanes' day which, by implication, was not
just) had decided to make his own peace with the Spartans since
the Athenian people would not. His envoy to the Spartans, returning with the peace treaty, is waylaid by a band of men from the
Athenian deme of Acharnai. He describes them to Dikaiopolis as
being old men, "veterans of Marathon, tough as oak or maple." In
part here, the mention of Marathon may just be a joke exaggerating the great age of these men: veterans of Marathon would have
been well into their eighties by the time of this play, if any still survived. But the Acharnians of the play's title are depicted as the true
old Athenians, the right sort, the best sort of Athenians; and the

fact that they come to agree with Dikaiopolis indicates that his (and Aristophanes') policy of seeking peace is the approach of which the truest of Athenians, those who fought at Marathon, would have approved. In *The Wasps*, Aristophanes goes further. He suggests that the Athenians not only deserve their empire because of their victories over the Persians, but that it would be right for the allies of Athens to pay for thousands of Athenian citizens to live a life of leisure to which "the trophies of Marathon give them the right." Here Marathon is seen not just as the most glorious achievement of the Athenians but as a benefit to all Greeks.

The theme is carried on in other plays by Aristophanes. In *The Knights*, Demos (the personified people of Athens) is offered various luxuries to which he is said to be entitled because "sword in hand, he saved Attica from the Median yoke at Marathon," and later in the play there is again reference to "the glory of Marathon." In the lost play *The Holkades* (merchant-ships) it was suggested that, among other supplies to be brought to Athens, there should be "a special bread roll for the old men, because of the trophy of Marathon." And in *Lysistrata*, performed in 411, seventy-nine years after Marathon, the old men of Athens, who oppose the attempt of the women to bring about peace, recall their prowess of old and proclaim that if they fail to bring the women to heel, "may the Marathon plain not boast my trophied victories." Marathon was fast on its way to becoming a cliché.

Around the same time, we find the same use of Marathon in a fragment of the sophist Kritias (later one of the hated "thirty tyrants" who ruled Athens for a year after her defeat in the Peloponnesian War). In a list of useful inventions made in different parts of Greece, each of which is simply mentioned by name, he concludes "but the potter's wheel, and glorious pottery, child of earth and oven, useful house ware, was invented by her who set up the trophy at Marathon." The victory at Marathon is now literally the defining event in Athenian history, since it can be used to name Athens. And again in this same period of the last quarter of the fifth century, we find scenes from the Battle of Marathon depicted in the friezes of the small but beautiful Temple of Nike (Victory) on the Akropolis.

It was in the fourth century, the heyday of Athenian patriotic oratory, that the Battle of Marathon truly became a cliché to be trotted out on every occasion to remind the Athenians of their former glory or spur them on to some policy the speaker was promoting. The noted orator Isokrates, in a speech he wrote on behalf of the younger Alkibiades, unworthy son of the great general and leader of the Peloponnesian War era, has him refer to his paternal and maternal ancestors (a much earlier Alkibiades and the great Kleisthenes, inventor of democracy as we shall see, respectively) who together "established that democratic form of government which so effectively trained the citizens in *aristeia* (excellence, literally "bestness") that single-handed they conquered in battle the barbarians who had attacked all Greece." This quote sums up perfectly the Athenian legend of Marathon: the association of the victory with the democracy; the victory was won single-handedly, a proof of the Athenians' supreme *aristeia*; and the victory as benefiting all of Greece.

Of course, to a great degree, as clichéd and hackneyed as references to it were becoming, the legend was right. As I shall argue in chapter 6, the victory at Marathon did benefit all of Greece; further, it is true that it was the democratic governing system that gave the Athenian citizen-militia hoplites the morale and (self)discipline to stand up to the Persians the way they did. But as we know, the claim that the Athenians had won at Marathon "single-handed" was not entirely true: the Plataians had served with the Athenians *pandemei* or in full force, about six hundred strong. Though the Athenians at times liked to ignore this to express the "we fought alone" notion of Athenian *aristeia*, the Plataian participation was in fact well remembered and formed another part of the battle's legend at Athens.

It was again Isokrates who particularly expressed this part of the legend in public words, in his speech written on behalf of the Plataians, the "Plataiikos." Twice in the speech Isokrates has the

37

Plataians remind the Athenians of their help at a crucial time in Athenian history. First they point out that they alone of all Greeks outside the Peloponnesos had shared the Athenians' peril: this was a clear reference to the campaign of 479 culminating in the battle of Plataia, a battle in which most of the men of central and northern Greece fought on the Persian side against the Spartan-led Peloponnesian League and the Athenians. A little later, though, the Plataians remind the Athenians that "we alone of all Greeks fought at your side for freedom": here the reference to Marathon is clear, for that was the only battle that Athenians and Plataians fought alone against the Persians. And the Athenians were grateful. They frequently aided the Plataians against their powerful and hostile neighbors the Thebans. On the two occasions when they could not prevent the Thebans from razing Plataia and driving the Plataians away—in 427, with Spartan help, and again in 373—the Athenians offered the fugitive Plataians refuge and both times, in gratitude specifically for Marathon, granted the Plataians a form of Athenian citizenship: on the first occasion, only after time had shown the Athenians could not restore the Plataians, in 404; the second time (in 373) at once.

The next generation of Athenian orators continued the Marathon theme in the same basic vein—Aischines and Demosthenes too harped on the achievements of the heroes of Marathon in their dispute with each other: Aischines in his speeches "On the Embassy" and "Against Ktesiphon," and Demosthenes in his speech "On the False Embassy," for example.

A special case, though, is the tradition of funeral orations. The most famous speech of this type is the speech of Perikles in book 2 of Thucydides' history; but it's very untypical, so much so that historians have often doubted it could be anything like what Perikles really said. Whereas Perikles' speech as it stands discusses the nature of Athenian society and politics at length, describing the city for which the honored dead were willing to die, the more typical orations spoke of Athens' tradition of military glory and gave plenty of emphasis to Marathon in doing so. The funeral oration of Lysias, for instance, from the early fourth century, dwells on Marathon. He suggested here that the Athenians deliberately fought the Persians alone, ashamed to have barbarians in their own country, and wanting the rest of the Greeks to owe them gratitude for driving the barbarians out rather than to owe other Greeks gratitude for their help in saving Athens. That's why they marched out, few in number, to face a multitude; and by being willing to put their own lives on the line, they earned the right to erect monuments admired throughout Greece and earned the goodwill of all Greeks who felt themselves to have been saved just as much as the Athenians.

This is a much exaggerated, and in some respects historically inaccurate, view of Marathon, but it's an exaggeration suited to the nature of the occasion, which called for extreme patriotism rather than careful recounting of the facts. Similarly, much later in the fourth century, Demosthenes emphasized in his funeral oration that the Athenians single-handedly repulsed a host gathered from an entire continent.

The Athenian legend of Marathon, then, emphasized Athens fighting alone, or virtually so; fighting on behalf of all Greece, not just the Athenians' own safety; and the huge disparity in size between the Persian or barbarian host, drawn from a whole continent, and the small but gallant Athenian force. In addition, the relationship between the Athenians' willingness to risk themselves, and the democracy in which they all shared and for which they took the risk, is often brought up. Athenian *aristeia* was, according to this legend, democratic *aristeia*, it was exercised to the benefit of all Greeks, and it was—as the term "bestness" requires—superior to the *aristeia* of others because the Athenians fought without allies. This was perhaps the most crucial part of the Marathon legend, because it contrasted the Athenians with their rivals and bugbears, the Spartans, who always brought allies to their battles. This Marathon legend was then used by non-Athenians too, either to praise or blame the Athenians.

A romantic painting depicting the Athenian runner, Philippides (or Pheidippides), arriving in Athens after his last twenty-six-mile run to announce the news of the Greek victory over the Persians at Marathon. This particular painting, one of many examples of the Marathon story in romantic art, was completed by Luc-Oliver Merson in 1869.

An example of each will illustrate this. The late fourth century philosopher Herakleides Pontikos, in a treatise arguing that pleasure and virtue are not incompatible, listed a variety of luxuries typically enjoyed by the Athenians and concluded "such were the men who won at Marathon, and alone overcame the power of all Asia." The influence of the Athenian oratorical Marathon legend is clear. On the other hand, the early third century historian Douris of Samos wrote about the (to his mind) disgraceful flattery the Athenians of his day showered on the Macedonian dynast Demetrios the Besieger, including composing and singing a hymn to him as if he were a god. Douris quoted the hymn in its entirety and then remarked "this was the song sung by the victors of Marathon (*Marathonomachoi*) . . . the men who slew uncounted myriads of barbarians." These uncounted myriads reflect the oratorical tradition of the vast size of the Persian army at Marathon. To Douris, therefore, the point was that later Athenians simply and disgracefully failed to live up to the example of their glorious ancestors. Marathon had become a stick to beat the degenerate later Athenians with.

After the decline of Athenian power and influence in the third century B.C.E., the urge to praise or blame the Athenians directly—whether by Athenian leaders themselves or by outside commentators—declined too. In Roman times Marathon was certainly remembered, but it was remembered simply as an example of the virtues of the old-time Athenians. The Attic orators of the fourth century still served as the main source for the ways in which Marathon was presented: for those Attic orators had become a standard part of the reading list of every educated man. So Roman imperial writers like Cornelius Nepos (in his biography of Miltiades), Plutarch, Lucian, Pausanias, and others refer to Marathon with emphasis on the vast numbers of Persians who fought there—nearly a quarter of a million in Nepos, for example; and as many as 600,000 in Justin—and the outstanding virtue of the Athenians who fought alone and won. Since praise of the antique Athenians was more or less a stock theme in these writers, however, interest tended to shift to picturesque details, real or imagined.

It was in the writings of Plutarch and Lucian that a new element of the Marathon legend first surfaced, 600 years or more after the event: the legend of the Marathon runner. The story is probably the best known part of the Marathon legend in modern times: the single runner, usually named Philippides, who ran from the battlefield straight to Athens to announce the victory and collapsed dead of exhaustion after getting out the words "we have won." Plutarch, in his essay "On the Glory of Athens" does attribute this story to the late fourth century B.C.E. writer Herakleides Pontikos, so it's possible (if that attribution is genuine) the story first arose in Athenian popular legend of the fourth century.

This statue of Philippides stands by the road to Marathon to commemorate both the battle and Philippides' heroic run.

At any rate, the runner, Philippides (or Pheidippides), was a real person, though in sober history his feat was much more impressive than a mere twenty-six-mile run, as we'll see.

THE MODERN LEGEND OF MARATHON

With the decline and end of the Roman Empire in the West, interest in the ancient Athenians and in Marathon naturally declined too. Knowledge of the battle survived in the Byzantine (or East Roman) Empire and was brought up by men of culture from time to time in essentially the same way as the classical Athenian orators had done, as a time-honored cliché. The battle was not entirely forgotten in the West either, and as interest in the ancient Greeks revived, so awareness of Marathon revived too; but there was no sense that the Battle of Marathon was anything very remarkable except, as usual, for its proof of ancient Athenian courage. And it was treated essentially in this same way by the earliest modern European historians of classical Greece, the likes of August Boeckh in Germany and Connop Thirlwall in Britain, and by the greatest of the early historians of the Greeks in the modern era, George Grote.

Grote devoted nearly thirty pages of volume 4 of his history to the Battle of Marathon, giving a detailed account of the battle insofar as the scholarship of his time was able to reconstruct it. He took into account the observations of the eighteenth and early nineteenth century travelers, such as Colonel William Leake, who had visited the site of Marathon, and gave a considered evaluation of the battle's importance to the Athenians and to the overall story of Greek resistance to Persian domination. But that is as far as he goes: he still sees the battle in the same light, essentially, as the ancient Athenians and Greeks themselves had seen it: a great achievement of the Athenians, an important stage in the Greek resistance to the Persians, and no more.

It was just three years after the publication of Grote's fourth volume, however, that a new and very different historical work was to bring about a fundamental reappraisal of the Battle of Marathon and its importance and establish the modern interest in and legend of Marathon as a "decisive battle in Western history": Edward Creasy's 1851 volume *The Fifteen Decisive Battles of the World: From Marathon to Waterloo*. As his title indicates, the Battle of Marathon was the first to be treated in Creasy's book, and the opening lines of the chapter on Marathon thus begin the book proper, giving a sense of the grand way in which Creasy viewed this battle:

> Two thousand three hundred and forty years ago, a council of Athenian Officers was summoned on the slope of one of the mountains that look over the plain of Marathon, on the eastern coast of Attica. The immediate subject of their meeting was to consider whether they should give battle to an enemy that lay encamped on the shore beneath them; but on the result of their deliberations depended, not merely the

43

fate of two armies, but the whole future progress of human civilization.

Creasy was, as numerous critics have pointed out, avowedly Eurocentric in his view of history. His fifteen battles are all European battles: great events in Asian warfare such as Genghis Khan's victories, Kublai Khan's conquest of China, the victories of Timur the Lame, or the battle of Sekigahara, whereby Ieyasu founded the Tokugawa Shogunate in Japan, are beyond his scope and probably beyond his ken. In fact a number of his decisive battles (five of the fifteen: Marathon, Arbela, Metaurus, Chalons, and Tours) seem chosen with a view to showing how the European peoples, to the good fortune of the world generally, beat back the attempts of "barbarian" Asiatic armies to break into or conquer Europe. If they had succeeded, inferior Asiatic ways would have overtaken Europe, is the implication; but by these hallowed victories Creasy discusses, the light of European culture was kept burning until in his day it could become a beacon to the world. I think that's a fair statement of Creasy's attitude, and it isn't one that would win much sympathy today.

Still, the fact that we may not agree with Creasy's view as to how or why a battle was decisive or important doesn't mean we must necessarily reject that battle's importance. We don't have to see Western civilization as some great boon to mankind, to believe that a particular event may have contributed greatly to making Western civilization what it is today. Neither should being aware of the darker side of Western history—the brutality and naked exploitation that were an undoubted part of Western imperialism, for example—blind us to the undoubted good in Western civilization. In any case, in the second half of the nineteenth century, Creasy's work was enormously popular and influential. It was an age, in fact, when the idea of the "decisive battle" was an appealing one.

During the era of so-called "cabinet warfare" between the "wars of religion" (mid-sixteenth to mid-seventeenth centuries) and the French Revolution, conflicts between the European nations had frequently been settled by wars, and wars had usually been decided by battles. As one ruler of the era put it: "I have lost a battle, I must pay with a province."

The notion that great battles could decide great issues was strengthened by the Napoleonic Wars, when a series of epic battles established Napoleon's France in control of Europe, and several equally epic battles, notably Leipzig and Waterloo, undid that control and restored the old order. The massive shock of the Napoleonic Wars, and the romantic glamour which attached to them as time passed, encouraged intellectuals to study warfare, producing what is still considered by most critics the greatest philosophical analysis of warfare, Clausewitz's *Vom Kriege* ("On War"). Though few would compare Creasy's work to Clausewitz's, it was a product of the same atmosphere of interest in warfare and how it influenced societies and civilizations.

The question for us is, why did Creasy begin with Marathon? It was not really an obvious choice. Given his Eurocentrism and the romantic philhellenism of the era, it was to be expected, perhaps, that Creasy would choose an ancient Greek battle as his starting point. But again, why Marathon? Since the Persian threat to Greece was only finally driven off by the battles of Salamis and Plataia in 480 and 479, one of those battles might have seemed a more natural starting point. And why start with a battle of the city-state Greeks at all? Why not begin with a battle of Alexander the Great, for example? Here one may suspect the influence of Grote, whose fourth volume Creasy had certainly read, and which he cites several times in his notes. To Grote, as a good English liberal, the Athenian democracy was a uniquely important political model for how a free people should govern themselves, and the Athenians' success in maintaining their freedom from Persian domination was thus vital. It was this that caused John Stuart Mill, who moved in the same liberal circles as Grote, to estimate that Marathon was more important to English history than the Battle of Hastings. Still, the Battle of Salamis might have seemed the obvious choice to highlight Athens' preservation of freedom and democracy, particularly since it was a naval battle and so might have been expected to appeal to a British historian—given Britain's long and distinguished naval history. Perhaps it's best again to let Creasy's own words explain his choice. He closes his account of Marathon with the following remarks:

> It was not indeed by one defeat, however signal, that the pride of Persia could be broken, and her dreams of universal empire dispelled. Ten years afterwards she renewed her attempts upon Europe on a grander scale of enterprise, and was repulsed by Greece with greater and reiterated loss. Larger forces and heavier slaughter than had been seen at Marathon signalized the conflicts of Greeks and Persians at Artemisium, Salamis, Plataea, and the Eurymedon. But mighty and momentous as these battles were, they rank not with Marathon in importance. They originated no new impulse. They turned back no current of fate. They were merely confirmatory of the already existing bias which Marathon had created. The day of Marathon is the critical epoch in the history of the two nations. It broke forever the spell of Persian invincibility, which had paralyzed men's minds. It generated among the Greeks the spirit which beat back Xerxes, and afterwards led on Xenophon, Agesilaus, and Alexander, in terrible retaliation through their Asiatic campaigns. It secured for mankind the intellectual treasures of Athens, the growth of free institutions, the liberal enlightenment of the Western world, and the gradual ascendency for many ages of the great principles of European civilization.

Creasy makes several key points here: it was Marathon that first "broke the spell" of Persian invincibility and showed the Greeks they could win; it was Marathon that "secured . . . the intellectual treasures of Athens" and "the liberal enlightenment of the Western world." Once again, I'll just reiterate that we don't have to follow him in his assessment of the value to the world of the ascendancy of European civilization (though some still may), in order to recognize the basic validity of the point he is making about the preservation of Athens, and therefore of the Athenians' later achievements. I shall argue in chapter 6 that these achievements were vital to the way our present Western civilization thinks, organizes its political life, and entertains itself, regardless of any grandiose concepts of the West's contribution to "the world." In other words, setting aside his Eurocentrism and Victorian prejudices, Creasy was right: the Battle of Marathon was a turning point, and his readers, both immediate and later, recognized as much.

It's worth just dwelling for a moment on the term "liberal enlightenment" in Creasy's text, because it helps to situate him in that liberal English milieu that found its spiritual ancestry in democratic Athens, the same liberal milieu in which Grote and John Stuart Mill moved. This liberal milieu contributed significantly to the democratizing of Britain between the great Reform Bills of the 1830s, the further reforms of Gladstonian liberalism in the 1880s, and the last great triumphs of liberal reform in the opening twelve years of the twentieth century. The legend of Marathon, as Creasy had set it out, played its role—by establishing a positive view of Athenian democracy and its excellence—in fostering the intellectual environment in which that democratizing could happen.

The later nineteenth century, which witnessed the great battles—Sadowa, Metz, Sedan—by which the Prussians ended Habsburg influence in Germany, broke the power of Second Empire France, and unified the German states into the new German Reich, was an era in which the concept of the decisive battle continued to thrive. Creasy's book remained popular, though there was a storm of historical debate around his choice of battles. Many writers have, over the years, revised or updated Creasy's list of battles. By and large, however, Marathon retained its position as the crucial battle with which Western history proper should begin.

In the second half of twentieth century, however, the notion of the decisive battle began to lose popularity. The tragic history of the First World War, in which battles on a scale and duration never witnessed before in human history, and with casualty lists that dwarfed all previous wars, led to no discernible result except the moving of the "front lines" a few useless miles one way or the other, began that process. World War II seemed to restore the decisive battle somewhat, with the brilliant German *blitzkrieg* victories of the opening stages, and the gigantic showdowns of Stalingrad and D-Day deciding the war's outcome. But since then, we have seen wars such as Korea, Vietnam, and more recently Iraq and Afghanistan, in which rare victories seem to bog down into interminable guerrilla wars, partisan operations, and/or insurrections that render victory in battle meaningless and war seemingly irrational, lasting victory unattainable. In the intellectual atmosphere generated by these less invigorating experiences of war, the notion of the decisive battle, the epoch-making event that turns history away from one path and onto another, has become unfashionable to say the least.

We mustn't let intellectual fashion decide our analysis of historical events, however. The present experience of battle as indecisive and leading to no useful result is only a phase of history, the result of a particular configuration of societies, and of the distribution of the means of destructive force. Our era's experience of warfare and battle can't properly detract from the reality and validity of the experiences of other eras, in which under different social, political, and military conditions, battles really were decisive. Still, it has to be said that the importance of Marathon, and of battles in general, has declined enormously in the past half century—in the estimation of academic historians, at any rate. Popular historians continue to write books about wars and decisive battles in the old mode and sell them to an interested public. And the proliferation of cable television has provided a niche for the same kind of military history to reach a popular audience: the History Channel, and its offshoot the Military History Channel. The History Channel has recently run its own series of shows on "Decisive Battles," for example, of which Marathon was one.

THE LEGEND OF THE MARATHON RUN

But in this same twentieth century interest in Marathon in any case shifted to, and was bolstered by, another aspect of the Marathon legend: the legend of the Marathon run. That legend was first made much of in Roman imperial times, as we've seen, by writers such as Plutarch and Lucian. The modern legend only goes back to 1896, though: the year of the first modern Olympic games. The roots of the Olympic movement lie in that same romantic nineteenth century philhellenism of which I've already spoken, together with the rising interest in sports, both as an activity and as a spectator event, in the late nineteenth century. Urban middle- and working-class clubs proliferated around Europe and America, dedicated to the practicing of one sport or another—football, baseball, rugby, tennis, and so on—and at times of multiple sports. So-called "athletics," that is the running and jumping and throwing sports the ancient Greeks had enjoyed, were very much part of this movement.

Intellectuals infused by philhellenism began to make much of the Greek passion for athletics, and to tell the story of the ancient athletic competitions. Eventually a movement arose dedicated to recreating those ancient Greek international athletic festivals, of which French aristocrat Baron Pierre de Coubertin became the leader. This movement was particularly struck by the so-called "Olympic truce" whereby participants in the Olympic games were exempt from the normal hostilities of whatever wars were current in Greece, especially as that truce was misunderstood as a total cessation of hostilities for the duration of the Olympic festival. It was hoped that a modern Olympic movement could gradually replace unhealthy international competition through violence and warfare, with a healthy athletic rivalry that would sponsor friendship in the place of hostility.

At any rate, in 1896 the movement succeeded in gathering

enough international support to organize an "Olympic Games" for the first time since antiquity. There could be only one location for these first games: Greece. But it was discovered to be impractical to hold them at Olympia itself—an archaeological site with no amenities for such an event—so the capital, Athens, was chosen. Thirteen modern nations (or fourteen if Hungary is counted separately from Austria, with which it was joined at the time) sent delegations of athletes, who competed in nine different sports. The games were considered a great success: the Panathenaic Stadium in Athens overflowed with spectators, and there was the largest international participation of any event up to that time.

But de Coubertin and his associates wanted to have a spectacular event with which to close the athletics (that is, track and field) portion of the games, something to catch the world's attention and really put the Olympics "on the map." It was the suggestion of Michel Breal, an associate of de Coubertin, to stage a new version of Philippides' legendary run from Marathon to Athens: the setting was perfect, since the race could actually start at Marathon and finish at the Olympic Stadium in Athens. The idea was enthusiastically taken up, and it proved a great success, particularly for sentimental, patriotic reasons. The Greek hosts of the games, though they had had hopes of medaling in various events, had failed to win any. The Marathon run would be their last chance to gain a gold medal in an athletic event that the ancient Greeks had invented. And as it turned out, an unknown and utterly unfancied Greek water-carrier named Spiridon Louis did in fact win the race in a time just under three hours, becoming an instant national hero. According to one piece of lore about that 1896 race, about which much has been written, the king of Greece offered Louis whatever he might want for an award; Louis only asked for a carriage to help him carry more water for his business. Louis was a true amateur runner and never competed in any kind of track event again, but his performance has been an inspiration to artists and athletes for more than a century.

From that point on the Marathon run became a fixture in the

This photo, taken in 1896, captures the first modern Olympic Marathon.

Spiridon Louis, the winner of the first modern Olympic Marathon in 1896, was a twenty-three-year-old water-carrier born just north of Athens. He was the only Greek medalist in the 1896 Olympic Games and became "a national hero.

Olympic Games, and a popular athletic event in its own right. Though it was some twenty years before the exact distance for a Marathon run was fixed, the event thrived and grew, until it has now entered the popular culture and even the English language. We speak of a "marathon effort," for example, to refer to any undertaking that takes immense energy and stamina to complete. Marathon races are held in various international competitions, and professional marathon runners can earn large sums of money. The concept of the marathon has expanded in modern athletics: we have "iron man" marathons in which the athletic feats required come much closer to the historical Philippides' real achievement: a run of 140 miles from Athens to Sparta, and the same distance back again, in just a few days. In truth all the modern recreations of the ancient Marathon run for professional athletes at athletic competitions, though they stem from a genuine ancient legend about an ancient Athenian athlete, bear little relation to the true historical Marathon "run": for that was, as we'll see in chapter 5, a speed march by the entire Athenian army from Marathon to Athens to save their city after the battle.

There are modern events that give a sense of that extraordinary afternoon in August of 490. But they are not the Marathon runs for professional athletes, who have met a qualifying time, at the Olympics and other international athletics festivals. It is rather in the modern, city Marathons—New York, Chicago, London, Boston, Tokyo—with their thousands and thousands of enthusiastic "amateur" runners—that is, runners who run for pure love of doing so, rather than as a profession. And this is not because ancient athletes were "amateurs" and so more like these enthusiasts than like modern professional athletes: the opposite is true; ancient athletes were professionals, and the "amateurism" of the early modern Olympics was a Victorian ideal that had nothing to do with ancient Greece. It is that the mass run—often in fact more of a speed walk—of the thousands of enthusiasts after the professionals have set off first and distanced themselves, truly recreates something of what the jogging speed-march of thousands of Athenian warriors from Marathon to Athens after the battle would have looked like.

This aspect of the modern Marathon run is depicted in a 2007 film, *The Spirit of the Marathon*, which follows a number of such running enthusiasts around the world as they train and tell their stories, and ultimately run in the Chicago Marathon. Surprisingly, though, this film is the most elaborate engagement of the movie industry with the legend of Marathon.

In light of Hollywood's longstanding interest in the ancient world, leading to such renowned films as *Ben Hur*, *Quo Vadis*, *Demetrius the Gladiator*, Stanley Kubrick's classic *Spartacus*, and many others; and in recent times to Ridley Scott's wonderful *Gladiator*, the visually stunning *Troy*, and the cartoonishly entertaining (and cartoon-based) *300*, about Thermopylai, it is surprising that there is no major movie treatment of the battle of Marathon proper. The one film that does deal with the battle as its main subject is, so far as I have been able to discover, a 1959 B-grade film called *La Bataille de Marathon* in Europe, but *The Giant of Marathon* in its American release. Directed by Jacques Tourneur with a mostly European cast, it starred the impressively muscled American B-list actor Steve Reeves, most famed for his title role in a series of "sword and sandal" epics about *Hercules*.

Amusingly, the film is a neat blending of the modern Marathon legends made popular by Creasy and de Coubertin respectively: that is, the decisive battle and the Marathon run. The hero of the film, played by Reeves, is none other than Philippides, reinvented as an all round athlete who becomes famous and popular at Athens by winning an Olympic victory in a sort of hybrid pentathlon event, involving throwing the javelin, swimming(!), a sort of shot put with a rough rock (perhaps based on the throwing competition won by Odysseus in Phaeacia in the *Odyssey*), wrestling, and finally the running for which the real Philippides was renowned. Thanks to his fame, Philippides is made commander of an elite (and fictional) Athenian military unit called the "Sacred Guard." This places him in the military and political debates about the coming invasion by the forces of the evil king Darius of Persia. He sides with Miltiades in arguing that Athens must fight and volunteers to go to seek Spartan aid. In the end, after the Greeks have defeated the Persian army, Philippides has to lead the Sacred Guard on a dash to Athens to save the city from being betrayed to the Persians while the army is away—which is where the Marathon run comes in. Amusing enough as a period piece, it is not a good film by any stretch of the imagination, yet it seems to be the sum total of popular treatment of the

Battle of Marathon in the film genre.

It would seem that the Battle of Marathon has all the elements that should appeal to Hollywood: a David versus Goliath story line (tiny Athens against the huge Persian Empire); an array of remarkable characters—King Darius, Miltiades, the war "archon" Kallimachos, the younger up-and-coming generals Themistokles and Aristides, among others; lots of action and intrigue; the remarkable run of Philippides; the great battle scene itself; and the romantic final dash of the victorious Athenian army. Perhaps in this new era of epic war films enhanced by computer and digital imaging, we may hope for a revival of the Marathon legend on the silver screen. Be that as it may, it's clear that the memory of the Athenians at Marathon, their stand for freedom, their defense of a truly popular form of democratic self-government, their making possible of the classical Greek culture we still admire and imitate, or simply that run over the iconic twenty-six-mile distance, is still green in the popular imagination 2,500 years after the event. And that interest in it isn't likely to disappear in any foreseeable future. The legend of Marathon lives on: let's see how and why and by whom this legendary battle was fought.

CHAPTER 1

THE ANCIENT GREEKS IN THE SEVENTH AND SIXTH CENTURIES B.C.E.

C LASSICAL GREEK CIVILIZATION BEGAN WITH HOMER. THE Homeric epics—the *Iliad* and the *Odyssey*—were in all likelihood originally composed in the second half of the eighth century B.C.E. They rapidly became, as it were, the "bible" of the ancient Greeks, especially the *Iliad* and remained so until they were replaced by the Christian Bible in the fourth century C.E. This is to say that during the seventh, sixth, and fifth centuries B.C.E. and later, Greek men were brought up on the Homeric epics, regarding the stories in them as portraying their cultural origins, and considering the values and ideals expressed in them as authoritative.

HOMER AND THE COMPETITIVE SPIRIT IN GREEK CULTURE

It's important for an understanding of ancient Greek culture to bear in mind that the Homeric epics were military epics: the *Iliad* was about warfare and the achievements of the greatest of all Greek warriors, Achilles; and the *Odyssey* was about a warrior's (Odysseus's) homecoming from long absence in war and his revenge on those who had wronged his "house" during his absence. From the Homeric epics, the Greeks learned to value above all the martial virtues and an intensely competitive spirit. For virtue, in Homer, is very much connected to martial prowess and competition for status and primacy. The heroes depicted in the Homeric epics strove to be the best, to demonstrate their *aristeia*, their "bestness." The Greeks learned from Homer to compete for honor and status, to strive to be the best at all times, and to perceive being the best in a very warlike, physical prowess kind of way. For example, the hero Achilles was universally acknowledged as being "the best of the Achaeans" (that is, Greeks). When we look into what qualities made him the best, we don't find any suggestion of moral goodness as it later—after Plato, and especially after Christianity—came to be understood: Achilles was the tallest, the strongest, the handsomest, the fastest runner, the best fighter, he owned the best war chariot with the fastest team of horses, and it was all this that made him "the best," not his moral character. His superlative excellence consisted in his outstanding physical and fighting characteristics, endowments, and qualities.

The urge to be best inherently fosters a competitive spirit. Best means better than others. For a Homeric leader, it was never enough to be good: one must be better than others. There was a constant sense of competing for relative status, and the way to prove one's *arete* (excellence, later understood as virtue) was by showing oneself better than others, by beating someone, whether it be an enemy warrior in a duel, or an allied warrior in achievement. Since allied warriors could not fight and kill each other, a form of competition that limited the danger of a lethal outcome was needed, and this was found in athletic competition.

The most noted example in the *Iliad* is the funeral games Achilles gave for Patroklos, at which the Greek warriors competed to show who was best at an array of physical contests: running, wrestling, spear fighting, archery, boxing, chariot racing. Prizes were awarded for outstanding achievement—winning or coming second or third—and those prizes were taken as symbols of honor

*A marble bust of Homer,
copied during Roman
times from a lost second
century B.C.E. original.*

and status. Similarly, prizes were awarded to the leading warriors for their achievements in war: the anger of Achilles that is the basis of the plot of the *Iliad* came about because the paramount King Agamemnon took away the prize Achilles had been awarded for his valor and thereby damaged his honor. Honor must be constantly protected and enhanced: when Odysseus, in the land of the Phaeacians, declared his unwillingness to participate in an athletic competition, he was taunted until he found himself obliged to protect his honor and show his "bestness" by outdoing all the Phaeacians in the throwing competition. The Greek term for competition was *agon*. It is the root of the English word "agony," and the "agonistic" (competitive) spirit that at all times infused Greek culture is one of the keys to understanding the nature of Greek society and the Greek way of life.

This competitiveness was not just an aristocratic preoccupation. A generation after Homer, the poet Hesiod composed his epic the *Works and Days* idealizing the way of life of the independent farming class in Greece. As the aristocratic "heroes," Hesiod's small farmers were depicted as infused by an intensely competitive spirit, though the competition was for them not so much about honor as about relative wealth. Hesiod stated that there were two kinds of *eris* or "strife," a good kind and a bad kind. The bad kind—the most normal meaning of *eris*—was the strife that could tear a community apart by unhealthy and violent striving for power and position. But the good kind of *eris* was the desire to better one's neighbors that caused potter to compete with potter and smith with smith to see who could be the most successful. Hesiod admonished farmers and artisans to work hard, to strive for success, and to outcompete each other. The aim, he stated, was to be able to buy one's neighbor's land, rather than having one's neighbor buy one's own land. This is a harsh competition indeed, for land and status were deeply connected in Greek culture and society, and the landless man was at the bottom of the social ladder.

Many of the most admired and most criticized aspects of classical Greek culture derive from this universal spirit of competition. On the one hand, the extraordinary military, political, and cultural achievements for which the ancient Greeks have been admired through history were motivated by mutual competition. On the other hand, the constant violence that marred Greek history—endless warfare between Greek cities and frequent civil strife within Greek cities—came from that same intense competitiveness.

Hesiod's emphasis on competition for ownership of land is particularly noteworthy. Greece is a very mountainous country, and up to 80 percent of its landmass is so rocky and mountainous as to be useless for farming purposes. Productive land was, as a result, a scarce and valuable commodity, and the competition for ownership or control of productive land was not just a peaceful competition among hard-working farmers. Much of the political history of the Greek city-states, with their chronic warfare against each other, is explained by rivalry for control of farmable land. Simply put, Greek states tended to develop strong and frequently hostile rivalries for control of border territories, with the result that border disputes were endemic throughout Greek history. Neighboring states in

Greece were almost always enemies rather than friends, because instead of sharing a history of cooperation they shared a history of border disputes and mutual warfare.

In addition, in the same pursuit of land, wealth, and thus power, larger Greek states often tried to dominate or incorporate smaller neighbors, resulting in hostile relations; and the larger states vied for regional predominance with each other, leading to inevitable warfare. Examples of these features of Greek inter-state relations are common and well known: neighbor states like Corinth and Megara, Eretria and Chalkis, Samos and Priene, to name just a few, had long-running border disputes that poisoned relations. Larger states like Argos and Thebes sought to dominate or incorporate smaller neighbors—Kleonai, Sikyon, or Epidaurus in the case of Argos; Plataia, Thespiai, or Tanagra in the case of Thebes—leading to frequent hostilities. And large states like Sparta and Argos, Athens and Thebes, vied for dominance in the Peloponnesos and central Greece respectively, causing centuries of mutual hostility and frequent warfare.

Just as individual Greeks, then, Greek states were involved in a constant competitive struggle to be best. And being best was measured by power, wealth, and above all the amount of territory and number of settlements a state controlled. The constant warfare between Greek states kept the Homeric value system always at the forefront of Greek life, and maintained the military virtues as the most important virtues in Greek moral thought. As destructive as this warfare for predominance could be, and frequently was, it had the effect of making the Greeks into tough fighters with a fierce determination to stand up for their own and their respective communities' independence. Throughout classical Greek history, Greeks fiercely resented being subordinated to others, having to obey the orders of others, and especially having to pay taxes or tribute (from resources never considered much more than adequate) to others.

By the time the Persian Empire arose in the middle of the sixth century B.C.E., and began to encroach on and try to subject the

Greeks and Greek lands, the Greeks had more than 150 years of mutual warfare behind them, inuring them to the hardships and dangers of battle and teaching them a very effective military system. On the other hand, the mutual hatreds of the Greeks were a weakness the Persians could and did attempt to exploit, in the classic strategy of "divide and rule." Again, therefore, I want to emphasize that the Homeric value system and the competitive and martial society and values it fostered were both a source of strength and a source of weakness for the Greeks, and it was very much open to question whether the strength or the weakness would prevail.

LEARNING FROM THE NEAR EAST

The Greeks, who eventually had to stand up to Persian pressure, though still guided in their thinking and values by Homer, had 200 years of further development since Homer's day behind them. During these centuries they had explored and learned from the other cultures and lands of the wider Mediterranean and near eastern world, had created highly organized and cohesive city-state structures within which a broad segment of the citizens shared political rights and input, had developed a unique culture of their own that gave them a sense of being a special people, and had evolved a military system that prized collective discipline, shared danger, and a mass formation based on thousands of men similarly equipped with strong defensive armor and determination to stand and fight.

By Homer's time, 300 years or more since the collapse of Greece's great Bronze Age civilization—the so-called Myceneans—Greece had long been an impoverished and underpopulated land largely cut off from contact with surrounding lands and peoples. Modern scholars often refer to this 300 or so years, from about 1050 to about 750 B.C.E., as Greece's "Dark Age." But by 750 important changes were afoot that were to transform Greece and the Greeks over the next 200 to 250 years.

For a start, the population of Greece was steadily rising in the eighth century: in fact rising at a rate that can almost be called a population explosion. Archaeological survey of Greece has shown that the number of permanent inhabited settlements in Greece was growing constantly and by leaps and bounds in the eighth and seventh centuries, and that the average size of these settlements was also growing. Clearly, more and bigger settlements would only be created to house a growing population. Yet already by 750 the population growth began to be felt to be a problem in the constricted terrain of Greece, with its limited food resources. So from about 750 onwards the Greeks began what historians call a "colonization movement." Bands of Greeks left their home communities to travel by ship out into the Mediterranean in search of new lands to settle. Hundreds of new Greek communities were founded as a result of this "movement": in the western Mediterranean, all around the eastern and southern coast of Sicily, along the southern and up the western coast of Italy, and along the southern coast of France; in the eastern Mediterranean, the region called Cyrenaica in modern Libya (after the first ancient Greek colony there, Cyrene), and the northern shore of the Aegean; and beyond the Mediterranean basin, all around the coasts of the Black Sea and its approaches. The Greek world was enormously expanded and enriched by this colonization movement, and tens of thousands, probably in fact hundreds of thousands of Greeks found new homes and settlements outside of Greece proper.

Yet the settlements in Greece proper continued to increase in number and size, indicating that the population growth outstripped the huge migration movement to the new colonies. We may wonder how this continual population growth was fueled and fed. We may also ask how the impoverished and inward looking Greeks of the "Dark Age" came to have, after 750, the maritime knowledge and skills to find overseas lands to settle and to move vast numbers of settlers to those new lands. The answer to both questions is the same: it involves Greek willingness and ability to learn from more

advanced neighbors to their east and south, and to develop themselves culturally, socially, and economically by what they learned.
Greece lay just beyond the great and ancient civilizations of the
Near and Middle East: the Egyptians, the Babylonians and Assyrians, the peoples of Syria and Palestine. For centuries the Greeks had
been almost entirely cut off from those civilizations, but during the
ninth and eighth centuries trading ships from the cities of the
Phoenicians—the cities of Tyre and Sidon, Byblos and Berytos
(Beirut) in the modern Lebanon—were exploring the western
Mediterranean and establishing trade routes and trading outposts
all the way to Spain and northwest Africa, to the Straits of Gibral-
tar and even beyond into the Atlantic. Phoenician ships sometimes
stopped in along the coasts of Greece looking for supplies and
engaging in trade for whatever local surplus products the Greeks
could produce, few and insignificant as such products were at first.

The Greeks were impressed by the knowledge and wealth of
these Phoenicians, as we can tell from Homer's frequent references
to Phoenician traders; and before long Greek adventurers began to
learn from the Phoenicians—constructing ships, sailing out into the
Aegean and Mediterranean waters, and tracking the Phoenicians
along their trade routes, east and west. Following the Phoenician
trade routes to the west, the Greeks found the relatively "uncivi-
lized," underpopulated, yet resource-rich lands of Sicily, Italy, and
southern France and were motivated to undertake the colonization
of those coasts as we have seen. Just as important if not more so,
though, tracking the Phoenicians back to their home ports in the
eastern Mediterranean brought the Greeks into direct contact with
the more advanced cultures of Egypt and western Asia for the first
time in centuries. The result was an extraordinary flowering of
Greek civilization and culture, as the Greeks eagerly learned from
the ancient civilizations of the east. As they learned, they adapted
and improved, thereby creating their own unique culture.

One of the first things the Greeks borrowed was the Phoenician writing system. Since the end of the Bronze Age, the Greeks had

had no writing. Contact with Phoenicians led to the discovery that these highly civilized easterners had a method of recording information by making special marks on pieces of papyrus-reed paper, or on wooden tablets coated with wax, or on clay tablets.

The Phoenician writing system was purely consonantal: there were no symbols for vowel sounds. A written document thus consisted of strings of consonants only, a sort of mnemonic device into which the reader had to insert, from memory or by deduction, the proper vowel sounds in order to make actual words that could be voiced. When some enterprising Greeks learned this writing system and tried to adapt it to the Greek language, they made a discovery and had an idea. The discovery was that certain symbols in the Phoenician writing system stood for consonant sounds not used in Greek; the idea was to use those symbols to represent vowel sounds instead. Thus was created the Greek alphabet, the world's first true alphabetic writing system, in the sense that the full range of sounds made in a language were recorded in writing, writing that could thus be read and voiced straight from the text as written. The importance of this adaptation the Greeks made from the Phoenician writing system can hardly be overstated: the Greek alphabet of between twenty-four and thirty letters (there were variant versions of it for the first few centuries) was so simple to learn that it made widespread literacy feasible for the first time. All modern Western alphabets, the Latin and Cyrillic alphabets just as much as the modern Greek alphabet, are direct descendants of the ancient Greek alphabet that was created around 800 B.C.E.

The way the Greeks did not simply borrow the Phoenician writing system but adapted and improved it was typical of how the Greeks learned from the advanced eastern cultures in this so-called "orientalizing" phase of Greek history, between about 750 and 600 B.C.E. Monumental stone architecture, sculpture, metallurgy, painting, agriculture, navigation, ship-building, religion: in all of these and still other disciplines, the Greeks borrowed ideas, techniques, methods, motifs, and know-how from Egypt and the Near East, and in each case they quickly developed and improved upon what they had borrowed and learned, making it their own. This urge to improve no doubt came, in part at least, from the intensely competitive nature of Greek culture already described: as individuals and as communities the Greeks were driven to be better than each other, to excel, and that drive for excellence led to a constant urge to try new things, to adapt and improve. In the words of archaeologist and historian Anthony Snodgrass, this era in Greek history was the "age of experiment," and it was the constant experimenting with new ideas and methods that created the society and culture of classical Greece.

Much of the attention paid by historians to this phase of Greek learning from the advanced civilizations of the Near East has tended, in many ways understandably, to focus on cultural matters: the development of Greek architecture, sculpture, and the decorative arts under the impact of Near Eastern models. Just as important, though, if not more so, was the economic development Greece went through under the impact of contact with the East. By following the Phoenician trade routes to the west, the Greeks opened up a whole new world of economic possibilities through acquiring the abundant natural resources available in the western Mediterranean region: grain, timber, and metals being no doubt the most important of these resources.

By colonizing extensively in the western Mediterranean, the Greeks carved out a guaranteed access to these resources, and developed secure trade routes, competing with and to some degree cutting out the Phoenician middlemen through whom they had first gained access to these trade goods. Indeed, in order to compete effectively with the Greeks, the Phoenicians too found it necessary to found permanent colonies in the western Mediterranean: Carthage, Tunis, and Utica in north Africa, for example, Motya and Panormos (Palermo) in western Sicily, and Gades (Cádiz) in Spain.

Following the Phoenicians to the east, the Greeks were able to compete with the Phoenicians in the role of middlemen in trading the raw products of the western Mediterranean for the highly desirable manufactured goods and other products of Egypt, Syria/Palestine, and Mesopotamia. And as they learned from these advanced civilizations, the Greeks were able more and more to trade products of their own—wine and olive oil, from their own developing cash-crop farming, but also manufactured goods, especially metal goods—as they began to outstrip their teachers in the refinement and quality of their manufactures. Greek pottery, jewelry, tools, and weapons began to be prized around the Mediterranean world, so that, by 600 at the latest, the Greeks were no longer just middlemen traders. A prime example of highly valued Greek manufactures are the carbonized steel tools and weapons that Greeks learned to make after about 700 B.C.E.

The growth of trade routes, access to abundant resources not just from the western Mediterranean but also, by the second half of the seventh century, from Egypt and the Black Sea region (grain, timber, metals, hides for leather, fish, and slaves), the development of more productive and wealth-generating cash crop farming, and the growth of manufacturing in ceramics and metal goods particularly: all of this economic development led to an enormous increase in the wealth of the Greeks, fueled the continuing growth of the Greek population, funded the expansion of settlements into genuine cities (Athens, Corinth, Miletos, Samos, and many others), and made possible the rise of a prosperous "middle class" of independent farmers with surplus income from their cash crops, artisans manufacturing all sorts of metal, ceramic, wooden, and leather products, and merchants and traders facilitating the exchange mechanisms that made all this possible.

THE AGE OF TYRANTS

This newly prosperous class of farmers, artisans, and traders began to play an important role in the political and military, as well as economic, life of their communities. Their surplus wealth made them able to afford the expense and time of military equipment and military service, and their economic independence and importance led them to demand a political say in the governing of their communities.

Taking this latter point first, the evidence—scanty as it is—indicates that in the first half of the seventh century, Greek communities were dominated and ruled by more or less hereditary aristocracies, the *Eupatridai* ("well-born ones") of Athens being the best known of them. Some of these aristocracies were very narrow, consisting essentially only of one extended family or *genos* ("clan"), such as the *Bakkhiadai* of Corinth or the *Penthilidai* of Mytilene; others consisted of a number of competing families or clans, as was the case with the Athenian Eupatrids. What these aristocracies had in common was their exclusive hold on power and predominance in their communities, and their disdain for those born outside the circle of aristocratic privilege. Hesiod had already complained in *Works and Days* (perhaps around 700 B.C.E.) about the arrogance, greed, and (as he saw it) injustice of these aristocrats. On the other hand, we get an excellent insight into the mindset and outlook of such aristocrats from the poetry of the Megarian aristocrat Theognis, writing (most likely) in the mid-sixth century, when the power and privileges of the aristocracies were very much on the wane. Prosperous farmers, artisans, and traders who were not in any way dependent on these aristocrats for their livelihoods and well-being naturally began to resent being subordinated to them in the rule of their communities. In expressing that dissatisfaction and doing something about it, they faced a problem: entrenched traditional aristocracies do not give up their power and privilege easily.

In order to bring about a change in the political structure of aristocratic control, this new "middle class" would need to find a way to pool its disparate interests and energies and bring about united action. That was not easy to do, but in many of the more prosperous and, in that sense and all its consequences, advanced Greek communities they found a way to do so. Powerful individual leaders began to arise, partly from within the aristocracies them-

The Ancient Greeks

selves, who united the numerous aspiring groups of the *demos*
("people") behind them. Their aim was, in essence, simply to seize
dominant power for themselves: recall again that in Greek society
being one of the better group was never enough, one wanted to be
the best! But in mobilizing various dissatisfied elements from outside the aristocracy in order to achieve that aim, they necessarily
had to serve to some degree the interests of the groups they had
mobilized; and in order to keep their grip on power once it was
achieved, they had to break the traditional power of the aristocrats.

Some of these powerful leaders were, to all appearances, not
merely power grabbers but genuine reformers. The Greeks invented
a new term to refer to these new, autocratic and usurping rulers:
tyrannos, a non-Greek word in origin (possibly adapted from a
Phoenician term for ruler), which is of course the origin of the English word "tyrant." It should be noted, however, that in early Greece
the term "tyrant" didn't carry the sense of "evil, harsh, unjust ruler"
it carries in English today. The early Greek tyrants were not all, in
effect, tyrannical. Some of them were actually remembered as mild,
just, and popular rulers. The term tyrant was invented originally
simply to refer to an autocratic usurper who did not hold power
according to traditional rules and norms, as opposed to a traditional
basileus ("king"), who did so and was thus limited by the traditional rules and customs of his society.

A number of these usurper tyrants, holding virtually unlimited
power in their communities for as long as their dominance lasted,
became famous and were long remembered in Greek historical
memory and legend. Among the most notable and successful were
Pheidon of Argos, reputedly the earliest of the tyrants (ca. 680-660);
Kypselos and his son Periandros at Corinth, who ruled altogether
about sixty years from around 650 until around 590; Kleisthenes of
Sikyon, who ruled for several decades in the early sixth century,
until at least 570; Theagenes of Megara and Thrasyboulos of Miletos, who both held power, so far as we can tell, in the second half
of the seventh century; Pittakos of Mytilene, who is said to have

held power for ten years before (uniquely) abdicating and returning to private life, most probably in the early sixth century; Polykrates of Samos, well-known to readers of Herodotos as a remarkable, powerful, and flashy ruler in the 530s and 520s; and Peisistratos and his sons at Athens, who held power from 548/7 until their ouster in 510. Many other tyrants are known of from this period of the seventh and sixth centuries, which is sometimes referred to as the "Age of Tyrants" after these characteristic despots. Of most of them, however, we know at best an anecdote or two, and many of them are no more to us than names. Historians have spilled much ink over the question of why so many tyrannies arose in just this period of four or five generations, and what the meaning or purpose of these tyrannies was. Despite the long-standing controversies, it seems to me that the matter is really very straightforward.

The profound economic, social, and cultural changes happening in the developing and urbanizing communities of Greece under the impact of contact with the wider Mediterranean and, especially, Near Eastern world were bound to have an effect on the political structures of the Greek communities. The old ways of doing things, the old elites with their traditional codes and outlooks could not continue to dominate their communities unchanged. But, as entrenched elites naturally tend to be, they were opposed to political change, which they felt could only come at their expense. And they were certainly right to fear that, since the rising new middle elements of society could not gain a substantial share in political power except at the expense of traditional aristocratic power.

It was the opposition of these entrenched elites to political change that made it necessary for those determined to force change to coalesce around powerful leaders who, by seizing supreme autocratic power, could break the hold of the entrenched elites and bring about the changes that were needed. The process differed from place to place, and by no means all of the tyrants even attempted to bring about reforms; but everywhere, even where tyrants arose largely out of aristocratic infighting as at Mytilene,

This is thought to be a bust of Herodotos of Halicarnassus, the author of The Histories.

the effect was to weaken the traditional aristocracies considerably. For whatever their personal aims and ambitions might be, the tyrants necessarily found themselves threatened by the traditional aristocrats who opposed their autocratic power, and so found it necessary to weaken the aristocrats in order to try to cling to power.

Herodotos tells a famous story concerning this. The Corinthian tyrant Periandros, finding his grip on power too weak for his comfort, sent an envoy to his friend the tyrant Thrasyboulos of Miletos to seek his advice as to how best to strengthen his grip on power. Thrasyboulos, rather than answering the envoy's question, took him for a stroll outside the city of Miletos. During this walk, Thrasyboulos questioned the envoy closely about conditions at Corinth and, to the envoy's amazement, used his walking stick to slash the tops off the tallest stalks of grain as they passed through the wheat fields. Finally they returned to Miletos, and Thrasyboulos sent Periandros's envoy back home to Corinth without offering any verbal advice. However, when Periandros heard a detailed account of Thrasyboulos's behavior from his envoy, he at once grasped the significance of the Milesian tyrant's behavior: by cutting off all the tallest stalks of grain, Thrasyboulos was advising Periandros to remove all the most prominent—in the sense of wealthiest and most influential—men in Corinth, since these were the men who might threaten his power. And this is in fact what not only Periandros and Thrasyboulos but most tyrants did. Aristocrats and other prominent men were exiled or killed, and much, or at times all, of their property was confiscated and either distributed among the tyrants' backers—usually poorer men—or used for other purposes.

Hindsight shows that the changes happening in the Greek world were trending towards a growth in the numbers, relative wealth, and political importance of what I have called, for want of a better term, the new "middle class" of independent farmers, artisans, and traders, though there was also a significant growth of newly rich men. Both the new rich and the "middle class" resented the aristocrats' exclusive hold on political power and sought to break it.

In addition, there was a process of state formation: the small, loosely knit, and often rather dispersed communities of earlier times were giving way to bigger, more tightly structured, urbanized communities that began to establish an idea of citizenship and systems of governance such that we can begin to call these communities "states." The process was uneven and didn't really take hold in central and northern Greece, but in the more advanced regions of southern and eastern Greece, and in the colonies, as urbanization and economic growth created *poleis* (cities), these political changes turned these cities into city-states. Here again the entrenched aristocracies, with their resistance to central authority and their insistence on the more or less independent power of their own *oikoi* (families, estates), were in the way. Both in order to facilitate the further development of the middle class and of new elites, and in order to allow the processes of centralization, unification, and elaboration of governing structures, the old aristocracies had to be weakened. And this is the role the tyrants played, whether as deliberate reformers who had some grasp of what was happening, or more accidentally as simple power-grabbers who helped bring about necessary change by accident. Of course, once the aristocracy was weakened and/or important reforms had been enacted, the rising middle class and new elites saw no further need for the tyrants; and it was rare, as a result, for tyrannical rule to last in any community for more than a few decades at most before being overthrown.

The Greece that emerged from the "Age of Tyrants" was no longer a Greece of poor, scattered, disunited communities dominated by entrenched aristocracies, but instead—at any rate in the more advanced regions just mentioned—a land of tightly unified city-states in which political participation (citizenship) had spread down the social scale to a broad middle segment of thousands of farmers and tradesmen. These city-state Greeks were proud of their citizenship, highly patriotic to and active participants in the governing processes of their city-states. They had developed codes of written laws, available for all literate citizens to read—and literacy had come to be a prized attainment for any self-respecting citizen, who did not want others to be able to look down on him. They had developed defined governing systems: annual magistrates to take care of the day to day business of the community, state councils to oversee the magistrates and make sure they didn't overstep their authority, and public meetings at which the mass of citizens could voice their concerns and opinions. They had developed a new system of warfare, based on self-equipped and self-motivated citizen militias. And since these militias and their style of warfare were crucial both in giving the middle classes the standing and power to take and hold their political role in the city-states, and in providing the disciplined and motivated force needed to stand up to the power of the Persian Empire, we should take a closer look at the new style of warfare and how it came about.

THE NEW HOPLITE WARFARE

The style of warfare depicted in the military epics of Homer, and the style of warfare described in considerable detail by the fifth century historians Herodotos and (especially) Thucydides, are fundamentally different, and the differences reflect key economic, social, and political changes. Homeric warfare is an aristocratic style of warfare. Though the *Iliad* depicts massed armies of Greeks and Trojans fighting each other in pitched battle, it is made clear that the majority of the soldiers in these armies were of little real importance. A clear distinction is made between the "front fighters" and the supporting mass of soldiers, and it's evident that the basis of the distinction is equipment. The "front fighter" wore a bronze helmet, cuirass, and greaves (shin protectors), and carried a large wooden shield covered with layers of ox-hide. This defensive equipment enabled him to stand in the front of battle and engage enemy warriors with confidence: the weapon of choice was a stout spear that could be used for either thrusting or throwing, though the sword was an important back-up weapon. In addition, the leading warriors owned chariots pulled by teams of two or four horses, on which they rode to and from battle and moved about the field of battle from one point of confrontation to another, in a way notably similar to the British chariotry depicted in books 4 and 5 of Caesar's *Gallic War*.

The expense of all of this equipment was great: the value of a plain panoply of armor is estimated as the worth of nine oxen (*Iliad* 6.234-236), meaning that only wealthy men could afford to equip themselves with this armor. And horse-breeding was throughout Greek history a hobby only the very richest could afford. The majority of soldiers, much more lightly armored and equipped, stood back and supported their "front fighting" aristocratic leaders with an array of missile weapons—bows and arrows, slings, stones—and pressed forward to offer close support only when the aristocrats had killed or driven off enemy "front fighters" and were driving back the enemy ranks.

Battles, under these circumstances, were loose, free-flowing, sporadic affairs. There was little in the way of order or discipline in the armies. Aristocratic "front fighters" singled each other out across "no man's land" and engaged in duels, while their entourages of companions and ordinary soldiers supported them with missiles and shouts. Soldiers surged to and fro as the fortunes of battle swayed. At times groups of warriors would pull out of the ranks for a rest; at other times they would mass closely in support of some leader engaged in a duel or trying to strip the equipment from a foe he had killed. Aristocrats moved freely about the field of battle, looking for suitable opponents, pulling out of a dangerous-looking confrontation, or throwing themselves into some melee that looked promising. Victory and defeat were effectively determined by the death or retreat of key leaders, the rest of the soldiers streaming forward or in retreat according to the success or failure of their leaders.

Battle was, in essence, a way for the aristocratic leaders to affirm their status in their communities, to build up their honor, and to prove their "bestness" (*aristeia*) at the expense of enemy leaders or in comparison to allied champions. Needless to say, societies conducting war in this manner could not have hoped to stand up to the huge, highly organized, and well-equipped and disciplined armies of an empire like that of the Persians. And it is worth noting that those parts of Greece that did not develop city-states and all the accompanying political and military changes—northern and central Greece, that is, where communities remained loosely organized and aristocratically dominated—surrendered to the Persians without a fight when the great invasion came.

In southern and eastern Greece, however, the economic and social changes of the seventh century led to a fundamentally different type of warfare. Three crucial things made the changes possible: the development of a new weaponry that was well suited to a more disciplined and collective style of warfare; the trade in metals from east and west that made metal goods both much more abundantly available in Greece, and consequently significantly cheaper to acquire; and the emergence of the prosperous middle class who were well-to-do enough to afford military equipment and had enough of a stake in society to be willing to lay their lives on the line for the common good. Although the bronze cuirass or corslet certainly developed and grew cheaper in this period of the seventh century, the crucial changes in equipment were the emergence of new shields, helmets, and spears.

Soon after 700 the "Argive shield"—so-called perhaps because it was invented at Argos—began to spread as the favored shield of Greek warriors. Whereas the Homeric ox-hide shield had been held by a central grip and a neck-strap and had offered only limited protection against strong spear thrusts, the new shield was heavier and stronger and held by a new type of grip. The Argive shield was made of a solid core of wood heavily reinforced with bronze: at the very least a bronze rim and a central boss, but most often a full facing of bronze. Perfectly round and approximately one meter in diameter, this wood and metal shield was too heavy and unwieldy to be manipulated by a central hand-grip, or carried by a neck-strap. Instead it was held by a double grip: in the center of the back face of the shield was a metal arm band (called the *porpax*) through which the left arm was passed up to the elbow, and at the rim of the shield was a hand grip called the *antilabe*. Holding the shield in this double grip, the left arm was fully occupied; but the shield was strong enough to offer excellent protection against all missile weapons and even very strong spear thrusts. The weight was a trial for the left arm even so, but the shield was made very concave in shape so that one could turn the left shoulder into the bowl of the shield and rest the rim, and so carry much of the weight, on one's shoulder. Since the left arm held the shield from its center to its right rim, nearly half of the shield projected out to the warrior's left, uselessly to the shield bearer but offering possible protection to a man standing close to his left. It was this feature that was to encourage Greek warriors to develop a formation (the phalanx) involving thousands of men standing together in neat lines with overlapping shields, as we shall see.

In this same period, after 700, a new type of helmet, the so-called Corinthian helmet, became increasingly popular until it became the standard helmet for Greek heavily armed infantry. This helmet, beaten out of a single sheet of bronze, covered the entire

The Chigi vase, which dates from the seventh century B.C.E., includes among its four friezes the earliest extant depiction of Greek hoplite phalanx.

head from the neck up, including most of the face. Cut-outs created eye holes and left the mouth and nostrils free. A felt cap and/or leather or felt lining was needed to cushion the helmet. When pulled down over the head it offered first rate protection for the whole head against any type of weapon. On the other hand, it limited vision to what was directly in front and muffled one's hearing considerably and thus was normally worn pushed up onto the crown of the head until the moments before battle itself, when it would be pulled down to cover the head and face as virtually the last thing a warrior would do before confronting the enemy. Finally, as opposed to the Homeric spear that, since it could be thrown as well as used for thrusting, must have been relatively light, a long and heavy spear used exclusively for thrusting was adopted. Usually made of cornel wood, the spear was over two meters (seven to eight feet) long. It had a metal head that could be as much as a foot long and a heavy counter-balancing bronze butt spike, designed in part to keep the balance point of the spear near the rear, and in part to enable even a broken spear to be used as a weapon.

Along with these three items, the fully armed Greek heavy

infantryman, or hoplite, wore bronze greaves over his shins, from ankle to knee; a bronze cuirass that covered the entire torso (though after about 550 corslets made of lighter materials became popular, since the shield offered such excellent protection to the torso); and he carried, as his secondary weapon, a short but heavy slashing sword, usually about eighteen inches or so in length. Equipped in this way, with greaves, cuirass, helmet, shield, spear, and sword, the Greek hoplite was carrying some sixty pounds or more of equipment about his person. The body armor and shield severely limited his mobility, making him relatively slow and ponderous; and the helmet greatly reduced his vision and hearing. To compensate for these disabilities, the warrior so equipped was to a great degree invulnerable to harm from a frontal attack. Face to face with a more lightly equipped warrior, he could ward off the enemy's blows with ease, catching them on his shield or helmet, and a thrust from his heavy spear—either over arm or under arm—was likely to do considerable damage.

It's possible that this panoply, which we first find in its complete form shortly after 700, was developed for aristocratic warriors and their duels: two champions facing each other in this armor could certainly have dueled very satisfactorily, and often with little real threat to the life of either. However, it must soon have become clear that a lightly armed man facing such a single hoplite alone could easily skip around him, past his shield and out of his range of vision, and then take him down from the side or rear by a blow of knife or other weapon to the neck or thighs.

Seen as equipment for individual warriors operating in the Homeric mode, then, the hoplite panoply was of limited usefulness. Such a warrior would need to have a group of companions protecting his flanks and rear in order to survive against more mobile soldiers. Thousands of warriors equipped with this panoply and operating together in a disciplined manner, however, offered an interesting opportunity. Before that opportunity could be realized, it was necessary for thousands of men in at least one Greek state to acquire this panoply. That was made possible by the lower cost of metal goods resulting from the developments of Greek trading networks and Greek economic specialization, in this case, in metal working; and by the growth of the middle class of prosperous small farmers and tradesmen, men who had enough surplus wealth to afford to equip themselves. Because Greek warriors did have to equip themselves: no Greek state and no Greek leader had the resources to equip thousands of warriors at its or his expense. However, since martial status and martial equipment were closely linked, and since higher martial status and prowess conferred higher honor and status in the community, the small farmers and tradesmen who could afford to do so did indeed equip themselves with the new armor and weaponry. Equipped with the best military gear, these men could and did begin to demand a greater voice in the political life of their communities, and it has plausibly been suggested that it was men newly outfitted with the hoplite panoply who formed a crucial element backing the rise of at least some of the early tyrants. In the longer term, one can legitimately argue that in the developing Greek city-states citizenship and ownership of weaponry went hand-in-hand.

In military terms, however, thousands of men with hoplite armor still constituted an undisciplined mass, and an unwieldy mass at that, unless one could find a tactical organization and sense of discipline that could create order and make the warriors more effective. We don't know exactly how this happened, and the process of its adoption will have been slow and uneven, but a new tactical order was created that turned these Greek hoplites into a highly disciplined and effective unit on the field of battle: the so-called phalanx formation. A hoplite phalanx in its fully developed form, as we see it in the battles described by Herodotos and Thucydides, was a rectangular mass of soldiers formed of precise lines and files of men. Since such a formation appears to be depicted on a painted Corinthian vase of the mid-seventh century, known as the Chigi Vase, we can presume that this tactical formation was invented a little before about 650 B.C.E. The keys to the formation were the overlapping left portion of the Argive shield, which provided cover to a man standing to the shield bearer's left, and the nature of the Greek terrain.

When thousands of men were formed up in neat lines one behind the other, so that the men in successive lines stood precisely behind a man in the line in front—forming files of men one behind the other as well as lines of men next to each other—the result was an organized unit of soldiers that presented an unbroken shield wall to an enemy in front, since each man in the front line was protected not only by his own shield but also, on his right side, by the projecting portion of the shield of the man to his right. The shields, and the other body armor, and the successive lines of men ready to step forward and fill any gap in the front line, made a phalanx of hoplites extremely hard to beat so long as its flanks could not be turned and its rear was secure. And since the Greek terrain consists of rather small and narrow plains divided from each other by mountain barriers and sea inlets, and cut by ravines, it was fairly easy to draw up a phalanx, whatever its size, in a place where it both had flat terrain to fight on, and natural barriers on either side protecting its vulnerable flanks.

A modern reconstruction of what a Greek phalanx would have looked like in action.

Several thousand men equipped as hoplites and drawn up in a phalanx could make a stand almost anywhere in Greece, by choosing the right bit of terrain; and so long as they held firm they were virtually unbeatable except by another better disciplined hoplite phalanx. This kind of warfare did not provide any scope for the individual heroics and derring-do of Homeric warfare. It was based instead on communal solidarity, on iron discipline, and on the dogged courage of standing one's ground under pressure, rather than the dashing courage of the dueling champion. This was an intrinsically egalitarian form of warfare, since every hoplite warrior was of roughly equal value, and each had the same task: to maintain his position in his line and file so as to keep the formation intact. It was ideally suited to the middle class of independently well-to-do Greeks of the city-states: it expressed perfectly their sense of belonging and commitment to their community and all it represented, and their willingness as stakeholders in their communities to make a stand in defense of the *polis*. When two such phalanxes met in battle, the fight was essentially a shoving match as the two front lines met and pressed their shields against each other and literally tried to push the enemy backwards. Thrusts of spears over or under the enemy's shield were certainly attempted but were clearly of limited effectiveness since we know that the casualties in most hoplite battles were light: the warriors were just too well protected to be vulnerable. On the other hand, if a hoplite phalanx on the right terrain confronted a lighter equipped force, it was liable simply to steamroll over and through that lighter force; and cavalry charges were useless against a hoplite phalanx so long as the charge came from in front (not from the side) and so long as the phalanx stood its ground. Confronted by the vast unbroken shield wall, the horses would simply balk and refuse to charge home against an obstacle they could see no way over or through.

It's clear that the phalanx formation must have been invented and introduced by some reformer. Forming a disciplined unit of precise lines and files and marching forward to fight in such a formation is a highly artificial activity. Men do not naturally align themselves in precise lines, or form disciplined ranks, as a glance at any crowd will show. Someone had to impose this order, just as every such artificial innovation in military tactics through history has been the work of a reformer: for example, the cohort formation in Roman warfare was imposed by Caius Marius and the drill and formations of modern warfare were invented and imposed in the late sixteenth and early seventeenth centuries by generals such as Maurice of Nassau and Gustavus Adolphus. In fourth century B.C.E. Greece we know that the new pike phalanx of the Macedonians was invented and imposed by King Philip II. There must have been an equally remarkable and inventive military reformer behind the first hoplite phalanx in Greek history, but we don't know who it was, nor when and where he established this remarkably successful military system. At a guess, it may have been one of the early tyrants who was responsible, perhaps Pheidon of Argos or Kypselos of Corinth, since two of the key pieces of hoplite equipment—the shield and the helmet—are associated with those cities.

Whoever first created the hoplite phalanx, it was an outstanding success, and by the middle of the sixth century it was the dominant military formation in Greek warfare and remained so for two centuries until the new military system of the great Macedonian kings Philip II and Alexander the Great. Besides its rapidly spreading popularity and success in Greek warfare itself, the excellence of the hoplite system of warfare is attested to by the popularity of Greek hoplites as mercenaries outside of Greece. The Egyptian Pharaohs Necho II and Psamtik II in the late seventh and early sixth centuries already employed numerous Greek hoplites in their armies, and by the mid-sixth century the Pharaoh Amasis reputedly relied on up to 30,000 Greek hoplites as the core of his army. The great Babylonian ruler Nebuchadnezzar is also known to have employed Greek mercenaries during his Palestinian campaigns in the 580s.

By the middle of the sixth century, then, when Persian power began its rise to dominance in the Middle and Near East, southern and eastern Greece were home to dozens of independent and mutually competitive city-states, which were flourishing politically, economically, militarily, and culturally. Politically, these city-states were built on a numerous middle class of citizens who enjoyed a limited but important degree of political participation in their own governance: magistrates and state councils continued to be drawn from the traditional aristocracies, though with increasing participation of newly wealthy families, but they were in some manner appointed by and responsible to the general citizenry, who voiced their concerns and opinions in more-or-less regular public meetings.

Economically, the Greeks had advanced beyond all recognition from their pastoralist and subsistence farming beginnings in the ninth and early eighth centuries. Specialized cash crop farming made agriculture far more productive and profitable, exchange mechanisms and trading networks enable the Greeks to dispose of their cash crops with ease and profit and to supply their various wants from imported goods purchased with the proceeds of their cash crops. Greek shippers and merchants plied the Mediterranean and Black Sea basins, rivaling and in some regions and respects supplanting the Phoenicians as the great middle men in east-west and north-south trade in these seas, and fueling continuing economic growth. And a prosperous and steadily more numerous class of artisans produced goods in metal, ceramic, wood, and leather. These goods not only satisfied a growing appetite for such products among the increasingly large and well-to-do population of the Greek lands themselves, but also were becoming more and more popular with the non-Greek peoples to east and west, north and south, thanks to the increasing skill of Greek artisans and quality of their products. Militarily, as we have just seen, the Greek middle class had formed the backbone of a new, egalitarian, citizen militia army that was—in its equipment, tactical formation, and discipline—of the highest quality; and Greek soldiers were increasingly sought after as mercenaries, as a result. Their status as self-equipped, heavily armed citizen militia soldiers was crucial to the political participation of these middle class Greeks in their own city-states.

CULTURAL DEVELOPMENTS

We have yet to look, however, at the cultural development of the Greeks, though we began this overview of who the Greeks were by considering two cultural giants: Homer and Hesiod. Though many Greek poets continued writing epic poetry after Hesiod, little of it survives, and the general assessment of its literary value has, with the exception of a few of the so-called "Homeric Hymns," been damning. Greek poetic culture moved away from epic composition to the creation of shorter lyric poetry. It's worth emphasizing that the word "lyric" must be understood literally: the poems written in this era (the seventh and sixth centuries) were actual song lyrics, intended to be sung to the accompaniment of a lyre (a stringed instrument, a sort of ancient guitar) or of a wind instrument called a *diaulos* which, though it's often translated as "flute," was actually a sort of double piped instrument, as if a man were playing two recorders or penny whistles at the same time. The poets of this era can be compared, then, not so much to modern literary poets such as T.S. Eliot or Allen Ginsberg but rather to songwriters such as Bob Dylan or Joni Mitchell. The music written by these early Greek poets has not, alas, survived; but we must always remember that their poetry was sung, and that their fame was spread around the Greek world by musical performances, not by the reading of their poems from the page.

The earliest of these new singer/poets whose name and fame has survived was Archilochos of Paros, who lived in the first half of the seventh century and wrote songs about his experiences in love, friendship, and warfare from a decidedly individual and at times controversial point of view. That isn't to say that his surviving poems are literally autobiographical, any more than a modern songwriter's songs are always and entirely autobiographical. But his songs reflected his own ideas and experience of life and the world, and we can understand from them the kind of life Archilochos lived, though not necessarily the actual events and experiences of his life.

After Archilochos, many other songwriters followed his example of writing songs reflecting their ideas, opinions, and experiences, and found enthusiastic audiences for their work. Terpandros and Arion of Lesbos became famed for their innovations in music, but by general consent the greatest of the new poets were Sappho and Alkaios of Mytilene on Lesbos, both active in the early sixth century; Alkman of Sparta in the second half of the seventh century; Stesichoros of Himera in Sicily, a younger contemporary of Alkman most probably; Mimnermos of Kolophon and Hipponax of Ephesos, active seemingly in the later seventh and early sixth centuries; Ibykos of Rhegion and Anakreon of Teos, who wrote in the second half of the sixth century; and Simonides of Keos and Pindar of Thebes, poets of the late sixth and early fifth centuries. Many other names could be brought up—Tyrtaios, Solon, Theognis, Bacchylides, and many more—but the point is that there was a flourishing culture of popular songwriters whose songs spread rapidly around the Greek world, performed at public festivals and private parties, giving evidence of a society that appreciated strong individualism and an often critical look at received ideas and customs.

For example, both Archilochos and Alkaios flouted conventions by proclaiming that they had thrown away their shields in battle, in order to make good their escape when their forces were defeated. The standard view insisted that it was a shame and a disgrace to lose one's shield, that the true warrior stood his ground and kept his shield, facing the enemy, and preferring death to flight and disgrace. Archilochos brazenly adopted an alternative view:

Some Saian guy enjoys my shield, for under a bush,
unwilling, I left it behind, though it was flawless.
But I saved myself. What do I care about that shield?
To heck with it! I can buy one again that's no worse.

The point, clearly, is that you only get one life, and to throw it away over a point of honor is silly. Greek audiences enjoyed and sang Archilochos's song, and appreciated the point he was making; but they didn't change their standard view that it was a shame to lose one's shield. It's a rare culture that is willing, even eager, to hear and appreciate criticisms of its cherished values and beliefs, especially from individuals who held no post of power or respect and claimed no authority other than their own personal opinions. Yet this is what many of the popular song writers of this era offered.

Perhaps even more startling than a case such as that of Archilochos and Alkaios undermining the traditional notion of military honor, since these were after all men—and in the case of Alkaios at least, an aristocrat—is the poet Sappho. For Sappho, remarkably, was a woman, whose voice was given a hearing in spite of the fundamentally patriarchal nature of her society. Sappho too questioned the prevailing martial view of honor and beauty. In a poem about love, she claimed that those who thought that the most beautiful sight to behold was a band of soldiers marching, or a squadron of cavalry, or ships at sea, or indeed all the war-chariots of Lydia, were wrong: the most beautiful sight is the face of the woman one loves, and she illustrates this by referring to the famed and war-causing beauty of Helen of Troy. Now obviously the people who regarded infantry or cavalry, warships or chariots, as the most beautiful sight were the men of her time, Greek upper- and middle-class men imbued with the martial ethos of Homer. Sappho not only dares to take them on and refute their view, but she disproves their ideas from their own revered mythic tradition: for Homer of course celebrated the very war that Helen's fabled beauty had brought about.

These archaic songwriters, then, composed their songs about everyday matters—love affairs, quarrels, parties, voyages, political in-fighting, soldiering—and were avidly listened to, becoming famous in their own days, and revered throughout subsequent Greek history. And perhaps the most remarkable thing about them is that they spoke entirely in their own voices and on their own authority. Hesiod had already dared to criticize the aristocracy of his day, and to voice his own ideas and views, but he claimed the authority of the Muses, god-desses of song, who had taught him how and what to sing. In Israel, prophets and religious reformers famously dared to criticize the rulers and policies of their day, but they claimed to be uttering not their own ideas, but the word of God. The archaic lyricists of Greece by and large made no such claim: they presented themselves to the audience as they were, Greek men and women (besides Sappho, there were Ko-rinna and Praxilla, for example) just like their listeners, worthy of a hearing simply for what they had to say as members of a free society in which the voice of the individual had a right to speak up.

The songs of these highly individualistic poets were an integral component of the popular culture of the wealthier element of Greek society. For well-to-do Greeks liked to get together when they could, groups of friends and relatives, to dine together and then enjoy a convivial evening of drinking wine and entertainment: the so-called *symposion*, literally "drinking together." The entertain-ment at these parties, which were a crucial part of Greek social life—filling the same role as going out to a restaurant, and then to a movie or concert or play or party in modern social life—might at times be provided by professional entertainers. Dancers, musicians, jugglers and acrobats, and the like were certainly brought in by wealthy patrons to entertain their guests at *symposia*. But almost al-ways, and often exclusively, the guests were expected to entertain each other, with a story, or a discussion of the latest political events or ideas, or with songs.

Ambitious and talented symposiasts might have a go at com-posing a song of their own to perform at a party, but more often (inevitably) it was the popular songs of the day that were sung. A guest might, when the lyre was passed to him, strike up a song by Archilochos or Anakreon, Sappho or Simonides, and so these songs became an integral part of Greek culture and the Greek consciousness. City-state Greeks, especially the upper class among them, traveled frequently to trade, to attend festivals, or simply to visit "guest-friends" (*xenoi*) in other communities, and they brought the latest songs and the names of the latest poets with them. And the poet/songwriters themselves traveled, at times widely: Arion held a famously successful concert tour of the colonies in Italy and Sicily, for example, as Herodotos tells us in a well-known story; Ibykos and Anakreon moved from community to community seeking patronage; Simonides and Pindar were seen everywhere in Greece plying their song-writing trade.

Besides essentially private performances, many songs were composed and performed at public events. Sappho was particularly famed for her wedding songs, performed by choruses of maidens or youths at weddings throughout Greece. Pindar and Simonides wrote choral songs to be performed by choirs of young men to praise athletic victors who had achieved fame by winning one or other of the events at the Olympic games (or Pythian games at Delphi, or Isthmian or Nemean games). Above all, there were the regularly recurring religious festivals, spaced throughout the Greek year, at which choruses of young men (or at times young women) sang and danced in honor of the gods. Alkman and Stesichoros were particularly famed for their choral songs written for such festivals. And these more grandiose choral songs shared the same characteristics of individualism and interest in everyday life as the personal lyrics: in one of Alkman's famous "Maiden Songs," for example, the girls of the chorus sing not only of mythical tales to honor the gods, but also of the gossip of their everyday lives—which girl is the most beautiful, who is in love with whom, and so on.

The ultimate expression of characteristic Greek individualism came in the sixth century, with the emergence of rational philosophizing. Beginning with Thales of Miletos in the 580s, a string of Greek thinkers, many of them from the cities of Ionia in eastern Greece (along the coast of Asia Minor), dared to question the traditional ideas of how the world was created and of what it was composed; of what life is about, and what god or the gods are like. Because so many of them were from Ionia, these philosophers are often referred to as the Ionian rationalists—a better term than the unhelpful "pre-Socratic philosophers" that's also in use, since it does express a key fact about them: their essential rationalism. These men were not satisfied with the traditional religious and mythic explanations for the way the world worked. Rather than appealing to the authority of god or the gods, they wanted to explain and understand the world on their own terms, through the use of their own reason. Thales observed that matter has three basic forms—solid, liquid, and gaseous; or as he put it, earth, water, and air—and theorized that the middle form, liquid, must be the most essential. Consequently, he also argued that all life must have its origins in water, that is in the sea, and that humans must have come originally from the sea. One of his pupils, Anaximandros, gathered data about the shape of the world, and on the basis of it produced the first known map of the world, which he engraved on a sheet of bronze.

In the later sixth century, Xenophanes of Kolophon dared to theorize about the gods, arguing that it was irrational for the Greeks to worship gods who looked and acted just like humans. Such anthropomorphism was absurd, he declared, and he suggested that if horses and cows could think and had hands to make statues, they would conceive of gods who looked just like horses and cows. Xenophanes argued instead for a perfect god, who as the epitome of perfection must be singular, one god, since the singular is more perfect than the plural. This perfect one god must be utterly unlike imperfect humans. Since corporeal forms are subject to change and decay, god (being perfect) could have no corporeal form, but must be pure mind, the essence of pure reason. This conception of god was, of course, to have a long subsequent history in Western and Near Eastern religion: Xenophanes stands at the beginning of monotheistic theology, and his ideas about god were borrowed—though mostly without any acknowledgment to be sure—by all three of the great monotheistic traditions of the West and Near East, Judaism, Christianity, and Islam, to name them in chronological order. Unlike the prophets and theologians of those religions, however, Xenophanes dared to present these ideas as the fruit of his own human reasoning: he claimed no divine mandate for his ideas, he did not claim to be the "mouthpiece of god."

At the end of the sixth century and beginning of the fifth, Herakleitos of Ephesos conceived of the principle of relativism. He expressed his views in brief gnomic remarks that he wrote down into a book, which he reputedly dedicated in the Temple of Artemis at Ephesos. Herakleitos observed that there is no ultimate reality that we can know of, because all things that we observe are constantly changing, constantly in flux: all things flow (*panta rhei*), as he phrased it. Change is therefore an essential feature of the world, of our reality: one cannot step into the same river twice, as he put it. And every person's reality is slightly different than every other person's, because all persons perceive reality from their own unique point of view. How one conceives of a thing, and therefore too what one names it, what one considers it to be, is dependent on one's position in relation to it: the way up, and the way down, are one and the same, in Herakleitos's words. Reality is therefore a relative, not an absolute; reality is change, not constant; humans cannot truly know reality, they can only know what they themselves perceive to be reality.

The high culture of Greece, literary and intellectual, was treading new paths then, impelled by the competitive spirit and individualism that were so characteristic of the Greeks. At the same time the Greeks were producing monumental stone temples of remarkable grace and sense of proportion, as well as size and impressiveness: the Temple of Artemis at Ephesos that came to be regarded as one of the wonders of the ancient world; the Temple of Hera on Samos, the Temple of Apollo at Didyma, and numerous other temples in mainland Greece and the western colonies.

The Greeks were creating statues of men and women that were becoming more and more anatomically correct, in their pursuit of a depiction of the physical ideals of manhood and young femininity. They produced paintings of a unique psychological sensitivity: we mostly have remaining to us the paintings on luxury vases to give us a sense of what Greek painting was capable of, but in the art of a master such as the famous Exekias one can see that our loss, in having virtually no larger scale Greek painting from this era, is a great one. Yet one Greek state stood outside all of this cultural effervescence in the sixthth century, and turned its back on economic, social, and political developments too; yet did so without dropping out of the mainstream of Greek life, instead making itself into one of the central bastions of Greekness. I refer, of course, to the Spartans, and no account of the ancient Greeks as they were on the eve of the Persian wars is complete without a description of this remarkable state and its history.

THE SPARTANS

In the eighth and seventh centuries, the Spartans were not so very different from the other developing Greek communities. The town of Sparta was created, probably around the beginning of the eighth century, when four villages on the east bank of the Eurotas river coalesced into a single community. One very unusual feature of Sparta may be explained by this origin: the Spartans throughout their history had a dual kingship, with two royal families—the Agiads and Eurypontids—each providing a king at any given time. Most likely, these were the dominant families of two of the villages that came together to make Sparta. From their position on some bluffs overlooking the Eurotas valley, the Spartans looked out over the two best agricultural plains of the region of Lakedaimon, the southeast corner of the Peloponnesos. From this position they were able to dominate and take control of these plains, and possessing them made the Spartans the biggest and most populous community in Lakedaimon. As a result, by the third quarter of the eighth century the Spartans had managed to unite and dominate all of Lakedaimon.

In uniting this region, the Spartans imposed on the rest of the Lakedaimonians—except for the village of Amyklai a few miles south of Sparta proper—one of two subordinate statuses. Free inhabitants of most other substantial towns and villages were left free, but made politically dependent on the Spartans, having no say in the governing of the *polis* of the Lakedaimonians, as the Spartans called their state. These free but politically subservient Lakedaimonians were called *perioikoi*, which means "those living round about"—meaning round about Sparta itself, the perspective always being from Sparta. The country people of Lakedaimon, and a few less favored towns, were reduced to a slave-like condition similar to that of medieval serfs: they were known as Helots. The Helots maintained a normal family life and lived in their own small communities but belonged to the Spartan masters who owned the land they farmed, and they were obliged to pay half of their produce to their Spartan masters, as well as perform other chores for them.

Such slave-like statuses and populations were not that unusual in early Greece, it should be noted. In Krete there were serf-like peoples called the *Klarotai*; Argos had an unfree population group called the *Gymnetes* (literally "naked ones"); and in Thessaly we hear of a serf population called the *Penestai*, for example. What came to be unusual at Sparta was the persistence and brutality of the serf-like status of the Helots and the degree of brutality to which they were subjected.

Although by uniting all of Lakedaimon in this way the Spartans had already created one of the larger states in Greece, they were not satisfied. In the last quarter of the eighth century, the Spartans began to invade and attempt to subordinate the neighboring region of the Peloponnesos to their west: Messenia. The Messenians controlled some of the better farmland in Greece, and with some of the highest annual rainfall in Greece (since rain-bearing winds in

Greece come mostly from the west), they had very favorable conditions for agriculture. Over the course of about twenty years of fighting, according to the Spartan poet Tyrtaios who lived in the mid-seventh century, the Spartans succeeded in gaining control of most of Messenia and reducing the bulk of Messenia's inhabitants to the status of Helots. These Messenian Helots, like their Lakedaimonian counterparts, did not own their own land and had to pay over to Spartan masters half of everything they produced, as Tyrtaios states it. After some obscure infighting at Sparta—in the course of which a group of Spartans were sent away to found the colony of Tarentum in southern Italy a little before 700—it seems that the bulk of the Messenian land was fairly evenly distributed among the free Spartans, each of whom thereby became a landowner who did not need to work for a living, having an ample income from the labors of his Messenian Helots.

The bitterness of the Messenians, reduced to this slave-like status of subservience and exploited by their Spartan masters, can be imagined. For a time, the Spartans lived very comfortably under this arrangement. They participated fully in the culture of the Greeks: Lakonian (that is, Spartan) pottery and bronze wares were widely prized in Greece and even the wider Mediterranean—though these wares were likely produced by *perioikoi* rather than Spartans proper. Two of the notable early poets, Alkman and Tyrtaios, were Spartans; and in Alkman's poetry we see a grace, a playfulness, a sense of the joy of life that were no longer to be found in the Sparta of the late sixth and fifth centuries.

In addition, the Spartans created, for themselves at any rate, a political system that was at the cutting edge of Greek political development in the first half of the seventh century. The exclusive hold on power and privilege of the traditional aristocracy was broken without ever having recourse to a tyrant. The aristocratic families did apparently retain the privilege of providing the members of the state council, the *gerousia* ("elders"), so called because the minimum age for membership was sixty. All the same, the members of the *gerousia*—except the two kings who were members *ex officio*—were elected by the ordinary Spartans from among those eligible; once elected, membership was for life. The *gerousia* seems to have directed Spartan policy and functioned as a kind of supreme court. But supreme authority in the Spartan state resided with an assembly of all Spartan citizens, who met at regular intervals and voted yea or nay to proposals presented to them by the *gerousia*. This was in its day a remarkably advanced system of participatory citizen governance, so far as it went—that is, among the Spartans proper, or Spartiates as the in-group of full citizens came to call themselves.

Around the third quarter of the seventh century, however, the Spartans went through a grave crisis that led to profound changes in their society, by which they transformed themselves into the dour militaristic people known from our fifth century sources and cut themselves off completely from all further cultural, economic, and political developments in the Greek world. This crisis was a great rebellion by the Messenian Helots in which the Messenians came very close to successfully reasserting their independence. The poet Tyrtaios, who lived through this rebellion, suggests that there may have been some defeatists at Sparta ready to relinquish control over Messenia, but Tyrtaios urged his fellow Spartans not to give in but to hold on to what their grandfathers had gained. In the end, the Spartans won and resubjected all of Messenia to their control.

In the aftermath of this rebellion that had so nearly proved successful, the Spartans reformed their way of life with one goal in mind: to make themselves into supreme warriors so that they could at all times keep the Helots in subjection, and thereby keep themselves free from the need for physical labor. To those in the modern era who still admire the Spartans, as many people have throughout history, it's worth emphasizing again what the "glorious" Spartan way of life was based on: ruthless exploitation of a conquered subordinate class and the avoidance of the need to engage in productive work. Spartan secrecy, and the successful myth of the lawgiver Lykourgos, who supposedly created the Spartan system at one go back in the mists of pre-history, make it impossible for us today to grasp the process and timing of the Spartans' self-reformation. But we can see the outcome of the process in the depictions of Spartans and the Spartan way of life in writings from the fifth century and later.

Every year the Spartiates elected from among themselves five magistrates called *Ephoroi* (Ephors, or "overseers"), who played a very important role in the reformed Spartan system. Each year, they presided at two religious ceremonies: in one, the two kings swore to the Ephors, as representatives of the Spartiates, that they would rule in accordance with the law, and the Ephors then swore on behalf of the Spartiates that they would maintain the kings in office, with all proper privileges and powers, so long as they upheld what they had sworn. By this, the Ephors were effectively made overseers and judges of the kings. The kings were accompanied by at least two Ephors when engaged in public business, who advised them, and might prosecute them if the kings were thought to have failed to live up to what was required. A number of such prosecutions are known from the fifth and fourth centuries, and a number of kings were actually deposed and exiled as a result.

In the other ceremony, the Ephors, again acting on behalf of the Spartiates, formally declared war on the Helots. Thus throughout its great period in the sixth, fifth, and fourth centuries the Spartan state was formally at war with the majority of its own population: the Helots outnumbered the Spartiates by as much as seven to one, or even more. The point of this annual declaration of war was to turn the Helots, juridically and religiously, into enemy aliens to whom, under the rules of war, anything could be done up to and including infliction of death. The Spartiates were at all times afraid of the possibility of a Helot rebellion and used naked terror and brutality to keep the Helots down.

The Spartiate way of life was exclusively modeled to produce outstanding soldiers who would stand ready, at a moment's notice, to take action against the Helots in defense of the Spartiates' privileges. When a Spartiate baby was born, it was inspected by the "eldest of the tribesmen" for physical soundness. A baby that showed any deformity or obvious weaknesses was taken from its parents and exposed to die on a hillside outside Sparta: the Spartan state would raise only healthy babies who could be expected to grow up to be strong warriors or, if girls, healthy mothers. Once it had passed inspection, the baby was raised by its mother until the age of seven. At that age, all Spartiate boys were removed from their homes and brought to live in barracks where they underwent the *agoge*, the Spartiate training system.

The training of the Spartiate boy instilled hardiness, indifference to cold, pain, and hunger, a rigid discipline, physical fitness and endurance, and familiarity with the weapons, armor, and tactics of the hoplite warrior and phalanx. The training system was brutal in the extreme, and the boys were carefully watched for any sign of weakness or indiscipline. Any such sign could result in the boy being deemed to have failed the *agoge*, in which case he would not be permitted full Spartiate citizenship on reaching adulthood: he would be considered throughout his life a *hypomeion* (lesser). Spartiate boys grew up under a military style of discipline: special officers were placed in charge of the boys and their training; every adult Spartiate was automatically senior to any boy and could give him orders; the older boys were, if no officers or adults were present, in command of the younger boys; and within the age classes of boys, those who did best in the *agoge* were made officers over the rest. Thus, there was always a chain of command, and a Spartiate boy was always under discipline. It's all too easy to imagine the rituals of hazing and bullying that inevitably will have been prevalent in these boys' barracks, and which were tolerated if not encouraged as part of the toughening up process.

The boys were fed only adequately, clothed sparingly, and given a single blanket and the right to cut reeds from the river bank to make bedding. As a result, they were nearly always hungry, often cold, and inevitably uncomfortable. But they were encouraged to supplement their food and so on by stealing whatever they could, with the proviso that they would, if caught, be subject to a severe beating as punishment. The point of this was that, as soldiers, they might often be required to live off the land in enemy territory, foraging for supplies and being killed by the enemy if caught. Thus they were taught as boys to steal and not get caught. At the festival of Artemis Orthia each year, at a temple just outside the town of Sparta, the boys underwent a special ritual of brutality. Cheeses were placed on the altar of the goddess, and the older boys lined up on the path to the altar armed with sticks. The younger boys had to "run the gauntlet" to pick cheeses from the altar. Whichever boy got the most cheeses, and thus absorbed the most punishment, was the winner.

At eighteen, the boys finally graduated from the *agoge* and became Spartiate warriors and citizens—if they were judged to have completed the *agoge* successfully. That judgment was expressed by the older Spartiates in a special way. Every Spartiate was required, in order to hold full citizenship, to be a member of a military dining group, called a *syssition* or *phidition*. Throughout his life, unless he was away on official service or had special leave to deal with some personal business or other, the Spartiate male dined with his mess group. The mess groups cut across the age class system of the *agoge*, tying Spartiates of different ages and generations together, and membership of a mess group was by invitation. A Spartiate youth who failed to be invited into a mess group was thereby adjudged to have performed inadequately during the *agoge* and permanently deprived of full Spartiate citizenship. As member of a mess group, the Spartiate was required to provide a set quantity of basic food stuffs for his nightly dinners, and failure to provide the monthly contribution would result in eviction from the mess group and loss of full citizenship.

The Spartan dinners were famously minimalist. The basic meal each evening consisted of a kind of stew, of which the main ingredients were beans, pig's blood, and barley, a rough peasant bread, and wine. There is a story of a man from the famously wealthy and luxurious city of Sybaris in southern Italy visiting Sparta and being invited to dine at a mess group. To his hosts' surprise, the Sybarite ate his dinner quite readily. When asked what he thought of the typical Spartan dinner, however, he replied that he finally now understood a matter that had always puzzled him: namely, why it was that Spartans were not afraid to die! With that to look forward to every evening, who would cling to life?

Graduating from the *agoge* did not mean that the Spartiate youth could leave the barracks and go home, however. From eighteen to thirty the Spartiates formed the "standing army" of the Spartan state, living in barracks under discipline ready to be mobilized for active service at any time. Even when there was no war on—something of a rarity in Spartan history—they would go out on maneuvers in the Lakedaimonian and Messenian countryside, where they were encouraged to harass any Helots who seemed less than fully cowed and subservient. In fact the boys who had stood the *agoge* the best were recruited into an elite unit called the *krypteia* (literally, "the secret band"), whose task was to move quietly around the Messenian countryside, staying under cover and observing the Helots. Unusually strong or assertive Helots were known to disappear mysteriously: it was understood that the *krypteia* had taken them and that they would never be seen again. The terrorizing of the Helots was a constant preoccupation of the Spartiates. Adult Spartiates were encouraged to marry young and start having children; but they could not live with their wives until, at the age of 30, their active service period was over and they could go home and take up a home life: if that was possible for men who had lived in barracks with male companionship since they were seven, and still had to dine with their mess mates every evening.

There was no room in Spartan life for inventive cultural activities, for intellectual activities, or anything of that sort. After

Alkman and Tyrtaios in the seventh century, Sparta never produced another poet that we hear of; Sparta produced no dramatists or philosophers; there were no Spartan historians or architects or sculptors, at any rate, none of great note, none during the era of Spartan dominance in the sixth to early fourth centuries. Culturally, Sparta died when it imposed the *agoge*, and entertainment and cultural life, such as it was, revolved around the "manly" activities of exercise and athletics (at which the Spartans excelled), hunting, and the chanting or singing of old traditional poems and songs, especially by Homer and Tyrtaios. Freedom of speech or thought were not prized at Sparta. Instead what was prized was rigid conformity: the Spartan system had been created, so the legend went, by the great hero Lykourgos and was perfect. No invention or deviation, nothing new, was wanted.

Of course, there was one thing the Spartans were supremely good at, not surprisingly since they spent their lives working to be good at it: hoplite warfare. The Spartan principle with regard to warfare is famous, and famously simple: conquer or die. Reputedly, when a Spartan set off for war, his mother or wife would hand him his shield with the words: come back with this, or on it. The meaning was, come back victorious, and so still carrying your shield; or dead, and so being carried on your shield. A Spartan who failed, who lost and/or ran, should not come back to Sparta at all: no one would receive him or talk to him. In a Greek community of city-states in which the hoplite warriors were citizen militia soldiers who took up arms only when the need arose, the Spartans stood out as professionals surrounded by amateurs, for the Spartans devoted themselves full-time to hoplite training. A famous anecdote illustrates this fact.

In the early fourth century, the Spartan king Agesilaos was commanding an army of Spartans and allies, of which the allies formed the overwhelming majority. Seeing this, the allied leaders complained to Agesilaos that only he was in command and argued that since they, the allies, supplied most of the soldiers, they should have a share in the command, turn and turn about. In answer, Agesilaos called an assembly of the entire army and addressed the troops. He instructed all men who were potters to sit down: many allied soldiers did so. Then Agesilaos gave the same command for all men who were carpenters, and smiths, and so on through the list of ways of making a living. Finally, all of the allies were seated, but the Spartans were still standing: then Agesilaos asked who present were soldiers, and the Spartans sat. Agesilaos turned to the allied leaders and told them that the Spartans didn't provide most of the soldiers in the army; they provided the *only* soldiers in the army, and that was why Spartans always held the command.

From the mid-sixth century on, in fact, for nearly 200 years the Spartans not only enjoyed a reputation for invincibility in warfare; they were never actually beaten in any major battle, until the battle of Leuktra in 371. In a series of campaigns throughout the Peloponnesos, the Spartans defeated one by one and forced to make alliances with Sparta every Peloponnesian city and community except the Argives The alliances were invariably very simple in form: the city or community in question bound itself to have "the same friends and enemies as the Lakedaimonians"; that is, they swore to follow the Spartan lead in foreign policy and warfare. In this way, by the end of the sixth century, the Spartans had established domination over the entire Peloponnesos and could call upon the military forces of every Peloponnesian state when they wished to, to fight alongside them in warfare. There was one exception: the Argives.

Though the Spartans had defeated the Argives in a great battle in mid-century and taken for themselves a substantial slice of Argive territory—the so-called Thyreatis—as spoil, the Spartans did not succeed in forcing the Argives into alliance. Other than that, their control over the Peloponnesos was complete by century's end, and this network of alliances under Spartan domination is referred to by historians as the Peloponnesian League. That's a bit of a misnomer, as there really was no league, just a system for Spartan predominance. The greatest virtue of the system from the Spartans' perspective was that, if the Helots were to rebel, there was no one in the entire Peloponnesos they could look to for help or alliance, since all were already allies of the Spartans. Beyond that, however, the Spartan alliance system was the greatest military structure in the Greek world: through it, the Spartans could easily mobilize 20,000 or more hoplites at need, in addition to the 9,000 Spartiates of this period and thousands of *perioikoi* capable of serving as hoplites.

Around 520 or so, as the power of Persia was spreading in Asia, a new young king came to the throne in the Agiad line at Sparta. His name was Kleomenes, and he proved to be a very remarkable, though in the end controversial, ruler. For some thirty years he was clearly the dominant personality at Sparta. Nearly every story Herodotos has to tell about the Spartans in this period, from 520 to 490, involves Kleomenes, usually in the leading role. We first meet him in 519, when he was apparently engaged in enrolling the Megarians, just outside the Peloponnesos, in Sparta's alliance system. He was approached by envoys from the Plataians in southern Boiotia who, under pressure from the expansionist Thebans, sought alliance with the Spartans as a protection. Instead of taking them as allies, however, Kleomenes, perhaps from Machiavellian motives, advised the Plataians to seek alliance with the Athenians, who were much nearer to Plataia. The Athenians agreed, beginning a centuries-long alliance with the Plataians, but also initiating bitter hostility with the powerful Thebans, which many suspect was Kleomenes' aim. Between 510 and about 506 Kleomenes was deeply involved in the events surrounding the ending of the Peisistratid tyranny at Athens, and the beginning of Athenian democracy; this will be discussed fully in chapter 3. It initiated a period of hostility between the Athenians and the Spartans and, within Sparta, an enmity between Kleomenes and his co-king from the Eurypontid line, Demaratos, an enmity which was to prove fateful. In 499 it was again Kleomenes who met with, and rejected the pleas of, the Ionian leader Aristagoras, when he sought Spartan aid for the Ionian revolt, as we shall see in chapter 4. Attempts to draw the Spartans far from the Peloponnesos and the threat of their Helots were never successful in this era.

Kleomenes' greatest achievement as king of Sparta came in a war against the Argives in 494. Sparta and Argos were old and perennial rivals and enemies. The Spartans had decisively bested the Argives in the middle of the sixth century, and a peace had been patched up after that Spartan victory. But every few decades the Argives would try the fortunes of war against the Spartans again, and in the 490s it was Kleomenes, as the dominant personality at Sparta, who took command against them. Rather than marching overland via the territory of Tegea in Arkadia, or through the Thyreatis, into Argive territory, Kleomenes showed his strategic ingenuity by gathering ships and taking his army to Argive territory by sea, landing on the coast of the Argolid near Nauplion. The men of Argos were taken by surprise and failed to contest Kleomenes' landing; but they brought their full hoplite force down to Nauplion and confronted Kleomenes' Spartan army there. For several days, the two armies drew up for battle every morning at a place called Sepeia, but neither side was willing to take the initiative of advancing against the enemy. After standing to for a few hours in phalanx formation, waiting for the Argives to make a move, Kleomenes would order his men to stand down and go off to camp to take some lunch. After a few days of this, though, he noticed that the Argives, as soon as he ordered his trumpeters to sound the signal for his men to go to lunch, would also stand down and head back to their camp. He took advantage of this by ordering his men that when the trumpeters sounded for lunch, instead of breaking formation they were to charge the Argives. Next day, when the signal for lunch sounded, the Argives lowered their shields and began to turn away, only to see the Spartan phalanx advancing to the attack. That took the Argives by surprise, and panic ensued: the Argives ran and Kleomenes won a crushing victory.

As usually happened in hoplite battles, most of the Argives got away: by dropping their shields, and getting their helmets and (perhaps) greaves off, they made themselves much lighter and more mobile than their still fully equipped enemies and so easily outran them. Hence the association in Greek thought between loss of one's shield and defeat, running away, and by implication also cowardice. In this instance, though, instead of running all the way to the city of Argos and taking refuge behind its walls, many of the fleeing Argives took refuge in a nearby sacred grove, one of those stands of primal trees and scrub, under the protection of a god or hero, which dotted the Greek landscape. We hear that as many as six thousand of the Argives found refuge in this grove, and Kleomenes determined to make his victory decisive by not letting these Argives escape. At first he lured many individual Argives out of the grove by learning their names from captured slaves, and calling them out on the pretext that their families had sent ransom for them. Any who came out were killed, but the rest of the Argives soon cottoned on to that trick and stopped coming out. Kleomenes didn't wish to offend the deity of the grove himself, nor to let the Argives in it alone; so he ordered his Helots to set fire to the grove, giving the Argives the choice of running out to be killed or staying to burn. Thus most of the six thousand Argives died, and this blow to Argive manpower was so devastating that it took Argos thirty years to recover. Surprisingly, despite having weakened the Argives so drastically, Kleomenes didn't try to capture the city of Argos itself, for which he was prosecuted by the Ephors before the *gerousia* when he returned home, but he managed to win acquittal with a religious explanation for his decision not to attack Argos. The Spartans were always particularly scrupulous about religious observances.

This victory at Sepeia in 494, then, marked the high point of Kleomenes' success and influence at Sparta. After this battle, it was the looming threat of Persia that began to preoccupy Greek leaders, as Miletos had fallen, the Ionian revolt was beaten, and the Persians visibly turned their attention to expanding their power across the Aegean into Greece. As leaders of the Peloponnesos, the attitude of the Spartans to Persia would be critical. If they decided to resist Persia, the forces they could command would make a stand against the Persian army possible; if they decided to submit, Persian conquest of Greece would seem inevitable. But submission was not in the Spartan character: their appalling education system at least had this virtue, that by its influence the Spartans would never tamely submit to anyone without a fight, and if it came to it they would go down fighting bravely to the end rather than surrender.

In 491 the Persian king, Darius, sent envoys throughout mainland Greece to demand earth and water, the formal tokens of surrender to Persian domination. Most Greek states offered the tokens, but the Spartans rejected the demand and would not permit their allies to offer the tokens either. When the Athenians, who had also refused to submit, learned that the Aiginetans, their enemies, had offered earth and water, though Sparta's allies, they (the Athenians) sent to Sparta to complain, and it was Kleomenes who took up this complaint. He now, under the far graver threat of Persian power, gave up his hostility towards the Athenians, and ordered the Aiginetans to rescind their tokens of surrender to Persia, and to give hostages to the Athenians to guarantee their future good (that is, anti-Persian) behavior.

Kleomenes had been used to getting his way at Sparta for decades, but now his co-king Demaratos intervened. The two men had been in conflict before, fifteen years earlier, in 506, over policy towards Athens, and it now became apparent that Demaratos was encouraging the Aiginetans to resist Kleomenes' demands. When Kleomenes visited Aigina in person, Aiginetan leaders told him to his face, according to Herodotos, they would obey only if both Spartan kings gave the order, which made it clear that Demaratos was behind their refusal. This is often seen as a personal conflict between two rival leaders; yet Kleomenes and Demaratos had been ruling jointly for the better part of twenty years by this time, and the one disagreement we hear of between them was long in the past. It seems more likely that the conflict was over policy, and that in encouraging the Aiginetans, Demaratos revealed his view that outright resistance to Persia was unwise. Kleomenes was not to be balked, however: despite the fact that Demaratos had been king for so long already, he raised questions about Demaratos's legitimacy, and bribed the oracle at Delphi to deny Demaratos's legitimate birth when the Spartans sent to ask advice.

As a result, Demaratos was deposed, and replaced as king by his cousin Leotychidas. And accompanied by Leotychidas, Kleomenes was able to visit Aigina and enforce his orders to rescind submission to Persia and give hostages. At first Demaratos remained at Sparta: he was being closely watched. But when Leotychidas taunted him for his loss of status, he managed to slip away, and fled to the court of the Persian king, where he became an adviser on Greek affairs and later (in 480) accompanied king Xerxes during the latter's invasion of Greece. Herodotos, who apparently knew some of Demaratos's descendants, treats him oddly sympathetically; but it seems clear in point of fact that Demaratos was nothing better than a traitor to Sparta and to the cause of Greek freedom. At best we may perhaps give him credit for believing that submission to Persia was the only safe course for Sparta and the Greeks.

Yet the Demaratos affair turned out to have a sting in its tail. For the moment, there was a clear agreement between the Athenians and the Spartans that they would collaborate in resisting Persian attack, symbolized by Kleomenes visiting Athens to "bury the hatchet" and leave the Aiginetan hostages in the Athenians' custody. But, not long afterwards, the fact that Kleomenes had bribed the Pythia at Delphi came out, fatally undermining his position at Sparta. Kleomenes was forced to run, fleeing to Thessaly, and then to Arkadia in the Peloponnesos. Thus when the Persians finally did invade and land in Attica, Kleomenes was not in charge at Sparta, and the Spartans dithered over what help to send and when, as we shall see. Kleomenes himself was eventually invited back to Sparta, but once there he was abruptly arrested as a madman, and came to a gruesome—and according to Herodotos's informants—self-inflicted end. Many historians have doubted this and suspected that Kleomenes' enemies got him out of the way. When the great Persian invasion of 480 occurred, it was, as a result, not Kleomenes but his half-brother Leonidas who led the Spartans. Meanwhile, in 490, the Athenians ended up facing the Persians alone. This whole affair illustrates the fragility of Greek co-operation, and of Spartan willingness to stand in support of other Greeks: the fate of individual leaders could radically change what the Spartans were or were not prepared to do.

This, then, was Greece on the eve of the Persian conflict: a vibrant, developing society of city-states and other communities, growing economically, expanding demographically, making ever new steps forward in political and cultural achievement. Yet a society that remained deeply fragile because of the endemic disunity that plagued it, disunity both among rival cities, and within them among rival leaders and factions. The greatest strength of the Greeks lay in their military system of hoplite warfare, based on the commitment and discipline of thousands of Greek citizen-warriors who stood ready, in principle, to take the field and lay their lives on the line, making a stand for their free way of life. But would they really do so? So much depended on what the Spartans, the supreme hoplite warriors and leaders of the strongest alliance system in Greece, would ultimately decide to do. Would they come out and fight? The eyes and hopes of all Greeks preferring to avoid subjection to Persia were on them, but, as it turned out, the decisive stands were not to be made by the Spartans after all.

CHAPTER 2

THE RISE OF THE
PERSIAN EMPIRE

O UTSIDE OF IRAN, IT'S LIKELY THAT TOO FEW PEOPLE KNOW the Persians once created and ruled the largest and most powerful empire the world had yet seen. The fame of the Persian Empire has been overshadowed by the greater and longer-lasting empire of the Romans, and the most widely known fact about the Persian Empire is probably the rather negative one that Alexander the Great defeated and conquered it. But between the middle of the sixth century B.C.E. and the arrival of Alexander in 334, the Persian Empire was for two centuries the greatest, richest, and most powerful state in the ancient world, larger and more powerful by far than such earlier empires as the Egyptian, Babylonian, and Assyrian. Despite the Greeks' insistence that Persians were cruel and corrupt, Persian rule seems, on the whole, to have been fairly mild and just in the eyes of most subject peoples, if only by comparison with earlier empires. By the time the Persian Empire took control of all of western Asia, there was a long tradition of empires in that part of the world, going back to third millennium Sumerian rulers such as Gudea of Lagash and Sargon of Akkad, to the early second millennium Babylonian Empire of the great Hammurabi and others, and above all, in the late second millennium and—in revived form—between about 800 and 612, to the mighty Assyrian Empire, the greatest of all these. Not insignificantly, these earlier empires had accustomed most peoples of western Asia to being ruled by an imperial power, making the job of conquest for the Persians much simpler.

GEOGRAPHY AND RELIGION OF THE PERSIAN EMPIRE

At its height, between about 510 and 480, the Persian Empire was a truly vast, multi-ethnic power. It covered all of western Asia from modern Pakistan, Afghanistan, and the former Soviet republics in central Asia (Turkmenistan, Tajikistan, Uzbekistan), to the Aegean and Mediterranean Seas in the west, including modern Turkey, Syria, Lebanon, and Israel/Palestine, and it extended into northeast Africa in modern Egypt, Libya, and the Sudan. It comprised basically four great cultural/linguistic zones. At its heart, and making up the eastern portion of the empire, were the lands occupied by various Iranian speaking peoples and tribes: the Persians themselves and their northern neighbors the Medes, and the Parthians, Baktrians, and Saka peoples inhabiting the rest of modern Iran and Afghanistan. These lands provided the military peoples who powered the empire, but there were relatively few and mostly small cities, and economically and culturally this part of the empire was less "advanced" than the other zones.

To the west of these imperial heartlands was a great zone dominated by Semitic peoples speaking one form or another of Aramaic, comprising Mesopotamia (modern Iraq), Syria, and Palestine. Urban "civilization" in this zone went back nearly three millennia, and it was this region that was the economic power house of the empire—the rich agriculture of Mesopotamia, the flourishing cities of that region and Syria/Palestine, and their great and old-established trading networks—as well as much of the administrative structure that kept the empire functioning. It was for this latter reason that Akkadian (the traditional language of

106

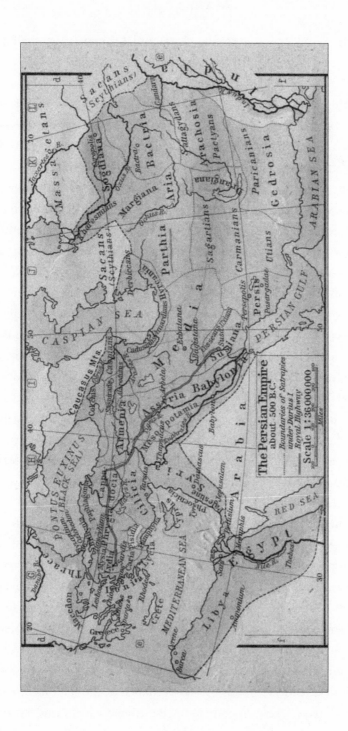

The Persian Empire
about 500 B.C.
—— Boundaries of Satrapies
under Darius I.
—— Royal Highway
Scale 1:35,000,000

Babylonia and its bureaucratic class) and Aramaic were the chief languages of imperial administration, rather than Persian as one might have expected.

Then there were two great extensions to the northwest and southwest, respectively. The former comprised Anatolia or Asia Minor (modern Turkey), a vast region inhabited in antiquity by many different ethnic/linguistic groups—Lydians, Karians, Lykians, Pisidians, Pamphylians, Phrygians, Mysians, Bithynians, Paphlago-nians, Kappadokians, Kilikians, Armenians, as well as the Greeks living along the west and north coasts—and offering a similar diversity in urbanization, level of "civilization," economic sophis-tication, and so on. The latter covered Egypt, ancient in civilization and immensely wealthy thanks to the rich agriculture of the Nile valley, with extensions south into the Sudan and west into Libya. Egypt was the last of these major zones to be acquired by the Per-sians and the most resistant to Persian power: the Egyptians re-belled frequently and often with significant though temporary success. There are rebellions on record for the mid-480s, the 450s and a particularly successful one at the end of the fifth century that led to Egypt's being independent for over fifty years before its reconquest in 343. The Egyptians always resented Persian rule, or indeed any outside interference, remembering their own long and glorious past.

The determined resistance of the Egyptians to Persian domi-nation was relatively unusual, though: by and large, most of the subject peoples remained quiet under Persian rule, apart from occasional local uprisings. Besides their reliance on established imperial traditions and administrative structures taken over from the older empires, the Persians' success in keeping their subjects quiet and at least reasonably submissive can be traced to several key elements in Persian rule. The Persians relied extensively on local elites for the actual "hands-on" governance of the regions of their empire. This is best known from the west, where local leaders were placed in charge of the various Greek cities along the coast, and a native dynastic family—the Hekatomnids—was allowed to rule over Karia. But the policy seems to have been empire-wide, and in allowing local elites to govern their home regions—under the supervision of Persian governors of the great provinces of the empire, of course—the Persians removed one likely source of disaffection: those local elites trusted by the Persians with local rule were not inclined to rebel and "bite the hand that fed them," as the saying goes. Further, the Persians established a system of highways—the best known being the great "royal road" described by Herodotos that led from Susa to Sardis, with an extension to the Aegean coast at Ephesos—that created an efficient system of communication from the imperial center to the outlying parts of the empire. Along these roads, which had regular way stations where food and lodging, and for imperial messengers a change of horses, were available, traveled the messengers and military forces of the empire, carrying information to and fro and delivering military force where it was needed. Finally, the Persians were tolerant of local customs, cultures, and religious traditions and did not attempt to impose their own customs or religion.

The Iranian peoples had a shared religious tradition that involved worship of a number of traditional deities, Mithra and Anahita being perhaps the most important. Mithra was associated particularly with the Sun, with light and fire, and with prophecy and therefore at times equated by the Greeks with Apollo. Anahita was a great goddess of life in all its forms, in whom the Greeks saw a likeness to Aphrodite or Artemis. Playing a key role in Iranian religion was a priestly tribe or caste known as the Magoi (or Magi), who were perhaps specifically Median in origin but seem to have enjoyed special prestige throughout the Iranian lands. They tended the sacred fire altars at which religious observances took place and in general devoted themselves to the religious traditions and rites of the Iranian gods. Herodotos has much to say about them, though it is not clear how well he understood their exact role or roles. In later popular traditions they came to be associated with magical rites and knowledge, to which in fact they gave their name.

The sixth century, however, the era in which the Persians rose to imperial power, was apparently also the era in which lived the great Iranian prophet Zarathustra or Zoroaster (as the Greeks called him), who taught new religious ideas of two opposed forces in the cosmos: a force of truth, justice, good, and light; and a force of lies, injustice, evil, and darkness. This dualistic world view was to be very influential in later Near Eastern and Western religious thought, and the Persian rulers from at least Darius the Great onwards attached themselves to this outlook, proclaiming themselves the favorites of the great god of light and truth Ahura Mazda, and the opponents of the Lie. But the Persian rulers were not exclusive or missionary about this: they were prepared to see in other peoples' chief deities—the Jewish Yahweh or the Greek Zeus Megistos, for example—versions of Ahura Mazda deserving of respect. That respect for local religious traditions was not the least factor in allowing the subject peoples to accept Persian rule. But we should consider how the Persians came to rule their vast empire, how they conquered it, and for that we must turn back to the last days of Assyrian imperial power.

CYRUS AND THE PERSIAN CONQUEST

One of the most momentous events in the history of the ancient near east was the sack of Nineveh, the capital city of the great Assyrian Empire, in 612 B.C.E. Since the Assyrians had dominated Mesopotamia (Iraq) and the surrounding lands to east (western Iran) and west (Syria and Palestine) for about six or seven centuries off and on, the destruction of Nineveh, and with it the utter collapse and disappearance of the Assyrian Empire, truly marked the end of an era and the beginning of new things.

The Assyrians, a martial and often brutal imperial people, were unlamented on the whole: indeed many of their former sub-

This monument to Cyrus the Great, which stands in Sydney's Olympic Park, is a replica of the original classical Persian stone carving. Sydney chose Cyrus, the first known ruler to have issued a human rights declaration, as a symbol of multiculturalism: the Emperor is depicted with a Jewish helmet, a Babylonian outfit, and a Persian beard.

jects, such as the Judaeans, were filled with glee at their downfall (see the biblical book of Nahum, for example). But the disappearance of this mighty and long enduring empire left a power vacuum in western Asia, and it was a question how this vacuum was to be filled, and by whom. The Assyrian Empire was destroyed by a coalition of two powers: the new empire of the

111

Medes in northern Iran and a revived Babylonian Empire in southern Mesopotamia under Chaldaean leadership. Of these, the Medes, led by their king Huwakhshatra (in Greek, Kyaxares), seem to have been militarily the more effective, indeed fearsome. But the Chaldaean ruler of Babylon, Nabopolassar, managed to hold his own in the alliance and to effect a division of western Asia into two spheres of power: the Median Empire covered Iran and part of Afghanistan, as well as northeastern Iraq and a part of eastern Anatolia; and the so-called Neo-Babylonian Empire held southern and part of northwestern Iraq, together with Syria and Palestine. In addition, the end of Assyrian power permitted a revival of Egypt under the Saite dynasty of Pharaohs: Necho, Psamtik (Greek: Psammetichos), and Ahmose (Greek: Amasis) most notably; and a new power arose in western Anatolia in the shape of the Lydian Empire of Gyges and his successors, especially Alyattes and Croesus.

After some initial warfare between the Babylonians and the Egyptians, and between the Medes and the Lydians, a balance of power seemed to develop among these four empires, with the Iranian Medes perhaps the strongest of the four but lacking the strength to engage the other three and conquer them. The capital of the Median Empire was at Ekbatana (Hamadan) in northern Iran, and the empire covered essentially Iranian lands and peoples; the attention of the Medes seems in fact to have been focused predominantly to south and east, to control their fellow Iranian peoples in Persia (Fars) and Baktria (Afghanistan).

Although the record is sparse and far from being clear it appears that Iranian speakers had entered the historically Iranian lands in a series of tribal movements culminating in the seventh century B.C.E. The Persians proper can be tracked in Assyrian sources, from the region of the upper Zagros mountains (in modern Kurdistan) moving south eastwards roughly along the border of modern Iran and Iraq to end in their historic homeland, the mountainous region of Fars just to the east of the Persian Gulf, by 600.

Meanwhile, various groups of semi-nomadic, horse-rearing Median tribes and clans had occupied northern, especially northwestern, Iran, where the upland plateaus were particularly favorable to their horse breeding and cattle herding way of life. These groups gradually coalesced into a united people under a succession of influential leaders: we hear of a Daiukku who fell afoul of Assyrian power a little before 700 and who is probably to be equated with a founding Median king named Deioces by Herodotos; and of a Khshathrita who came into conflict with the Assyrians in the early seventh century. In the second half of the seventh century, Herodotos knows of a King Phraortes (a genuine name, the Greek spelling of Median Frawartish), who apparently expanded Median power to the east and south.

At any rate, King Huwakhshatra or Kyaxares, ruling from about 625 until 585, controlled all of Media and most of the neighboring Iranian peoples: the Parsa (Persians) to the south, the Parthawa (Parthians) to the northeast, and the Bakhtrish (Bactrians) to the east. Late in his reign, Kyaxares fought a war in eastern Anatolia against the Lydian king Alyattes. The war ended indecisively after a great battle was interrupted by a solar eclipse, and the two kings made a compromise peace, establishing the river Halys as the border between their respective realms, and marrying Alyattes' daughter Aryenis to Cyaxares' son Ishtuwegu (Astyages) to cement the peace. This eclipse has been identified as that of 28th May 585, providing one of the few fixed chronological points in Median history.

In addition, Babylonian sources establish that it was Huwakhshatra/Kyaxares who sacked Nineveh in 612, and the Babylonian Nabonidus Chronicle establishes 550 as the year in which the Median king Ishtuwegu (Astyages) was overthrown by the Persian Kurash (Cyrus). The former fits well with the dates given above for Kyaxares, based on Herodotos, while the latter also fits with Herodotos's chronology of the rise of Persian power. The result of all this is a rising Median Empire developing in the early to mid-seventh century under rulers named Khshathrita and Frawartish and coming to dominate the Iranian lands by the second half of the century; the Median Empire, at its height, was one of the great powers of the Middle and Near East between about 625 and 550 under the two kings known to the Greeks as Kyaxares and Astyages.

The Persians (Parsa) in their homeland of Fars were, during the reigns of the last two great Median kings, no more than a subordinate people under Median domination, though an important one. The Persians had their own ruling family, descending from a legendary founder named Hakhamanish (Achaimenes in Greek), which split into two branches about the beginning of the sixth century. The most important branch, at first, became kings of Anshan, a city and region in northern Fars, under Median domination. A cylinder seal of the great conqueror Cyrus (Kurash in Persian) from Babylonia gives his ancestry: "son of Kanbujiya (Cambyses), great king, king of Anshan, grandson of Kurash (Cyrus), great king, king of Anshan, great-grandson of Chishpish (Teispes), great king, king of Anshan." That gives at least three generations of kings of Anshan before Cyrus the Conqueror, showing that the Persian rulers of Anshan were old in power already by the accession of Cyrus to the throne of Anshan in 560. The importance of these local Persian rulers to their Median overlords is clearly established by a crucial fact: the Median king Astyages married his daughter Mandane to Cambyses of Anshan, so that Cyrus the Conqueror was the Median king's grandson. The importance of these Persians within the Median Empire is probably based on military realities: the Medes were outstanding cavalry fighters, perhaps the best in the ancient world in their day, in great part because of the quality of the horses they bred. But they needed first-rate infantry, too, to maintain their empire, and, besides the native Median infantry, the Persians provided archers and javelineers who were among the best infantry available to the Medes.

The origin of the Persian Empire lay in the rebellion of Cyrus against his grandfather and overlord Astyages in 550 B.C.E. (the date is established by the contemporary Nabonidus Chronicle from Babylonia). The reason for this rebellion, other than the simple desire for power, is unclear. Herodotos tells a yarn about Astyages' dreams, which led him to fear his daughter's unborn child and attempt to have the babe killed: the story is, of course, a classic folktale of the Moses/Oedipus/Snow White type, and in Cyrus's case it is shown to be unhistorical by its incorrect information about Cyrus's father. As Herodotos has it, Astyages was first impelled by his dream to marry off Mandane to an undistinguished Persian, whose child could be no threat (Cambyses was in fact, as we know, a powerful subordinate ruler, king of Anshan). Growing fearful of the child even so, Astyages (in Herodotus's story) ordered his right-hand man, Harpagos, to kill Cyrus; but Harpagos could not bring himself to do so and instead fostered the boy with a shepherd couple. In the end, of course, the boy was recognized by his regal manner and appearance and reinstated to his home. Harpagos, all the same, was punished by Astyages, who killed the general's own son and served the boy up to him roasted for dinner—a hideous punishment for which Harpagos never forgave the king, and incidentally another classic folktale (see, for example, the Greek stories of Tantalos and Pelops, or Atreus and Thyestes). This story provides a notional explanation for the hostility to Astyages of both Cyrus, who rebels against his grandfather and overlord, and Harpagos, who betrays Astyages and sides with Cyrus, but as the story is clearly unhistorical, we actually know of no good reason for Cyrus's rebellion and Harpagos's betrayal.

What we do know is that Cyrus did rebel, persuaded the Persians to support him in rebelling against the Median king, and fought against the Median army in several engagements; and that the conflict was decided by Harpagos the Mede's decision to change sides, bringing part of the Median army over to Cyrus with him. Astyages was then defeated and captured, and by what was essentially an internal coup, the Median Empire became the Persian Empire. Thus far, there was nothing very remarkable about

Cyrus's and the Persians' rise to power: they simply managed to take over an already functioning empire, in part thanks to the treachery of a military leader of that empire. This origin of Persian power helps to explain the habitual Greek melding of Persians and Medes and, in fact, their frequent custom of referring to the Persian Empire as "the Mede." Indeed, in part no doubt thanks to the important role of Harpagos and his Median forces in enabling Cyrus's success, the Medes were treated almost as partners in empire, more than subjects, at any rate, early in the history of the Persian Empire. But Cyrus was not content simply to have seized control of the Median Empire: the Persian ascendancy in Iranian lands and culture unleashed a wave of new expansionism that saw the Persian Empire become the greatest empire in the history of the Middle East to that time.

The first step in this new expansionism was not initiated by Cyrus. The Lydian king Croesus, with his fabulous wealth, having established firm control over all of western and central Asia Minor, including the Ionian Greek cities on the coast, decided to attack the Persian Empire first, in 546. Herodotos explained Croesus's aggression as motivated by a desire to avenge the fall of his brother-in-law Astyages who had married Croesus's sister Aryenis. More plausibly, Croesus saw the internal turmoil in the Median/Persian Empire simply as an opportunity to expand his own power beyond the Halys boundary to which his father Alyattes had been obliged to agree. Herodotos has a characteristic story about Croesus's decision: the Lydian king supposedly sought the advice of the famous Oracle of Apollo at Delphi before deciding definitely to go to war. Croesus's envoy asked the Oracle what would happen if Croesus went to war against the Persians. The Pythia (priestess of the Oracle) replied if Croesus attacked the Persians, he would destroy a mighty empire. That sounded good to Croesus, and to war he went. But of course, he had failed to ask *which* empire he would destroy, his own or the Persians'.

Cyrus mobilized his army and met the Lydian army in eastern Anatolia. A great battle was fought, fairly late in the summer, at which the honors were even: the Lydian cavalry fought, we hear, superbly and kept Croesus's army in the fight, though the Persians had superior numbers. After the drawn battle, Croesus decided that the season was too far advanced to campaign much more, and he marched back home to Lydia and sent his army home for the winter. Here we observe the difference between a great military leader and a merely good one. Giving Croesus time to get well under way, Cyrus did not march home for the winter but followed Croesus to Sardis, arriving there shortly after Croesus's army had been dismissed to their homes. Croesus managed to summon his Lydian troops from the plains around Sardis but had to fight a battle outside Sardis, desperately outnumbered. Though the Lydian cavalry again fought heroically, Cyrus had an answer for that too. The Lydian horses were completely unfamiliar with camels, and Cyrus had noted in the earlier battle that they disliked the smell of those animals and veered away from them. He therefore mounted many of his men on camels and sent them against the Lydian cavalry, who couldn't force their horses to go near those unfamiliar and evil-smelling beasts. The Lydians dismounted and continued the fight on foot, but the outcome was unavoidable: Cyrus's army was victorious, and Croesus and his men were forced to seek refuge on the citadel of Sardis. Still, all was not lost: the acropolis of Sardis, with its massive fortification walls, was considered impregnable, with good reason; and Croesus hoped to hold out until the spring when his army and allies would mobilize and come to his rescue.

Cyrus was determined not to let it come to that. Many of his soldiers lived in mountainous regions of Iran, and they were experienced climbers. He set them to exploring the steep cliffs of the Sardian acropolis for a way up. As often, the solution was found at the most precipitous and seemingly most impregnable part of the citadel. Whereas the Lydians were guarding the walls of the acropolis carefully, at the one spot where it seemed impossible that enemy soldiers could approach, the Lydian guard was lax, and it was exactly there that a small band of Cyrus's mountaineers did in fact climb up and break into the citadel. Once some of his men were inside the Sardian acropolis, Cyrus launched an all-out attack on the walls, and within hours Sardis was his. Croesus was captured and probably killed, although Herodotos knew of a legend that his life was spared at the last moment and he became a valued adviser of Cyrus and later of Cyrus's son Cambyses. All of Anatolia was incorporated into the Persian Empire, including the Ionian Greek cities along the west coast. After lingering for a while to establish firmly his control over the former Lydian Empire, Cyrus marched his army away and gave thought to the next stage of imperial expansion: he had his eyes on the Babylonian Empire.

The Babylonian Empire was ruled at this time by an elderly king named Nabonidus, whose family came from northern Mesopotamia. The two great Chaldaean rulers, Nabopolassar and Nebuchadnezzar, had made Babylonia into a formidable power but had never really won full acceptance from the native Babylonians. Nebuchadnezzar's sons, much weaker men than their great father, were overthrown, and the elderly general Nabonidus came to power. At first he was quite well received, but his religious policies soon began to meet with disfavor. He was seen as insufficiently committed to the traditional gods of Babylon and Akkad. His mother had been priestess of the moon god Sin at his temple in Harran in northern Mesopotamia. The temple had been destroyed during the wars between the Assyrians and the Medes, and it was the ambition of Nabonidus's life to restore it and his mother's god Sin to their former splendor and honor.

The Babylonian priests resented the enormous resources Nabonidus committed to this distant temple in the far north, and Nabonidus increased that dissatisfaction with other policies. He decided to extend Babylonian power by a campaign deep into Arabia and remained there for years, missing the annual New Year ceremony in Babylon that meant so much to the Babylonian priests. Further, as the threat of Persian attack increased after 545, he did not return to Babylon, though he did give orders that the statues of the gods of the cities of Akkad and Sumeria be brought into Babylon for safekeeping, which did not endear him to the peoples of those cities. During his absence in Arabia, Babylon was ruled by his son Belshazzar, he of the famous feast in the biblical book of Daniel.

In the 590s and 580s King Nebuchadnezzar had campaigned in Palestine, conquering Judaea, sacking Jerusalem, and transporting much of its population to Babylonia, the famous Babylonian exile of Psalm 137: "By the waters of Babylon, there we sat down and wept, when we remembered Zion." Now, while the Babylonians looked nervously to the north and east, wondering when Cyrus would strike, the Jewish exiles at Babylon awaited the Persian attack with hope. The Persians moved in 539 and conquered Babylonia quite quickly and with relative ease. As with his conquest of Media, Cyrus was helped by an enemy leader: the governor of an important province of Babylonia east of the Tigris, named Ugbaru, went over to the Persians with his forces. It even seems that it was Ugbaru who first captured Babylon itself for Cyrus, while the Persian king was operating further to the north. Nabonidus, who had returned to Babylon after a near ten-year absence in Arabia, fled from the city, but was captured. To appease the various religious groupings, the statues of the gods that Nabonidus had caused to be brought to Babylon were returned to their temples, the Jews were permitted to return to Jerusalem and eventually to rebuild their temple, and Cyrus observed the rituals of the Babylonian god Marduk. With the conquest of Babylon, Cyrus now controlled Asia from Afghanistan to the Mediterranean and Aegean seas and held three of the four kingdoms that had divided the east after the fall of the Assyrian Empire: only Egypt under Pharaoh Amasis remained independent of Persian control. For the remainder of his reign, Cyrus seems to have focused his attention on consolidation and on extending the Empire eastward into central Asia. It was there that he died, in battle against a nomadic tribe, in 530.

It was left, consequently, to Cyrus's son and successor Cambyses to decide what, if anything, to do about Egypt. It was Cambyses' unfortunate fate to live under the shadow of his remarkable father. Not only a great conqueror, who had built the largest empire the ancient world had known, Cyrus was also apparently a likeable man. The Persians remembered him, Herodotos tells us, as a father. Cambyses had to try to live up to his father's reputation, but he evidently lacked his father's charisma. Deficient in the ability to make himself popular, at least he wanted to show he was his father's true heir as a military leader; that he too could conquer new lands to add to the Persian Empire. Egypt was the obvious target: the Assyrians, late in their history, had conquered Egypt; surely the Persians could too. And indeed they could. Cambyses was clearly a capable enough military leader, as he conquered Egypt with apparent ease. A great battle was fought near the Pelousiac branch of the Nile, the branch nearest to Palestine, in which the Persians were victorious. Herodotos later visited the battle site and reported finding it still covered with the bones and skulls of the men who died there: he claimed to be able to tell immediately what skull was Persian and which was Egyptian, by the thickness of the bone. It should be noted that breaking into Egypt from Palestine has never been easy: many armies through history have failed to do so, in the face of a determined defense. So Cambyses certainly deserves credit for leading the Persians successfully through the Egyptian defense and into Egypt, adding the last of the four successor Empires of the Assyrians to the Persian Empire. He didn't long outlive his victory, though.

DARIUS AND THE ORGANIZATION OF THE PERSIAN EMPIRE

By 522 Cambyses was dead, his end coming under mysterious circumstances. Whether it was a wound, or an illness, or murder or suicide, or even the anger of the Egyptian bull god Apis that carried

Cambyses off, as different versions have it, we really can't say. But he was succeeded, briefly, by his younger brother Bardiya or, in the Greek sources, Smerdis. The reign of Smerdis was violently ended by a conspiracy of leading Persian nobles, who claimed that the man ruling as Smerdis son of Cyrus was in fact an impostor, the real Smerdis having been killed some time previously on the orders of his brother Cambyses. Herodotos tells the story in great detail, but for a long time his veracity was doubted by scholars who wondered how he could have known what happened in the palaces of the Persian king, at the highest level of Persian society. In the mid-nineteenth century, however, the British soldier, diplomat, and scholar Henry Rawlinson investigated a great rock carving at Bisutun in northern Iran, not very far from Ekbatana (Hamadan), which included a great inscription in three different languages. Two of them were indecipherable at first, but the third proved to be old Persian, a language known from the Zorastrian sacred writings (the "Avesta") still in use. Translated, the text proved to be a kind of "autobiography" by the new King Darayawaush (Darius) himself,

Darius as depicted on a fourth century Greek vase.

in which he told in all essentials the same story about Smerdis as Herodotos, proving Herodotos had access to excellent Persian sources.

Briefly, seven great Persian nobles, of whom Darius was one, reached the conclusion that Smerdis was an impostor, though one suspects that in fact they simply disapproved of the way Smerdis was ruling. At any rate, they agreed together to remove the young king, or pseudo-king if one believes their claim, and replace him with another member of the Achaemenid royal clan. This was to be Darius himself, who was a distant cousin of Cambyses, descended according to his own account from the same Chishpish (Teispes) who was Cyrus's great-grandfather. The seven grandees—Otanes, Megabyxos, Gobryas, Intaphernes, Hydarnes, and Ardumanish in addition to Darius—forced their way into the palace, apparently near Ekbatana, where Smerdis was residing and killed him. Darius became king in his stead, perhaps not just because he was an Achaemenid and cousin of Cambyses, but because he had been Cambyses' "spearbearer," an important office that made him known to and trusted by the Persian army that Cambyses was leading home from Egypt when he died. Certainly strong military backing from the Persian "royal army" was crucial to Darius, because his accession to the throne was not widely accepted at first. A whole string of rebellions broke out around the empire in the years 521 and 520, and Darius and his supporters were virtually obliged to conquer the Persian Empire anew.

The trouble began almost immediately after Darius's seizure of the throne, at the beginning of the fall of 522, in two of the older states of the Middle East, which were used to being powers in their own right and clearly resented subordination to the Persians: Elam and Babylonia. The trouble in Elam was apparently quickly quashed by a demonstration of force, but in Babylonia a pretender calling himself Nebuchadnezzar and claiming to be the son of Nabonidus managed to take control of southern Mesopotamia, and by early October documents in Babylon were being dated by his reign. Darius had to lead his army to Babylonia and engage in some hard campaigning to recover control: he forced a crossing of the Tigris on inflated animal skins, and in mid December won a great battle that enabled him to enter Babylon. Meanwhile, however, the trouble had spread. Media rose in rebellion under a Median ruler named (according to Darius) Frawartish (Phraortes), but who called himself Khshathrita of the seed of Huwakhshatra: that is, he assumed the name of the mid-seventh century Median king who had united Media and first fought successfully against the Assyrians, and he claimed to be a descendant of the great Kyaxares. This was clearly meant to be a national Median attempt to recover dominance in the Perso-Median Empire—for that's what the Persian Empire really was. With Darius in trouble, national uprisings began throughout the empire. Rebellions occurred in Armenia, Assyria, Elam once more, Egypt, Parthia, and in the Saka lands. Most damagingly, perhaps, Darius could not even hold the Persian homeland: a certain Wahyazdata proclaimed himself to be Bardiya (Smerdis) and took control of Cyrus's capital city Parsagarda (Pasargadai), from where he dispatched forces into neighboring Arachosia, intent to extend his power.

To face all these uprisings Darius had part, at least, of the royal army of Cambyses—though he admits it was a small army at best—and his six co-conspirators, drawn from some of the most powerful Persian families; in addition, his father Wishtaspa (Hystaspes), who was still alive and governing the province of Hyrkania, naturally supported his son, and the governor of the vital eastern province of Baktria—named Dadarshish—also declared for Darius. It has to be said that Darius acted with great energy and efficacy in the face of all these difficulties and showed himself to be an outstanding leader. Hydarnes was sent with a force of Medes to contain the uprising in Media, and another force was dispatched to Armenia to contain the trouble there. Darius himself made another demonstration in Elam, causing the rebels there to submit and hand over their leader for execution.

In the spring of 521 Darius advanced into Media and won a

great battle against Frawartish/ Khshathrita at Kundurush, near Bisutun, which broke the back of the Median uprising. Flying columns were sent from Media into Armenia, to help put down the revolt there, and into Hyrkania where Darius's father had managed to hold out against Parthian and Hyrkanian rebel attacks, and was now able to go over to a counter-offensive. An army of Persian and Median troops was then sent, under a general named Artawardiya (Artavasdes) to attack the pretender Wahyazdata (or Bardiya as he claimed to be) in Persis. With the help of the governor of Arachosia, who had chosen loyalty to Darius, Wahyazdata was defeated in a series of battles, the crucial ones in late May and early June in Fars (Persis) itself enabling Darius to take back full control of the Persian homeland. With Media and Persia under his control, Darius was now firmly on the throne and only mopping-up operations remained.

Dadarshish in Baktria had been successful in subduing Saka and other rebels in the far east, Hystaspes had recovered control of Hyrkania and Parthia, renewed revolts in Elam and Babylonia were easily suppressed by Gobryas and Intaphernes, and by the end of the year 521 the Empire had mostly been restored to order. In his autobiographical inscription at Bisutun, carved on a cliff face near the site of his greatest and most crucial victory at Kundurush, Darius proudly proclaimed that he won nineteen battles and held captive nine "false kings" in one year. Even allowing for some exaggeration, and for Darius claiming credit for his subordinates' victories, it was an amazing achievement.

Darius had certainly shown himself to be a worthy heir to the great conqueror Cyrus, and in essence he held the throne of the Persian Empire by right of conquest, having, as noted above, basically been obliged to reconquer almost the whole empire. He still had campaigning to do to consolidate Persian power in the east. In 519 he operated against the so-called "pointed hat Saka" in the Caspian region, and in subsequent years brought his army to Gandara (apparently the basin of the Kabul river) and further into modern

Pakistan, apparently conquering the lands on the western side of the Indus river and incorporating them into the empire as a new province named Hindush after the river that was now the empire's south-eastern border. There is also some evidence to suggest that Darius may have visited Egypt about 517, though this is unclear. Persian power was extended southwards and westwards, however, into Kush (Ethiopia) and Put (Libya), in the latter case impinging on the Greeks who inhabited the Cyrenaica region of Libya. The Greek city of Barke there was captured and its population sent to Susa for Darius' judgment, according to Herodotos.

By about 514, the eastern and southern boundaries of the empire could be considered satisfactorily settled, and Darius turned his attention to the west. He had already had occasion to intervene there indirectly in about 519, because the governor at Sardis, Oroites, had not declared loyalty to Darius and had taken advantage of the time of troubles to kill the governor Mitrobates at Daskyleion in northern Asia Minor. After that, Oroites ignored Darius's messengers, or even killed them, so he would clearly need to be brought to book. A special envoy named Bagaios persuaded Oroites' Persian guards to rebel against him in Darius's name, and Oroites was killed. Subsequently one of the Seven, Otanes, was sent to take control of the former Lydian lands, and he extended Persian power westwards slightly by capturing Samos—whose great tyrant Polykrates had already been trapped and killed by Oroites—and inducing Chios and Lesbos to submit. About 513 or 512 Darius visited the western part of the empire himself, bringing with him a great royal army, for it was his intention to extend Persian power further west into Europe. His immediate aim was the conquest of Thrace, that is, roughly modern Bulgaria and Romania south of the Danube—though it seems Darius planned to cross that great river and extend his conquests as far as possible on the north bank. Besides the royal army he brought with him, built as always around a solid core of Persians and Medes, the peoples of Asia Minor, not least the Ionian Greeks, were required to contribute contingents. In the case of the Greeks, it was their naval power that was wanted.

Darius did not wish his great army to have to linger at the Bosporus for days or weeks while it was slowly ferried across from Asia to Europe. Consequently a Greek engineer, Mandrokles of Samos, had been commissioned in advance to construct a bridge across the Bosporus for the army to cross. Mandrokles constructed a pontoon bridge, stringing Greek warships across the narrow strait, lashed together and firmly anchored, and building a roadway over the ships that thus acted as pontoons. This was no easy feat, as the current flowing through the Bosporus from the Black Sea towards the Aegean is strong, and in summer the prevailing winds tend to blow in the same direction as the current. Nevertheless, the project succeeded, thanks to the warships contributed by the Ionian cities, and the army crossed safely and quickly.

The Ionian warships then broke up the bridge and sailed into the Black Sea to the mouth of the Danube, and up the river Danube to rendezvous with Darius at an agreed point along the river's course. Darius and the army marched through Thrace and won the submission of the various Thracian tribes without too much difficulty, reaching the Danube and the meeting with the Ionian ships as arranged. There the ships once again were formed into a bridge, this time across the Danube. The various contingents of the Ionian fleet were commanded in person by the local rulers—in Greek eyes tyrants—the Persian governors had placed in control of each city, Histiaios of Miletos being the most important of them, as Miletos was the largest and wealthiest of the cities. When Darius and his army crossed the Danube to attack the Skythians who lived on the northern side, he left the Ionians at the Danube with orders to remove the northern third or so of the bridge, but keep the rest intact and wait for Darius and his army to return, when the bridge would be completed again for his army to recross. The Persian army then vanished into the interior and the Ionians waited.

In seeking to conquer the Skythians, however, Darius had bitten off more than he could chew. These semi-nomadic tribesmen did not stay around to fight Darius's army: they took all their possessions and disappeared into the interior of Romania and Ukraine, removing all supplies and poisoning wells as they went. Darius and his army marched far and wide searching for the enemy, but apart from harassing bands of horsemen who disappeared as soon as they were attacked by substantial forces, there was no enemy to be found. Meanwhile the army's supply situation was becoming critical, with the food rapidly dwindling and good drinking water hard to find. Darius was forced to turn back with nothing accomplished and head back to his bridge; and the question now was whether he could avoid the fate that Cyrus had met against similar nomads in central Asia, and whether the Ionian fleet and the bridge they formed would still be waiting for him. Skythian cavalry had apparently shown up at the Danube bridge, and tried to persuade the Ionians to leave, according to Herodotos. But realizing that their positions as rulers of their respective cities were dependent on Darius's power, the Ionian leaders chose to stay and await the king. It was with relief, therefore, after much hard marching and some suffering, that Darius and his men, on reaching the Danube, found the Greeks and the bridge still there, and were able to cross back into Thrace.

After this abortive but by no means disastrous Skythian campaign, then, Darius decided that his western border was in good shape and he could return. He had added a great new province, Thrace, to the empire, and he left a substantial army under a governor named Megabazos with orders to extend Persian power further westwards as possible. Megabazos extended his province as far as the river Strymon, and cajoled the king of Macedonia to the west of the Strymon, King Amyntas, to submit to Persian power, which thereby advanced into northern Greece for the first time. Darius, with the rest of his army, marched down to the Hellespont and there crossed back to Asia. He went to Sardis, where he stayed for perhaps a year or more, settling the western part of the empire

*The stone relief of Darius
at Behistun/Bisutun.*

and receiving reports from Megabazos. Then, perhaps around 510, Darius returned to the center of his empire and effectively retired from active campaigning, dedicating the remainder of his life to the task of organizing the empire in a thorough and efficient manner. He left his half-brother Artaphernes as governor at Sardis and thus effectively in control of the western frontier of the empire, and by and large trusted him to maintain the west secure, and perhaps judiciously extend Persian power a little further westwards if and when opportunities occurred.

Darius had by most calculations already achieved much, enough perhaps to earn his common sobriquet of "Darius the Great," but his main achievements were in fact carried out over the next twenty years of peaceful governance. He completely reorganized the empire and set it on a business-like footing. According to Herodotos, the Persian nobility despised him for this rather than admiring his work—they supposedly referred to Cyrus as a father,

Cambyses as a master, but Darius as a mere shopkeeper—but in truth it was Darius's work more than anyone's that enabled the empire to function smoothly and last for another 150 or more years, until Alexander the Great took it over. As Herodotos tells it Darius divided the empire into twenty well-defined provinces (the number varied later as new provinces were occasionally added by conquest or division), each under a military and political governor called a satrap (khshathrapan), and each paying a defined tribute to the imperial treasury. Persia (Parsa) is often added as a twenty-first province, but it was not a tribute paying satrapy like the others. The list as Herodotos presents it is:

1. the Ionians and neighboing peoples, tribute 400 talents of silver;
2. the Lydians and neighbors, tribute 500 talents;
3. the Hellespontine region, tribute 300 talents;
4. Kilikia, tribute 500 talents and 360 horses;
5. Syria and Palestine, including Phoenicia, tribute 350 talents;
6. Egypt and Libya, tribute 700 talents;
7. Gandara and surrounding peoples, tribute 170 talents;
8. Susiane, tribute 300 talents;
9. Babylonia and Assyria, tribute 1000 talents and 500 eunuchs;
10. Media, tribute 450 talents;
11. the Caspian region, tribute 200 talents;
12. Baktria, tribute 360 talents;
13. Armenia, tribute 400 talents;
14. the Sagartians and neighbors, tribute 600 talents;
15. the Saka, 250 talents;
16. Parthia, tribute 300 talents;
17. the Parikanioi, tribute 400 talents;
18. the Matiene region, tribute 200 talents;
19. the Moschoi and neighbors, tribute 300 talents;

20. the Indians, tribute 360 talents of gold (worth about 4,680 talents of silver).

The total annual tribute thus amounted to over 14,500 talents of silver, a truly stupendous sum. It isn't really possible to express ancient sums of money usefully in modern terms, but a comparison may help. The Athenians at the height of their power in the mid-fifth century received an annual tribute from their allies of not quite 400 talents. From this they were able to build and maintain the most powerful fleet in the ancient world, to conduct mostly successful warfare against the Persians and (at times) the Spartans, to build some of the most expensive and widely admired buildings in the ancient world (most famously the Parthenon), and to create a reserve fund that by 432 B.C.E. amounted to 10,000 talents. The annual tribute received by the Persian kings was more than thirty times that received by the Athenians, that enabled them to do all these things. Stupendous is hardly a sufficient term to describe the size of this tribute income.

Having organized the empire in this way, and made the satraps responsible for taking in and forwarding the tribute as well as for the internal security and borders of their respective satrapies, Darius had available immense resources to carry out any plans he had of imperial consolidation and so on. Herodotos's list is on the whole reliable: we have various lists of subject peoples from monumental inscriptions by Darius, and we have a great depiction of the peoples of empire offering tribute carved on the walls of Darius's *apadana* (audience hall) at Persepolis; and although there is some variation (probably in large part due to a distinction between subject peoples on the one hand, and provinces on the other) these sources on the whole corroborate Herodotos sufficiently well.

Besides organizing his empire efficiently in this way, Darius was concerned to leave behind monuments that would secure his memory, and to give the empire suitably impressive capital cities.

As far as the latter goes, under Cyrus the capital had apparently been at Pasargadai (Parsagarda), where Cyrus was buried in an impressive tomb that was visited by Alexander the Great and can still be seen, and that continued to function as an important imperial and ceremonial center; likewise the Median capital Ekbatana continued to serve as a capital and royal seat; and Babylon too played an important role as an imperial administrative center and occasional royal seat. But Darius built two new imperial capitals, one of which became (according to Greek sources) the main center of his rule: Susa and Persepolis. Both were extensively excavated before the Islamic regime post-Khomeini ended such activities in Iran, and the remains that were published as a result are impressive in the extreme. Vast resources were clearly expended in building immense royal complexes at these two sites. Susa was the main capital, from which Darius ruled; Persepolis, in the heart of Persia, was a summer palace and a nod to old Persian sensibilities, and was made particularly important also by the building nearby at Naqsh-i-Rustam of a huge tomb complex for Darius and his successors.

Most important of all, perhaps, was a careful organization of the Persian royal army. Darius was proud of his own record of military achievement, and his military skills. In his tomb inscription at Naqsih-i-Rustam his first boast, after he had named himself as the favorite of the great god Ahura Mazda and announced that he ruled by the favor of Ahura Mazda, was of his military skill: "as an archer, I am a good archer, both on horse and on foot; as a spearman, I am a good spearman, both on horse and on foot." The Persian king was a military monarch and must demonstrate the personal prowess of the Persian fighting man. The weapons of the Persians, as indicated here, were the bow and the throwing spear, or javelin. His personal weapons accompanied the king at all times, and his personal bow and spear bearers were important and highly trusted political and military advisers.

The Persian and Median core of the army was organized into

This glazed tile depiction of Persian infantry— possibly Darius's Immortals —dates from around 500 B.C.E. in a frieze from Darius's palace at Susa.

structured units according to equipment. The most important unit, was the imperial guard, 10,000 strong and known to the Greeks as the "Immortals," because they supposedly were always kept exactly at the number 10,000, any man who died or retired being instantly replaced. The Immortals wore the standard long robes, trousers, and high felt caps of the Persian and Median warrior; but over these garments they wore a light armor of scales, like fish scales, and they carried long spears with golden apples in place of butt spikes and, of course, the ubiquitous bow and arrows that were the most characteristic Persian weapon. Their shields were light and of a sort of reinforced wicker effective at stopping or diverting arrows and thrown spears, and they also carried curved swords, like scimitars. The other Persian infantry regiments were similarly equipped, but most of them without the scale armor and with shorter throwing spears.

The Persians, born and bred in the mountains, prized mobility and fought as light infantry. They were superbly disciplined, and in battle their main tactic was to rush to within easy bowshot of the enemy (perhaps 100 meters or so) and halt there, setting up their wicker shields into a great shield wall from behind which they fired rapid volleys of arrows into the enemy formation. Each soldier carried a quiver full of dozens of arrows, and the effect of these arrows raining down, fired by a composite bow (the so-called Skythian bow) which had considerable range and fired with great force, could be devastating. Speed of fire was crucial, and the Persian archer could fire an arrow every few seconds. When the arrows had done their work of wounding, killing, disrupting, and demoralizing the enemy, the Persians set the bows aside, took up their shields, and charged home with the spear, which was hurled at the enemy from close range, and then the sword, which was used to finish the enemy off. Special support units also existed—slingers and other types of infantry, mostly from the subject peoples—to skirmish and scout and forage, and so on.

Very important to the Persian system of battle, too, were the cavalry, mostly from Media. Dressed and equipped like the infantry, they rode into battle, where they had four key functions. Before battle, they rode around the enemy forces as they approached and encamped, harassing and trying to disrupt their columns of march and supply lines. They could do this very effectively, as Herodotos's account of the battle of Plataia shows. In the build up to and early stages of the battle, they rode up to and along the front of the enemy formation as it was being drawn up and readied, charging in units, each unit in turn riding close to the enemy formation and then wheeling, firing arrows and/or hurling javelins, and then charging away for the next unit to come up. In this way a constant barrage of arrows and spears could be maintained, and the effect on the nerves of the enemy from the constant cavalry charges must have been wearing.

At times, these tactics alone might break the enemy and turn them to flight. Once the Persian infantry advanced to within bowshot, the cavalry withdrew to the wings of the army, where their task was to attempt to outflank the enemy force on one or both sides, and so attack them in rear as the infantry attacked from in front. Finally, when the enemy broke and fled, the job of the cavalry was to pursue, kill as many as possible, and keep the enemy from regrouping to fight again. Cooperating in this way, the Persian and Median infantry and cavalry conquered all of western Asia, as we have seen, and won a deserved reputation as fearsome and invincible warriors.

One other element of land warfare remains to be discussed, the matter of sieges. In conquering and holding an empire, one cannot afford to be stymied by fortifications. Ancient siege technology at this time was fairly simple: there was little in the way of artillery, except the bow, and complex siege engines were not used. Scaling ladders and mining (under enemy walls, to tunnel into the enemy city or make part of the wall collapse) had been known to and used by the Assyrians. The Persians, however, particularly favored the siege ramp. The standard Persian army included large forces drawn from the subject peoples, of limited use for the hard fighting by and large. But this meant that there was usually plentiful manpower that could be ordered to dig up and carry, or fell and carry, earth, stones and trees in vast quantities to build a ramp that would gradually mount up, in an easy slope, to the tops of the enemy walls. Archers and slingers gave covering fire to the men building the ramp as they got closer to the enemy walls. Once the ramp was complete, the Persian infantry could just charge up it and over the enemy walls into their city. A notable example of such a Persian siege ramp has been excavated by archaeologists at Paphos on Cyprus.

The Persian army, then, in its fully developed form under Darius, was a true army of combined arms—elite infantry and cavalry forces trained to cooperate with each other, and a variety of support units including "sappers" for siege operations. The Greeks, with their tunics and custom of exercising naked, found the voluminous Persian clothing, especially the trousers, absurd and even "womanish"; and with their own heavy armor and shields, and stout thrusting spears, they came to despise the Persian light infantry and Median cavalry. But that disdain arose only after their victories in the Persian invasions. Before the battles of Marathon and Plataia, the Greeks feared the Persian infantry, were awed by the Median cavalry, and found the Persian garb to be fearful rather than ludicrous. Down to the time of Marathon, there were a number of military confrontations between Persians and Greeks, as we shall see, and the Persians invariably came away victorious. The Greeks of the sixth and early fifth centuries did not despise the Persians and Medes, far from it: they respected and feared them, and they had every reason to do so. It is all the more remarkable that they dared, in the end, to stand up to the Persians; and it was no mean feat for the Greeks finally to win. The Persians and Medes were among the outstanding military peoples and systems in history.

Herodotos, though writing in the mid-fifth century, still shows how deeply the Greeks respected the Persians, their culture, their fighting abilities, and their power. He never speaks of the Persian leadership, nobility, and army with anything but respect, and shows a proper appreciation of their courage, their discipline, and their military system. His account of the education system of the Persian noble has often been cited with approval. According to Herodotos, the Persian was taught three basic things: to ride a horse, to shoot the bow, and to tell the truth. This was a simple and noble education, he thought, and that there is much truth to it is evidenced by Darius's self account quoted above, in which he emphasized his abilities as a horseman and as an archer. It should be noted that truth also played a major role in Darius's self-presentation, and in Persian religion. The Persians of Darius's time believed in a form of Zoroastrianism, though they were not doctrinaire or missionary about their religion. In Zoroastrianism, the cosmos is ruled by two opposed deities—Ahura Mazda, the great god of truth, light, and goodness; and Ahriman, the god of dark, the lie, and evil—who are in constant conflict with each other. Humans must choose sides in this conflict, and all good humans will naturally side with Ahura Mazda and fight for truth and light. Darius constantly referred to Ahura Mazda as his patron and benefactor in his inscriptions, and constantly characterized his enemies as proponents of the Lie.

So long as they maintained this rather simple and noble value system, and a considerable degree of toleration for their subjects' values, cultures, and religions, Persian rule was not seen as very irksome in most of western Asia. To some it was even welcome. In the biblical book of Isaiah the Persian king Cyrus was hailed as "the Lord's anointed" (that is, Messiah!) thanks to his policy of permitting the exiled Jews of Babylon to return home, and his edict authorizing the rebuilding of the temple in Jerusalem. And in the book of Esther, the king Xerxes, who to the Greeks seemed the epitome of arrogance, cruelty, and treachery appeared as the mild and honest Ahasuerus, who almost wronged the Jews due to being misled, but treated them kindly as soon as the deception was exposed. There is a great divide, however, between the simple, honest, and noble way of life Herodotos attributes to the early Persians, and the tales of luxury and arrogance that later Greeks came to attribute to the Persians. Whence the difference? Perhaps the Persians had changed: Herodotos certainly seemed to think that they were changing for the worse, under the influence of imperial power and the wealth and luxury it made possible. Though Herodotos and other Greeks can be suspected of anti-Persian bias, of course, it would hardly be surprising if a certain decadence really did come to infect Persian culture after a generation or two of imperial power and wealth

At the very end of his history, Herodotos tells one of his characteristic stories, this one about Cyrus and the Persians. As he tells it, late in Cyrus's reign, the Persians sent a delegation to their king with a request. Since they now owned all of western Asia, it seemed inappropriate to them that they should continue to live in a poor, harsh, mountainous country while many of their subjects lived in much easier, climatically more favored lands. They proposed to the king that they should seize the most pleasant of the lands they controlled and all move there, forcing the current inhabitants out.

Cyrus replied that they could do so if they wished, but they must then be prepared to lose their power and become a subject people again. For soft lands, he claimed, breed soft people; it was the hard and poor nature of their homeland that had made the Persians a tough and conquering people, and they could not expect to remain so if they moved to a soft country. Impressed by this view, says Herodotos, the Persians decided to remain in their own country. But Darius, in fact, did move to Susa, in the land of the ancient Elamites, a flatter, richer land with a softer, warmer climate. And many Persians moved from their homeland to Susa, or to the various satrapies, and took up lives of comfort and luxury there. Herodotos's story, I think, is intended to hint at the reasons for Persian decline and Greek victory in his day: it was now the Greeks who had the virtues, bred in a poor, hard, mountainous country, that the Persians used to have but had lost. But in 500 such ideas lay in the future: as the Persian threat loomed over Greece, no one took the Persians lightly or thought of them as being in decline.

CHAPTER 3

THE ATHENIAN CITY-STATE
ABOUT 500 B.C.E.

I N THE DECADES BEFORE 600 B.C.E., ATHENS WAS BY NO MEANS a very unusual city-state, certainly not one of the leading or most powerful city-states in the Greek world. Yet by 500, little more than a century later, Athens was politically and culturally one of the most advanced city-states in the Greek world, and militarily one of the most powerful and important. Much had obviously changed in the course of the sixth century, and without those changes it's hardly conceivable that the Athenians could even have tried to stand up to the Persian Empire, as they eventually did. The foundations of the Athenians' greatness in the fifth century were laid in the sixth century, especially in some dramatic and trans-forming events in the last decade of that century.

EARLY ATHENS

In 600 the Athenians were a rather middling community, standing out from the general run of Greek city-states in only two respects: the developing Athenian city-state was larger than all but the very largest Greek city-states, and unlike many advanced Greek city-states, Athens had never yet undergone a period of rule by a tyrant. With regard to size, Athens was the largest settlement in the territory of Attica (see map 4), and the Athenians had managed by 600 to bring pretty much all of Attica into their city-state, a territory of some 1,000 sqare miles (about 2,400 square kilometers). The unification of Attica into one city-state was no foregone conclusion: the region of Boiotia to the north of Attica, for example, never achieved unification into one city-state, and there was no obvious geographic or other reason why the communities of Attica should have unified while those of Boiotia did not. Attica could easily have housed four or five or even more independent and rival city-states—in addition to Athens, for example, communities like Eleusis, Marathon, Thorikos, and conceivably even Acharnai and others could have become separate little states—and in that case the great city-state of the Athenians that we know would never have come about. By unifying all of Attica, the Athenians created a city-state that matched or exceeded in size all other Greek city-states except Sparta, and that made the Athenians potentially powerful and important. In 600, though, the unification of Attica was still very fragile and incomplete. The way in which the Athenians completed that unification made them the remarkable and powerful state they became, as we'll see.

The fact that the Athenians had avoided rule by a tyrant down to 600 might be thought of as a good thing for them, but it was not necessarily so. The tyrants of early Greece were progressive, reforming leaders—at least the best of them were—who helped their communities break down various entrenched groups and customs that stood in the way of cultural and political advances. Except for the Spartans, all the most important and highly developed city-states in Greece had experienced tyrannies by 600—the Corinthians, the Milesians, the Argives, and the Sikyonians, for example—and emerged stronger and more unified from that experience. A powerful aristocrat named Kylon did try to make himself tyrant at Athens, probably in 632, but was prevented by the opposition of a very influential aristocratic family called the Alkmaionidai, with

The Athenian Akropolis, with the late fifth century Parthenon.

the backing of much of the common folk. The dispute that arose out of the episode damaged the power and standing of the Alkmaionid family too, though: some of Kylon's supporters were massacred even though they had sought sanctuary at one of the altars or temples on the Akropolis, and the Oracle of Apollo at Delphi was induced to place the Alkmaionid family, and their head Megakles, under a religious curse as a result. That "curse of the Alkmaionidai" was to resonate through Athenian history. Meanwhile Athens remained down to 600 a community dominated by a number of rival aristocratic clans and leaders, and with little in the way of centralized political/religious institutions or popular participation in political life to give it cohesion and strength. It was in fact very much still an old-style Greek community, and this is evidenced by the fact that Athens produced no notable poets or other cultural figures before 600, and played no role in the great colonizing movement that was spreading Greek settlements around the Mediterranean and Black Seas.

One progressive change did come out of the internal disputes at Athens after Kylon's attempted tyranny, though: the Athenians successfully pressured the controlling aristocratic families—the

Eupatridai or "well born ones"—to agree to write down the laws of the community and set them up in a public place where any literate citizen could read them. This happened, according to tradition, in 621, and it was an aristocrat called Drakon who was given the task of writing down the laws. His laws don't survive, except for his law about homicide, which was to be influential through subsequent history for the distinction it made between deliberate murder and involuntary manslaughter. But it seems that most Athenians, when they learned from Drakon what their laws were, became very dissatisfied with those laws. The traditional laws were considered too harsh—or "Draconian," as harsh laws have been called ever since—and agitation arose to change the laws. Soon after 600, this agitation led to the appointing of a new "law establisher," whose revision of the laws of the Athenians, and through them of Athenian society and politics, began the process that turned the Athenians into the most advanced state in Greece. His name was Solon, he was appointed chief magistrate (or *archon*) of Athens in 594, and he was given extraordinary power to revise the laws and settle the conflicts that were roiling Athens. He came to be revered, thanks to his new law code, as one of the "Seven Wise Men" of early Greece, and as the most important reformer in Athenian history.

THE REFORMS OF SOLON

The political agitation at Athens was focused on two major issues: political participation and ownership of land. Down to Solon's archonship, participation in the political life of the Athenian community had been limited to or controlled by the traditional aristocracy, the *Eupatridai*. Every year nine magistrates, the archons, were appointed—we are not sure how, but possibly by some form of election—and only men from Eupatrid families were eligible to become archons. Since these archons were the executive officers and chief judges of the community, the day to day governing of the community was in their hands. After their year in office, archons became life members of a state council that came to be called the "Areopagos Council," after the Areopagos hill on which they met, near the Akropolis. The Areopagos Council seems to have been in effect the ruling organ of the community: overseeing the annual magistrates, setting policy, and acting as a kind of "supreme court" on major political and social issues and trials. Since it was made up of former archons, it was an aristocratic council—its members exclusively from Eupatrid families—and all of the leading and successful politicians of the community were members. Its prestige was thus great. Furthermore, Athenian citizenship, such as it was at that time, seems to have been exercised through membership of groups called "phratries": notionally kinship groups, but in reality religio-social organizations through which communal, religious, and military participation, as well as whatever limited political activity was open to "commoners," was organized; and membership of the phratries was apparently controlled by the Eupatrid families. Thus the traditional aristocracy had a firm grip on the political life of the community. Yet Greece was changing, economically, socially, and militarily, as we have seen, and Athens was not exempt. There was a substantial class of men who were not from Eupatrid families yet were well-to-do or even wealthy—thanks to farming, manufacturing, and/or trading activities—and who resented their exclusion from magistracies and the state council, and the Eupatrid control of active political participation.

As to land ownership, this seems to have been a matter that was very much in dispute. Traditionally, it has been supposed that the aristocratic families owned most of the land, which was worked for them by tenants who paid as rent one sixth of their produce, these tenants thus being known as *hektemoroi* or "one-sixth share men." By this supposition, the dispute Solon faced is seen as a demand by the tenants or sharecroppers for redistribution of the land, dispossessing the *Eupatridai* of much of their estates and granting that seized land to the families who worked it; with the

Eupatrid families naturally resisting this demand and insisting on the *hektemoroi* continuing as tenants and paying their rents. This view of the matter sees the issues of Solon's day as very similar to disputes about land ownership in the fourth century B.C.E. and later, which is what our sources writing in that period (especially Aristotle) thought to be the case.

But in accepting this view, we may be accepting an anachronistic view of the issue, and one which doesn't entirely accord with some remarks of Solon himself: for Solon was a poet as well as reformer, and some of his poetry about his reforms still survives. The traditional view, in effect, takes the concept of private ownership of land, land as private property, for granted. But private ownership of land—as natural as it seemed to fourth century Greeks and seems to us today—is not found in all human societies, and shouldn't be treated as a given, therefore. We know of many societies in which much of the land was communally owned, or in which the very concept of ownership of land was missing. For example, in medieval Britain huge tracts of land were "common lands," controlled and used by village communities collectively; and in north America and Australia before the European takeover, many of the aboriginal peoples had no concept of ownership of the land, but simply had tribal territories where the members of tribes lived and hunted. It's worth considering whether and to what degree private ownership of the land was already established in Attica before Solon's day.

Archaeological exploration of Attica, and Greece more generally, has shown that most settlements in Greece were abandoned at the end of the Bronze Age, between about 1100 and 1000 B.C.E. The population of Greece, for whatever reasons, evidently declined dramatically, and it's thought that much of the remaining population took up a sort of semi-nomadic sheep herding lifestyle known as transhumant pastoralism: moving each year between summer pastures in the mountains and winter pastures in the coastal plains, and keeping no permanent settlements to live in as a result.

Beginning about 800 B.C.E. the style of life turned more

towards agriculture and living in permanent settlements again, leading to the classical Greek civilization of the sixth to the third centuries B.C.E. with which we are familiar. This means that Attica, in
particular, was mostly empty of permanent settlements as late as
750 B.C.E., and the few permanent settlements that remained—like
Athens itself—were small and poor. Under these conditions, with
most of Attica being used only seasonally by wandering shepherds
with their flocks, the majority of the land of Attica lay waste, and
was owned by no one. It isn't at all obvious or inevitable that, when
and as groups of people began to resettle the land of Attica and
bring it back into agricultural use between about 750 and 600, they
did so by taking parcels of land as private property at once. Turning waste land into productive farmland takes time and a considerable investment of effort and capital. Tools are needed, seeds,
food supplies to feed those doing the work until the land starts to
yield crops. Some of that capital may have been provided by
wealthy leaders, who may have felt they had a claim to the lands
brought into agriculture, as a result; but it's also likely that much
of this process was achieved by communal efforts and mutual aid,
and that the lands being turned into farms were thought of as communal lands rather than private property, initially.

In other words, the issue Solon confronted was very likely that
of the process of the agricultural lands of Attica being turned from
communal lands into privately owned lands. He termed this part of
his reform program the *seisachtheia,* which seems to mean "throwing off a burden"; and in one of his poems he speaks of freeing the
land of Attica that had been enslaved by boundary markers set
down by the rich.

> Regarding this I call to witness in the court of time
> the mother of the Olympian gods, greatest and best,
> black Earth herself, for I once removed from her
> the boundary markers everywhere fixed in her:
> before, she was enslaved; now she is free.

Solon's language in this and other poems, in which he speaks of the excessive greed of the rich, makes sense if what was happening is that the wealthy, aristocratic families were claiming that essentially common lands which, as the leaders of the community, they had to some degree controlled, were now their private property; that the "one sixth share" the farmers paid was not a contribution to some sort of communal reserve held, for example, by the phratries, but a rent paid to them, the aristocratic "owners"; that the *hektemoroi* were, therefore, their tenants. By way of comparison, one can point to the "Enclosure Acts" in eighteenth century England, through which the English upper class took the common lands of England into private ownership; or the American Homestead Act, which allowed European settlers to turn formerly communally controlled tribal lands of the native peoples into privately owned farms. One might even guess that it was the aim of the *Eupatridai* to turn the *hektemoroi* into a kind of unfree serf class, like the Helots of Sparta and the *Penestai* of Thessaly. As against these claims by the rich aristocrats, we can see the *hektemoroi* resisting, refusing any longer to pay the one sixth share (and being enslaved by the rich for doing so!), and arguing that if the land was to be private property, it should be the property of the families that actually lived on and farmed it.

Solon was thus confronted with a choice: whether Attica was to be a land of large estates owned by wealthy aristocrats and farmed by a "serf" class, or a land of small farms owned and worked by independent and moderately well-to-do farmers. He chose the latter, and in doing so laid the basis for the later Athenian democracy. Because the numerous, independent, and well-to-do middle class of small farmers that resulted from his *seisachtheia* formed the backbone of the Athenian *demos* (people) that eventually established the world's first democratic governing system.

In dealing with the issue of political access and input, Solon's solution followed the same line: just as he had broken the Eupatrid attempt to have exclusive ownership of the land, he ended the exclusive Eupatrid control of politics. Instead of the rule that only persons belonging to the right descent groups could participate in politics, Solon instituted four property classes—in essence, the very rich, the wealthy, the well-to-do, and the poor—and made the top two property classes eligible to hold the magistracies and thus become members of the Areopagos Council. This opened the archonships and the Council to non-Eupatrid Athenians who owned enough property, and permitted upward mobility in politics since anyone who could gain sufficient wealth could be enrolled in one of the upper property classes and thus become eligible for magistracies and Council. There was a good deal more to Solon's reform program, but these are the essential parts of it. By them, Solon did not create democracy, but he made democracy a possibility. Had he chosen to side with the *Eupatridai* and enforce their claims, the democratic Athens of the fifth and fourth centuries that we know and revere as the cradle of our culture and political ideas could never have come about.

Solon's reform program seems to have pleased hardly anyone. The *Eupatridai* were furious at the loss of their exclusive privileges and of their claims to the land; the rest of the Athenians felt that Solon had not gone far enough, leaving the aristocracy still with substantial estates, and the rich still with a dominant position in political life. In the same poem in which he claimed to have freed the earth, Solon likened himself to a "wolf turning about among many dogs"; and he spoke in another poem of having taken a middle position, holding his sturdy shield over both parties, the people and the rich and powerful, giving too much power and privilege to no one group but trying to protect the proper rights of all. But despite this widespread dissatisfaction, Solon's fundamental settlement of landownership and spreading of political participation took hold, and became crucial parts of the Athenian socio-political order, establishing Solon in the minds of later Athenians as their greatest lawgiver and founder of their political system.

THE PEISISTRATID TYRANNY

After Solon, the main problem that continued to beset the developing Athenian state was lack of cohesion, the still incomplete unification of Attica into one state. Political life in post-Solon Athens revolved, according to Herodotos and Aristotle, around three factions that were based in separate regions of Attica, reflecting a tendency to place regional ties and loyalties above any sense of common Athenian identity. These factions were: the *Pedieis*, that is the men who lived in the Athenian plain (*to pedion*) around the city of Athens itself, led by a Eupatrid named Lykourgos; the *Paralioi*, the men of the coastal region of southern Attica (called the *paralia*), led by the head of the Alkmaionid family, Megakles (grandson of the first Megakles); and the *Hyperakrioi*, the men of eastern Attica (from the perspective of Athens, from "beyond the hills"—the Pentele range—which is what *hyperakrioi* means), led by Peisistratos. These three factions competed with each other during the 570s and 560s, with Lykourgos and the *Pedieis*, having the advantage of living at and around the political center (Athens) itself, generally on top. A short lived alliance between Megakles and Peisistratos enabled the latter to take charge of Athens briefly as tyrant around 560 or so: they found an exceptionally tall and beautiful woman named Phye, dressed her up in the traditional gear of the goddess Athena, and put it about that Athena herself was bringing Peisistratos to the Akropolis to install him as ruler.

One hundred years later Herodotos still laughed at the gullibility of the Athenians in falling for this scheme. To cement the alliance Peisistratos married a daughter of Megakles, but the pact quickly fell apart when Peisistratos did not want to father Megakles' grandsons to be his heirs, having grown sons of his own to succeed him, and so "did not have sex with her in the normal way," as Herodotos delicately phrased it. Megakles then allied with Lykourgos' faction to drive Peisistratos out, and the two seem to have run Athens fairly peacefully for the next ten years. But in 548/7

Peisistratos returned with a large army of mercenaries and allies, defeated the forces of his rivals at Pallene in central Attica, where the road from Marathon crosses into the plain of Athens, and made himself tyrant of Athens until his death in 528, to be succeeded by his son Hippias for another seventeen years or so.

Though the Peisistratid tyranny emerged from the regional disunity of Attica and represented the victory of one of the regional factions, Peisistratos as tyrant rose above this regionalism and made it a key part of his policy to work at a fuller unification of Attica. In fact, in spite of the evil reputation tyranny acquired as a system of rule, Peisistratos was remembered as a moderate and popular ruler who did good things for Athens, and with good reason. With the cooperation of his sons, he pursued a variety of policies that improved the conditions of life in Athens and Attica, that strengthened the unification of Attica, and that brought Athens more into the mainstream of Greek culture and economic life.

For example, he encouraged agriculture in Attica, using a 5 percent tax on agricultural produce to establish a fund to provide capital for men to bring marginal lands into cultivation. He estab-

The Panathenaic Stadium at Athens, as reconstructed for the 1896 Olympic Games.

lished a system of impartial traveling judges, who went around the so-called "demes" (local villages and regions) of Attica to settle lawsuits and arbitrate disputes without the litigants having to go to the trouble and expense of traveling to the city of Athens. He improved the water supply of Athens, creating a great fountain house and bringing an abundant source of water into the heart of the city. He used religion to promote unification, bringing the local cults of Attica—such as the cult of Artemis at Brauron in eastern Attica, and the mysteries of Demeter at Eleusis in northern Attica—under central control and making them cults of all Athenians. Above all, he built up the festival of Athena, the *Panathenaia*, into a unifying festival for all Athenians.

In addition, to these policies aimed at improving conditions at home, Peisistratos sought to give Athens a higher profile in the Greek world. He built up the so-called "great *Panathenaia*" held every fourth year into an interstate festival for all Greeks, on the model of the Olympic and Pythian games. Contestants from every part of the Greek world came to compete in the contests at the festival, with the winners receiving valuable prizes of Attic olive oil—which enjoyed wide repute for its high quality—presented in special prize amphoras. These contests were not just athletic: there were contests in music and poetry too, notably a contest in recitation of the Homeric epics. Through this latter contest, the Peisistratids promoted the collation of variant versions of Homer and the careful sifting of them to produce the first authoritative texts of the two great epics. It is this Peisistratid edition of the Homeric epics that is commonly thought to underlie the texts we still use today.

Further, Athens entered more fully into the world of Greek trade and colonization. Since the late seventh century the Athenians had exported fine pottery and olive oil around the Greek world, but under Peisistratos and his sons the Athenians developed an interest in the valuable and important Black Sea trade. The products of that region—timber, grain, hides, slaves, metals, and fish—were prized all around the Greek world. Through colonization of the shores of the Black Sea and its approaches, the cities of Miletos and Megara had acquired a dominant position in this trade. Peisistratos promoted Athenian colonizing ventures at the mouth of the Hellespont (modern Dardanelles), the first narrow bottleneck in the route between the Aegean and Black Seas. At Sigeion, on the Asian side near ancient Troy, and on the long peninsula making up the northern side of the Hellespont—called by Greeks the Thracian *Chersonnesos*—Athenian settlements established outposts through which the Athenians could gain a secure entry into the Black Sea trade. As the city of Athens grew through the economic stimulus of Peisistratid peace and development policies, it was becoming important to be able to import grain and timber and other raw materials of which the Black Sea region was a rich source.

Through the rule of Peisistratos and, after his death, of his sons Hippias and Hipparchos, Athens grew more united, prosperous, and prominent in Greek affairs. But the very success of the tyranny began to undermine it. Throughout the Greek world, by the late sixth century, tyranny was going out of fashion, and in Athens itself prominent aristocratic families like the Alkmaionidai and the Philaidai (the family of the great Miltiades) were growing tired of Peisistratid domination; and the middle class of Athenians had developed to the point where it was ready to take an active political role.

In 514 the tyrant Hippias's brother Hipparchos was assassinated as a result of a sexual intrigue—the famous Harmodios and Aristogeiton affair. In the typical homo-erotic upper class culture of the time, relationships of a mentoring and sexual nature were common between mature men in their late twenties or older, and handsome youths in their late teens and early twenties. Harmodios was just such a handsome aristocratic youth, and he caught the eye of Hipparchos, who had a taste for such relationships. But Harmodios already had an older lover, Aristogeiton, and he rejected Hipparchos's advances. With the arrogance of long power, Hipparchos resented this and responded by publicly insulting

Harmodios's family; and it was that insult that led Harmodios and Aristogeiton to kill him. His brother's death brought out a vengeful strain of paranoia in Hippias: he assumed that this assassination must be part of a wider conspiracy against his rule, and instituted something of a "reign of terror," with torture and executions of those suspected of disloyalty. In this way the popular tyranny founded by Peisistratos became deeply unpopular; but it was still a strongly rooted tyranny that could not be easily overthrown. It was the head of the Alkmaionid family, which had been obliged to flee into exile, who found a way to get rid of the tyrant.

KLEISTHENES AND THE INVENTION OF DEMOCRACY

Kleisthenes the Alkmaionid deserves to be much more famous in Western civilization than he is, for it was Kleisthenes who first brought about the fall of the Peisistratid tyranny, and then—much more importantly—established the democratic system of government that was Athens' most important legacy to the modern world. Kleisthenes, that is to say, was effectively the inventor of democracy, and yet his name is virtually unknown outside of a narrow circle of professional scholars of ancient Greece and Rome. His first problem was to end Hippias's tyranny, and he and his supporters lacked the strength to do this by their own military action: they had tried in 513, after Hipparchos's killing, and failed. Kleisthenes, however, had considerable influence at the great Oracle of Apollo at Delphi, the single most sacred and important religious sanctuary in the Greek world.

Some decades earlier an earthquake had destroyed the temple of Apollo at Delphi, and the wealthy Alkmaionidai had taken the contract for rebuilding the temple. Though this contract called for a temple built of local limestone, the Alkmaionids had, at their own expense, provided a facade of expensive Parian marble, winning them the gratitude of the Oracle's priests. Using this gratitude, Kleisthenes persuaded the Oracle to instruct the Spartans, whenever they sent a delegation to consult Apollo—and the Spartans were particularly scrupulous about religion and consulting the will of the gods—that the god required them to free the Athenians. In 511/10 this repeated refrain finally moved the Spartans, reluctantly, to action: they sent a small expeditionary force under a minor Spartan officer to tell Hippias he should resign his tyranny. Hippias's forces drove these Spartans off with ease; but that, of course, set Spartan military prestige on the line and committed the Spartans seriously to overthrowing Hippias.

As a result of this blow to their prestige, the Spartans now sent a large-scale expedition led by the most influential Spartan of this time, King Kleomenes, to attack Hippias and bring down his rule. The Peisistratids and their supporters took refuge on the Akropolis and withstood a siege, but when Hippias tried to smuggle his grandchildren to safety they were intercepted and captured, and in order to get them back unharmed Hippias was forced to agree to give up power and leave Athens with his whole family. The Peisistratids went into exile at Sigeion in the Troad, and Athens was left a free state after some 38 years of tyranny.

Since Peisistratos had never abolished or even materially altered the Solonic governing system, allowing it to continue to function under his directing oversight, the magistrates and Areopagos Council were able to continue governing Athens without any serious hiccup. Still, after such a long tyranny, there was naturally uncertainty over who would govern Athens in the longer term, and how. In particular, it seems that divisions immediately arose between the leading, wealthy families that had remained peacefully in Athens under the Peisistratid rule, and those who had returned from exile with Hippias's removal. The latter group was led by Kleisthenes, and in the initial political infighting, they had the worst of it. It was this defeat in the traditional aristocratic politics of the years immediately after Hippias that led Kleisthenes, in 508, to devise a new political strategy. In the words of Herodotos, he took the people into his faction.

Herodotos's narrative, with his typical emphasis on individual leaders and their personal motivations, is deceptively simple. It's obvious, when one looks at the details of Kleisthenes' reforms as they emerge from Aristotle's account and from the Athenian government of the 490s and 480s, that Kleisthenes offered the Athenian *demos* (people) a wide-ranging set of proposals for changing the Athenian political system, a set of proposals that can hardly have been thought up on the spur of the moment, nor motivated simply by a desire to best his political opponents of the moment. And it's equally obvious that, in taking up Kleisthenes' offer and backing his proposals, the Athenian people were ready, even eager for change. In the face of the Athenians' acceptance of Kleisthenes' reform proposals, the leader of the conservative aristocrats, the archon for 508/7, Isagoras, turned to the Spartans for help. He was a personal friend of the Spartan king Kleomenes, and knew that the essentially oligarchic Spartans would not approve of the radical reforms Kleisthenes was bringing about at Athens.

Kleomenes responded to Isagoras's appeal by invoking the ancient "curse of the Alkmaionidai," ordering those under the curse to leave Athens. Apparently not wanting to be seen as the cause of a Spartan military intervention at Athens, Kleisthenes obeyed and left Athens. But Isagoras and Kleomenes were not content with this victory. Kleomenes now came to Athens with a small Spartan force and ordered everyone associated with the Alkmaionids and their curse to be exiled: we are told that 700 families were forced to flee from Attica, and that even the bones of their dead were dug up and flung out of Athenian territory. So far so good, but Kleomenes and Isagoras now proceeded to overreach. In their determination to place power at Athens firmly in the hands of Isagoras and his supporters, they ordered the state Council—presumably, that is, the Areopagos Council—to disband, reportedly intending to purge it and establish a new more loyal Council made up of 300 supporters of Isagoras. But the Council refused to disband, and instead called on the Athenian people to rise up in support of their Council and their own rights.

To the great surprise and dismay of Isagoras and Kleomenes, the Athenian people responded to this appeal forcefully and in great number. In the face of armed Athenians pouring into the streets in defense of the Council, Kleomenes and Isagoras and their supporters withdrew to the Akropolis and barricaded themselves in. They most likely expected the public tumult to die down fairly soon, as popular anger subsided and people drifted back to their homes and daily routines. The opposite happened: the people organized a siege of the Akropolis, keeping a careful guard on the gates, more and more men streaming in to join as word of the siege spread, even camping out overnight around the Akropolis with their arms to ensure that there could be no escape for the besieged.

After a few days of this, faced with inadequate water and lack of supplies, Kleomenes was forced to negotiate a withdrawal from Athens. He and his Spartans had to leave their weapons behind and return to Sparta in ignominy, leaving their Athenian allies to the judgment of the Athenian people—though Kleomenes did succeed in smuggling out his terrified friend Isagoras. Kleisthenes and the rest of the Alkmaionids and their supporters were recalled to Athens, and the reform program Kleisthenes had proposed was enacted. This was the birth of Athenian democracy: a reform package created by a rogue aristocrat, and a popular uprising against those from within Athens and without who tried to prevent that reform package from being enacted.

Kleisthenes' reforms of the Athenian governing system were complex, intricate; they reached deep into Athenian society in a variety of ways, and they cannot—despite the impression created by our sources and at times accepted at face value by historians—have been enacted and put into effect in a mere matter of weeks or months. We should more likely think of a process taking up a year or two, perhaps even longer, which has been telescoped by our sources into a single act of reform. The outcome of all the reforming, in whatever way and whenever it was carried out, is not in doubt however. Kleisthenes and the Athenian people created a system of government in which the free inhabitants of Attica were defined as citizens of the Athenian city-state with roughly equal political rights, duties, and privileges, and in which, as roughly equal Athenian citizens, the people ruled the state in the most direct and immediate sense. The Athenian form of democracy was what is called a "direct participatory" democracy: there was no distinction between the people and the government, because the people *were* the government. The basic principles of the system were two: the fundamental political equality of all citizens, which the Greeks called *isonomia* (equality before or under the law); and the right of all citizens to meet in decision making assemblies, and to discuss, debate, and decide public policy freely and with essential equality in those assemblies, which the Greeks called *isegoria* (equality of meeting in and addressing the assembly).

The principle that the citizens *were* the state and governed themselves directly was not new to democratic Athens: that notion, expressed by the way Greeks always referred to states as a collective noun—for example, the Corinthians or the Megarians, never Corinth or Megara—was already well established in Greek political life. What was new with democratic Athens was the widespread diffusion of citizenship, making not some minority or elite group the sovereign body in the state, but the Athenian people (that is, the free male inhabitants who formed the citizen group) as a whole. And this is why ultimately it was the term *demokrateia* (rule by the people) that came to be most widely used to describe this system. To be sure ancient Athens was, like every other ancient society, a slave owning society and slaves—who were virtually all imported foreigners, some Greek, but most from non-Greek peoples—did not enjoy citizen rights and so did not form part of the *demos*, the people seen as a political entity. And like all ancient societies too, Athens was patriarchal in nature, meaning that women did not enjoy active citizen rights. But that is merely to say that Athens was not a modern society. The point of lasting interest about the Athenian state was how remarkably widespread political rights were, with apparently every free-born male inhabitant fully enfranchised under Kleisthenes' reforms; and how fully and actively the citizens participated in the government of their community, making their democracy a true case of self-government by the citizens.

Of course, establishing the principle that the *demos*, the people as a whole, should be sovereign is one thing; actualizing it, putting it into practice, is another. And it was the process of making popular government a reality that was complicated and required a whole program of detailed, well thought out reforms. The crucial thing that needed to be done was to weave the citizen as political participant and the citizen as warrior into the fabric of the Athenian city-state in a way that would at the same time complete the unification of all of Attica and its inhabitants as the Athenian city-state.

That was a tall order, but Kleisthenes' solution to that problem was so elegant and successful, that there was never afterwards any issue as to how citizenship at Athens was defined, nor any trace of the old regionalist disunity. To achieve this effect, Kleisthenes created ten new subdivisions of the Athenian people, called *phylai* (usually, if misleadingly, translated as "tribes"), and grouped Athenian citizens into these *phylai* in such a way that each tribe was a microcosm of Attica and of the Athenian people. Each tribe was divided into thirds (*trittyes* in the Greek), and one third of each tribe came from each of the three regions of Attica. That is to say, every tribe was made up for one third of men from the plain of Athens itself (*Pedieis*), one third of men from the southern coastal region (*Paralioi*), and one third of men from central and eastern Attica (*Hyperakrioi*). In this way, citizens from all three regions of Attica were obliged to work together in the religious, political, and military functioning of the state. The *phylai* had an important role in state cult, were the organizing units of the Athenian hoplite phalanx (that is, army), and were a crucial division of the people for important political purposes. In this way men from every part of Attica learned to stop thinking of themselves as belonging to a particular region, and to think of themselves simply as Athenians instead.

The basic constituent parts of the *phylai* were not the *trittyes*, however, but the "demes" or local communities of which those "thirds" were made up. All around Attica there were numerous small towns, villages, and rural communities in which a substantial proportion of the "Athenians" actually lived—the population of Athens itself making up less than half of the Athenian people at this time. Kleisthenes designated all such communities as demes, and in addition divided the city of Athens and its suburbs into a number of demes also. In each of the three regions of Attica, the local demes were divided into ten groups in such a way as to ensure that each group had roughly the same population. These thirty groups of demes, ten in each region, were of course the *trittyes* or thirds of the *phylai*, and each of these "tribes" was thus made up of the populations of demes from all regions of Attica. And it was these demes that were made the basis for Athenian citizenship.

Every free Athenian was registered in the local deme in which he and/or his family lived, and it was made the responsibility of the local demes to maintain their lists of citizens for the future: striking off the names of deceased members, and adding the names of sons of deme members as they reached adulthood, membership of a deme being made hereditary regardless of changes in domicile. Each deme was given its own democratic government: an assembly of the demesmen, and magistrates (*demarchoi*) responsible to the assembly. In this way, the people of Athens were themselves placed in charge of determining who were and were not Athenian citizens, and so who got to participate in the politics and governance of Athens. The phratries continued to play an important part in witnessing to their members' eligibility for enrollment as citizens, but they were no longer controlled by the aristocracy, and the deme assemblies had the final say.

With all free-born inhabitants of Attica enrolled as citizens, mechanisms were needed to establish firmly the people's gover-

nance of the community. The traditional state Council, the Areopagos, was upper class in make-up, indeed still predominantly
aristocratic. It retained significant powers of a primarily judicial
and investigative nature—examining qualifications for magistracies
and wrongdoing by magistrates, for example—but its most important functions in the day to day governance and oversight of the
community and its affairs were taken from it and given to a new
state Council, the *Boule* (Council) of the 500, so-named because it
had 500 members. This *Boule* was carefully designed to form a representative sample of the Athenian people. It was made up of ten
groups of councilors, fifty from each of the ten tribes. The councilors were appointed by the demes, each deme appointing a number of councilors proportionate to its population. All Athenian
citizens in good standing and over thirty were eligible to serve. The
names of those eligible and willing to serve were placed into a lottery in each deme, and the requisite number of councilors were thus
selected by lot. In this way the *Boule* truly was an accurate representative cross section of the Athenian people.

It is worth pausing on the size of the sample for a moment,
and a comparative example can be illuminating in this regard. The
500 councilors of Athens represented a citizen body of between
about 30,000 and 50,000 men, according to the best estimates by
historians of Athenian demography. The USA too has a representative council of sorts: the Congress, which has a total of 535 members—100 in the Senate and 435 in the House of Representatives.
But those 535 members serve a citizen body of some 228 million
(227,719,424 according to the US Census Bureau's 2007 estimate)!
We can see that Kleisthenes' aim in creating such a large council, apportioned carefully so as to give each locality and community a proportionate representation, and using a lottery system to ensure
randomness of selection, really was to produce a body that was as
nearly a perfect random sample of the Athenian people as it was
possible to create.

This democratic *Boule* oversaw the day-to-day functioning of the government and magistrates, and in particular discussed issues of public importance in a preliminary way, and on the basis of doing that prepared and set the agenda for the popular assembly meetings. It was not, however, a decision-making, executive council: all major decisions must be referred to and made by the assembly of Athenian citizens. To make the actual functioning of the Council as democratic and equal as possible, the working of the Council was closely tied to the ten tribes. The Athenian state calendar, essentially based on and around religious cults and festivals, was made up of twelve lunar months totaling 354 days, which required an intercalary month to be inserted every few years to bring the lunar year into alignment with the solar year of 365 days.

In addition to this standard religiously based calendar, Kleisthenes instituted a new political year of ten units, called "prytanies," each of which was associated with one of the ten tribes. Thus each of the ten *phylai* in turn presided over the Athenian system for a thirty-six-day "political month." This was seen most particularly in relation to the *Boule*: the fifty representatives of the tribe which was associated with a given *prytany* formed in effect an executive committee of the Council for that thirty-six-day period. Every day the fifty councilors who held the *prytany* selected one of their members by lot to serve as presiding officer of the Council for that twenty-four-hour period. He was required to spend the entire twenty-four-hour period at the *Tholos*, a state building next to the Council House on the edge of the Athenian *agora* (central town square), and had to select seven or eight fellow members of his tribal contingent to watch with him. In this way, there was at all times a sub-committee of the *Boule* available in the heart of Athens to accept and begin to deal with any public business that might arise. Further, in order to ensure that no tribe would regularly hold the *prytany* during a particularly busy or important part of the year, the order of the tribal "prytanies" was reset each year by a process of allotment.

The main role of the Council was to preside over the regular assembly meetings. Assembly meetings were to be held a minimum of four times during each "prytany," that is every nine days, and it was the duty of the council to set the agenda for each popular assembly meeting, and of the tribal contingent holding the "prytany" to preside. The agenda for assembly meetings was advertised in advance, and in particular important policy proposals or proposed laws were published days in advance on whitened boards which were displayed for all citizens to read in the *agora* of Athens, at a monument in front of the Council chamber that was set up to honor the ten "tribal heroes." For Kleisthenes had obtained divine sanction for his reorganization of the Athenian citizen body by submitting a list of one hundred names of traditional heroes of Athenian myth and cult to the Oracle of Apollo at Delphi, asking Apollo to select the ten heroes who would give their names to the new Athenian *phylai*. All Athenians who were willing and free to do so, then, met every nine days in open assembly—or more frequently if there was important business that could not wait until the next regular assembly meeting—and there discussed, debated, and formally decided all matters of public business and policy. The people's vote was binding: the magistrates were required to enforce and be guided by the people's publicly expressed will, and the *Boule* was there to oversee the magistrates and ensure that they conducted themselves in accordance with the people's publicly expressed will.

For certain important forms of public business, a quorum of 6,000 citizens was required to be present at the assembly, indicating that the Athenians could and did expect a sixth or more of the citizen body to be present at the assembly on any given occasion. That is a high proportion of participation, given that there were forty or more such assembly meetings throughout the year. Athenians were, under the Kleisthenic system, active participants in self-governance, that is to say.

The same point can be made with respect to the *Boule*. Service on the Council was for one year only, and after a year on the Council one was ineligible to serve again until ten years had passed; and no Athenian could serve more than twice. Since 500 Councilors were empaneled each year, it is clear that over the course of a standard twenty-five-year generation, some 12,000 or more Athenian citizens must have served a year or two on the Council: more than a quarter of the available citizens of any given generation. This meant that there was a large segment of the citizen body that had detailed experience of public business from serving on the Council; and that the Athenian citizens, through consultation of the whitened boards at the Monument of the Ten Heroes, came to assembly meetings well informed and well prepared to debate and vote.

Through this Council and the regular assembly meetings, then, Kleisthenes created a genuinely popular governing system, one in which the people literally were the government in the fullest sense. Calling this system "direct participatory democracy" is no misnomer. It should be noted how much the system relied on allotment: the Athenians distrusted elections—as favoring the wealthy and prominent candidates over the average citizen—and insisted as much as possible on random allocations of duties and responsibilities. Eventually, numerous boards of overseers for all sorts of public business were set up to conduct public business at Athens, and so far as possible the principle of allotment was always maintained. Initially, under Kleisthenes' laws, the nine annual Archons were still elected and still held important powers, and the Areopagos Council still offered an organ of upper class oversight of public affairs; but that was to be changed by further reforms in 487 and in the 460s, as we know from Aristotle's treatise on the Athenian constitution.

So the democracy was not completed by Kleisthenes, but there can really be no doubt that his constitution was democratic, and that he was therefore the inventor of democracy. An important aspect of the Athenian democracy created by Kleisthenes remains to be discussed, however. The Athenian citizen was not just a political participant and part of the sovereign state assembly; he was also, and very importantly, a warrior who fought in battle to protect and advance his state and its interests. Greek warfare was, as we've seen, a citizen militia style of warfare, and in an important sense it was his role as a warrior who risked his life for the state that justified the citizen's right to a roughly equal political participation and voice.

Under Kleisthenes' reform, the Athenian hoplite phalanx was intimately tied to the new system of the ten *phylai*. It was the tribes that maintained a register of the citizens eligible for military service, and especially of those citizens well off enough to equip themselves and serve as hoplite warriors. The Athenian phalanx was made up, after Kleisthenes, of ten *taxeis* (regiments) provided by the ten *phylai*. The men of each tribe thus served and fought together, cementing their mutual co-operation and sense of unity. Further, Kleisthenes had created a new state magistracy in connection with this: each tribe annually elected a *strategos* (general) to organize and command the tribe's *taxis* of the phalanx. The ten annual *strategoi* not only commanded their tribal regiments in war, but also formed the military council of the Athenian commander in chief, who was at this time (and down to 487) still the *polemarchos* (war archon). Over subsequent decades, in fact, as the prestige of the traditional archons waned and their powers were curtailed, the ten *strategoi* grew in importance to become the chief executive magistrates of the Athenian city-state. Serving together in this hoplite phalanx under generals they had themselves elected proved to be one of the crucial factors binding the Athenians to their new governing system, and giving them the self-confidence to make the democratic government a practical reality.

There were other minor details to the Kleisthenic system, but one important fail-safe mechanism deserves full description. Kleisthenes' reforms came out of the aftermath of a near forty-year tyranny at Athens, and the danger of another leader trying to seize autocratic power was of great concern. To counter this, Kleisthenes created an institution known as *ostrakismos*, the origin of the English word ostracism.

Every year, at a designated assembly meeting, the assembled Athenian citizens would be asked by the presiding councilors whether there was, in their opinion, some prominent leader in Athens whose power seemed too great, such as to make him a threat to the democracy, a potential tyrant in effect. If that assembly's response was that yes, there was such a dangerous leader, a special assembly meeting would be called to vote on the question of who it was that represented a danger to the state. This special assembly was one of those requiring a quorum of 6,000 voters to be present; and if the quorum was met, the man who received the most votes was exiled from Athens for a ten-year period, but without loss of property or other civic rights, nor with any dishonor to himself or his family. The aim was simply to remove dangerous leaders from the political process for a ten year "cooling off" period. Though Aristotle tells us that ostracism was instituted by Kleisthenes, he adds that it was only after more than fifteen years had passed that the Athenians first ostracized a fellow citizen: Hipparchos the son of Charmos in 487. Some historians have doubted that ostracism was a Kleisthenic innovation, due to this long interval between invention and implementation, which they find implausible. However, apart from a flurry of five successive ostracisms in the 480s (Hipparchos in 487, then Megakles, Xanthippos, a man whose name is lost, and Aristides in the immediately following years), ostracisms seem to have been fairly rare.

We know of Themistokles in 472, Kimon in 462, Thucydides son of Melesias about 440, and Hyperbolos in 418. It's conceivable that lots of other Athenians were ostracized in intervening years of whom we don't happen to hear, but not very likely. It was in fact rare for the Athenians both to agree that there was a leader who represented a danger to the democracy, and to subsequently show up in sufficient numbers to complete an ostracism. So it isn't really very surprising that it should have taken years for the first ostracism to occur. And there is a late tradition that in fact Kleisthenes was the first Athenian to be ostracized, a victim of his own political success and his own reform. We can't be sure that was true, but it would explain Kleisthenes' otherwise puzzling disappearance from Athenian political life immediately after his reforms.

A final point worth making about Kleisthenes is to explain his surprising obscurity: why is the inventor of democracy not more famous for his achievement? The answer is found in Athenian politics at the end of the fifth century. Between 431 and 404 the Athenians fought and, famously, lost a great war against the Spartans and various allies, the so-called Peloponnesian War. As part of the peace deal imposed by the Spartans, the Athenian democracy was overthrown and replaced by a narrow oligarchic regime known as the "Thirty Tyrants." But after only a year the Athenians rose up, overthrew the Thirty, and re-instituted their democracy, and in doing so they established a commission to look into the constitutional laws of Athens, to create a coherent and ordered structure of constitutional law out of the law-establishing activities of Drakon, Solon, Kleisthenes, and Ephialtes (in the late 460s), and in general the Athenian people's numerous ad hoc laws and decrees over the years. The constitution established by this commission in 399 was in its greatest part a systematized version of the Kleisthenic constitution as reformed by Ephialtes: we are well informed about it through Aristotle's "Constitution of the Athenians" and by fragments of the inscribed laws themselves. But one of the criticisms aimed at the Athenian democracy during the late 5th century was that it was new, that it was a departure from the proper and ancient *patrios politeia* (ancestral constitution) of the Athenians.

Ancient Greek city-states, like virtually all human societies, revered tradition, and this criticism was therefore a powerful one. It seemed necessary, as a result, to establish that the democratic constitution re-established in 399 was the Athenian *patrios politeia*, and the reforming activities of Ephialtes (sixty years earlier) and Kleisthenes (one hundred years earlier) were too recent to make this argument effectively. Consequently it was the law-giving of Solon, a venerable 200 years earlier, that was singled out as the key to the establishment of democracy at Athens, and the constitutional code set up in 399 was referred to as the *Solonos nomoi*: the laws of Solon. That is how Solon, whose role was certainly important but who did not in fact create a democracy, as we have seen, came to be revered as the founder of democracy, and Kleisthenes came to be largely forgotten.

There is still, in modern times, a tendency to minimize the importance of Kleisthenes. Some historians insist that his aim was simply to further his own political power, not to create democracy. But one wonders in that case why Kleisthenes would have taken the trouble to create the ten new tribes, the Council of the 500, to establish the requirement of frequent sovereign assembly meetings throughout the year, and so on. He could have won popular backing for his own power without needing to institute such far reaching and fundamental reforms, surely. On the other hand, it is argued that he was primarily interested in unifying Attica, and that the democracy that emerged from his reforms was an incidental effect. Again, though, it must be said that, while completing the unification of Attica was clearly an important aspect of Kleisthenes' program, the *Boule* and the numerous and regular assembly meetings were not necessary to unifying Attica, but were clearly aimed at popular governance. One must insist, finally, that Kleisthenes really was and meant to be the creator of a democratic governing system. And again, the reforms instituted by Kleisthenes cannot have been the work of mere weeks or even months. It must have taken a few years to carry out all the necessary work and get the system "up and running." The 139 demes had to be established and defined, geographically and otherwise, and local deme governing structures created. The demes had to register their constituent members, and thereby create the first ever register of Athenian citizens.

Based on that deme registration, demes had to be apportioned into *trittyes* in a way that was geographically workable, while at the same time assuring that these "thirds" were of roughly equal size, population wise. The "thirds" then had to be assigned to tribes. The new official year had to be defined, and the tribes, through the demes, had to enroll their groups of 50 councilors to collectively form the new *Boule* of the 500. The *phylai* had to establish membership lists from the registers of their constituent demes, and determine which members were eligible for hoplite service. When one thinks about all of these complex administrative activities, I think it is indeed clear that this process must have taken considerable time to work out in detail and put into effect: several years at a minimum. The Athenians were not left to do all of this undisturbed and at peace.

THE DEFENSE OF DEMOCRATIC ATHENS

The Spartan king Kleomenes, livid at his humiliation by the Athenians, called out the Spartan army and summoned allied contingents from all around the Peloponnesos with the aim of nipping the nascent Athenian democracy in the bud. In addition, he persuaded regional rivals of the Athenians, the Thebans and Chalkidians, to cooperate with his intended invasion of Attica by themselves invading Attica at the same time from the north and north east respectively. Invaded simultaneously from three directions by three major enemy forces then, the Athenian experiment in democracy really did seem likely to be ended before it had properly begun. The Athenian leaders correctly saw that it was the Peloponnesian army approaching from the west that was the main danger, and they called on all Athenians of hoplite status to come together to meet this invasion, marching out to confront the Spartans and their allies in the plain of Eleusis. At the same time, they sent messengers to Sardis to the Persian satrap there, Artaphernes, with a desperate plea for help: the Persians seemed to be the only power strong enough to assist them against the danger that was threatening.

However, it seems Kleomenes had not told the allies he had summoned to join his army what his aim was, nor even fully informed his Spartan co-king Demaratos. When it became clear that the goal was to attack the Athenians and overthrow their new self-governance system, dissension arose in the Spartan camp. The strongest, and so most independent, of Sparta's allies were the Corinthians; and the Corinthians had a long standing friendship with the Athenians, based on common hostility towards their mutual neighbor Megara and their mutual trading and maritime rival Aigina. The Corinthians refused to join in an attack on Athens, and marched back home. They seem to have done this with the approval of Kleomenes' co-king Demaratos, who himself left the expeditionary force and returned home with some of the Spartans. Emboldened by this, the rest of the allied contingents decided to head for home too; and before the fearful Athenians' astonished eyes, the entire Peloponnesian army simply melted away without a blow being struck.

Meanwhile Kleomenes' allies the Thebans and Chalkidians had already invaded Attica and were ravaging the borderlands to the north and northeast, and the Athenians at once turned to deal with these enemies. They first moved to confront the Chalkidians, who had apparently penetrated deeper into Attica. The Thebans, however, learned of their intention and marched to the Chalkidians' aid. Learning of this in their turn, the Athenians shifted course and confronted the Thebans. A sharp battle was fought, apparently early in the morning, in which the Athenians won a clear victory, driving the Thebans out of Attica in flight, killing many, and capturing more than 700 prisoners. They then turned in the afternoon to deal with the Chalkidians, who had escaped back across the Euboian channel to their home territory on the island of Euboia.

But the Athenians wanted revenge for the unprovoked attack and invasion of Attica. They crossed over to Euboia in pursuit, brought the Chalkidians to battle on the afternoon of the same day as the Theban battle, and again won an overwhelming victory, even capturing the city of Chalkis itself. Herodotos, our source for all this, comments that these events showed the beneficial effects of political equality (*isegoria*). Before this time, he remarks, when the

Athenians were governed by tyrants, they were in no way out-standing in warfare; but now that they were free, they were vastly superior to their neighbors in battle. This showed that when they were fighting for a master, they did not try very hard; but now that they were free and fighting for their own interests, every man put out his best effort and they proved more than a match for their opponents. Having captured Chalkis, the Athenians avenged the unprovoked invasion of Attica by exiling the ruling aristocracy of Chalkis, known as the *Hippobotai* or "horse-rearers," confiscating their estates, and dividing that land into 4,000 allotments that were granted to poor Athenians.

These 4,000 Athenians living on allotments in Chalkis retained their Athenian citizenship, and in effect formed a perma-nent Athenian garrison at Chalkis. They were still there more than fifteen years later at the time of the Marathon campaign, and still ten years after that at the time of Xerxes' invasion of Greece in 480. The numerous Theban and Chalkidian prisoners of war were ran-somed for 200 drachmas per man, and out of the proceeds the Athenians built a great monument to their first democratic military success.

Their troubles were not yet over, though. Kleomenes remained enraged at his defeat by the Athenians. In order to prevent a deba-cle like that at Eleusis from happening again, the Spartans decreed that in future military operations only one of their two kings would go at the head of any expedition, avoiding the danger of divided command. In addition, they established a system of holding con-gresses of allied leaders before major military undertakings, to in-form the allies of what was planned and ensure allied support.

The first such congress was now held, probably in spring of 506, at which Kleomenes introduced the former Athenian tyrant Hippias and proposed a Peloponnesian expedition to re-install Hip-pias in control of Athens, talking at length (according to Herodotos) about the danger posed by democratic Athens, and the trick whereby the Alkmaionids, through the Delphic Oracle, had

wrongly induced the Spartans to depose Hippias. At first none of
the allies dared to object; but finally it was again the Corinthians
who stood by their Athenian friends and argued that it would be
wrong for the Spartans, of all people, to impose on a Greek city a
tyrant. After the Corinthians had dared to make this argument, the
rest of the allies chimed in, and Kleomenes and the Spartans reluctantly let the matter drop. So far, then—partly thanks to the staunch
friendship of the Corinthians, and partly thanks to their own military efforts—the Athenians had seen off the initial threats to their
new democracy. But there was still the matter of Persia.

It will be recalled that when Attica was invaded from three
directions and there seemed no hope that the Athenians could save
themselves, an embassy had been sent to the Persian governor Artaphernes at Sardis to ask for Persian help. Artaphernes had replied
that the Persians were willing to help the Athenians, but only if the
Athenians formally accepted Persian overlordship by offering to
king Darius the symbolic tokens of submission: earth and water,
symbolizing that the land and waters of Attica belonged to the king.
In their desperation, and according to Herodotos on their own initiative, the Athenian ambassadors agreed to this demand, only to
return home to find the crisis over, Athens safe, and Persian help no
longer needed or desired. Their agreement to offer submission to
the king was met with a storm of criticism and repudiated. Scholars have speculated to what degree Kleisthenes was involved in this:
it is assumed that, as the Athenian leader of the day, he must have
been behind the embassy to Sardis; and that as a widely traveled
and cosmopolitan man, he must have known the Persians would
demand earth and water and instructed the ambassadors to agree.
This is all speculation, however: we don't know that it was Kleisthenes' idea to ask for Persian help, we don't know that he would
have known to expect the demand for earth and water, we certainly
don't know that it was he who told the ambassadors to agree
to such a demand if necessary. All that we do know is that this
embassy first drew the Athenians into the orbit of Persian imperial

ambition. When Sparta's allies vetoed Kleomenes' project to restore Hippias as tyrant of Athens, the old man made his way to Sardis and sought Artaphernes' help to recover power. And, angry at the Athenians' about face on their offer of submission, Artaphernes reputedly agreed to help Hippias.

When an Athenian embassy arrived to excuse their change of mind and ask the satrap not to support Hippias, Artaphernes ordered the Athenians to take back Hippias as their tyrant, saying that only so could they have Persia's friendship. This the Athenians refused to do, and as a result the relations between the Persian Empire and the new Athenian democracy were now decidedly hostile. Still, nothing might have come of that hostility, were it not for the great Ionian revolt that was soon to take place.

On the eve of the beginning of outright conflict between Persia and the Greeks, then, Athens stood as a reformed society with a new and largely untested political system. Beginning with the reforms of Solon at the beginning of the 6th century, and culminating in Kleisthenes' reforms at the end of the century, Athens had grown from an incompletely united and rather backward community of no great military, cultural, or political importance, into a state that was at the cutting edge of political development and a military power to be reckoned with. The great test of Athenian democracy was still to come: could this new and remarkable political and social system produce the strength, resilience, determination, and leadership needed to stand up to the power of the mighty Persian Empire? The odds seemed decidedly against it, but confident in their new freedoms and communal cohesion and empowerment, the Athenians stood ready to meet the test.

CHAPTER 4

THE GROWTH
OF CONFLICT BETWEEN
PERSIANS AND GREEKS

R ELATIONS BETWEEN THE PERSIAN EMPIRE AND THE GREEKS
started out as they were to continue; on the whole, badly.
When Cyrus came to be at war with the Lydian Empire of
Croesus in 546, he discovered—how we don't know—that Croesus's
empire included, on its western seaboard, a number of important
city-states whose inhabitants, not Lydians but Greeks, had only relatively recently been subdued by the Lydians. He calculated that
these city-states might feel hostility towards their Lydian overlord,
and that he might turn such hostility to his advantage. As we've
seen, he sent messengers to the Greek cities of western Anatolia
inviting them to secede from Lydian domination and become his
friends. As it turned out, Greek sentiments towards Croesus were
by no means hostile—in fact Croesus was a fairly mild ruler and
the Greeks were inclined to admire him—and in any case the
Ionian Greeks were impressed by Croesus's power and wealth and
expected him to win. Thus they turned down Cyrus's invitation—
until it was too late. Only when it was clear that Croesus had lost
did the Greek cities send representatives to Cyrus reminding him
of his offer of friendship and saying that they would now like to

take him up on it. Cyrus, according to Herodotos, responded with a charming fable: a pipe-player once saw some fish in the sea and played his pipes to them in the hopes that they would come to the shore. The fish ignored his playing, so he took a net, cast it into the sea, and caught them. When he had hauled the net on land and saw the fish flopping about he said: "you need not dance for me now, since you were unwilling to dance for me when I played my pipes." In other words, Cyrus let the Ionian Greeks know that they had missed their opportunity, and they would now dance to his tune whether they liked it or not.

PERSIA AND THE GREEKS

The Greeks returned to their cities, closed their gates, and manned their walls hoping to see off the Persian threat. But Cyrus's general Harpagos captured the cities of Ionia one by one through the use of siege ramps, and so the Greek cities of the Anatolian coast came under Persian rule. On the whole, the Persians did not treat these eastern Greek cities badly. Each city was placed under the rule of a trusted local leader—from the Greek perspective, a tyrant—who reported to the Persian satrap at Sardis. And of course the Greeks had to pay tribute to the Persian king, but Persian tribute payments were not excessively burdensome. In fact, the Ionian cities enjoyed several decades of relative peace and prosperity under Persian rule during the second half of the sixth century. Of course, many eastern Greeks lamented the loss of their freedom. Some, rather than accept Persian rule, had chosen exile from their homeland, as individuals or *en masse*.

Most of the people of Phokaia, for example, took to their ships and migrated to the western Mediterranean, founding a new settlement called Alalia on the north coast of Corsica. Many of the people of Teos migrated to their colony of Abdera on the coast of Thrace in the north Aegean. And many individual Greeks left Ionia and moved to the western colonial regions in southern Italy and

Sicily, for example, the philosopher Pythagoras and many of his followers. Another philosopher, Xenophanes of Kolophon, who was twenty-five years old when Harpagos the Mede appeared in Ionia, spent by his own account sixty-seven years tossed about the lands of Greece, especially the cities of Sicily. In one of his surviving fragments he talks of meetings of Ionians in the west, and the natural question that arose at such meetings: how old were you when the Mede came?

The Mede, as the Greeks referred to Persians and Medes alike, became a figure of dread to the Greeks. The superb cavalry of the Medes, the numerous and highly disciplined infantry of the Persians with their deadly archery, and above all the siege technology of these easterners—which rendered ineffective the expensive fortification walls with which the Greeks surrounded their cities—made Cyrus's great empire seem irresistible and invincible. And that impression will only have been increased by the stories that spread of the conquest of the Babylonian Empire, and eventually of Egypt. Many Greeks themselves fought in these wars of conquest, as mercenary soldiers both in Persian service and—probably in much greater numbers—in service with the Babylonians and Egyptians. Their soldiers' tales provided the bulk of such information as the Greek world had about the Persians at first, and whether they fought on the Persian side or the losing sides, they naturally exaggerated the power and skill of the conquering "Mede." Another thing the Greeks certainly exaggerated was their own importance in the eyes of the Persians.

Herodotos's charming history is full of the stories of Greeks who entered Persian service, whether voluntarily or through capture, and of Greek encounters with Persians. In these stories the Greeks always play an important role as advisers or agents or warners of the king and other leading Persians. Examples are the Greek doctor Demokedes of Kroton, who supposedly cured King Darius of a badly dislocated ankle and the king's wife Atossa of an ulcerated breast, becoming a valued and trusted member of the royal court as a result; and the Milesian tyrant Histiaios who reputedly saved Darius and his army from being cut off north of the Danube, and became one of the king's most valued and trusted advisers as a result. Other examples are numerous, particularly in the account of Xerxes' campaign against Greece: the sage and crucial advice of numerous Greeks dancing attendance on the great king and his marshals is constantly high-lighted. I don't suggest that there is not a factual basis to these stories, only that the value and importance of these Greeks are seen through their own eyes in Herodotos's narrative, and naturally exaggerated, and that to the king and other Persians things may have looked rather different.

A truer sense of how the Persians viewed the Greeks, at any rate before the Ionian revolt, can be gotten from another story Herodotos tells about Cyrus. Reputedly, entreated for help against "the Mede" by the Ionian Greeks, the Spartans sent an embassy to Cyrus warning him that he should leave the Greek cities in peace, because the Spartans would not permit him to harm the Greeks. Understandably astonished at this message, Cyrus turned to his advisers and asked, in effect, who on earth the Spartans were. Informed about them, he then replied to the Spartan ambassadors that he would never be afraid of any men who set aside areas in their cities where they met together to lie and deceive each other. He was referring either to the Greek system of politics, their collective debate and decision making seeming to him foolish and deceitful, or to Greek markets, with their haggling over quality and price of merchandise, or both. The point, at any rate, is that to Cyrus the mainland Greeks were largely unknown and unimportant, and their views were negligible.

To the Persian kings Cyrus and Cambyses, in fact, and likely to Darius too before the shock of the Ionian revolt, the Greeks were a peripheral people of rather little account. Of far more importance to them were the Iranian peoples, who formed alongside the Persians themselves the core of the empire, and the great, ancient, and wealthy peoples of Mesopotamia and Egypt, whose civilization and resources were enormously influential and valuable. Much of the time, in truth, the Persian kings must have been only barely aware of the Greeks, and certainly won't have given them much thought. It was only to the Persian satraps in Asia Minor that the Greeks, that troublesome people inhabiting the western coast, were important. To these Persian governors it was plain that their western border was highly unsatisfactory. The conquest of the Lydian Empire had only brought with it control over the relative handful of Greek cities on the coast of the Asian mainland.

Immediately off shore lay the great islands of (south to north) Rhodes, Samos, Chios, and Lesbos, along with numerous smaller islands; strung out eastwards across the Aegean lay dozens more Greek islands, including the great islands of Krete and Euboia; and then there was the Greek mainland with its numerous city-states and ethnic states. The Ionian Greeks within the Persian Empire were in constant contact and interaction with all of these free Greeks, and the inevitable result was to foment dissatisfaction among the Ionian Greeks with their subject status. As a supremely self-confident ruling people of a still expanding empire, the Persians naturally had no thought of settling this troublesome border issue by retreating and leaving the Ionian Greek cities their freedom. The solution was naturally sought in further westward expansion, bringing more and more Greeks under Persian control.

The main power in the eastern Aegean in this era, the third quarter of the sixth century, was the tyranny of Polykrates of Samos. Herodotos has much to say about this colorful and remarkable ruler, whose fleet patrolled the eastern Aegean in a distinctly predatory manner, seemingly managing to intercept every valuable or interesting cargo that passed through these waters. Polykrates was far from being a mere pirate, however. He was a patron of the arts, paying huge sums to bring the great poets Anakreon of Teos and Ibykos of Rhegion to his court, as well as the noted doctor Demokedes of Kroton. He promoted great public works: the massive temple of Hera that rivaled the Artemision at Ephesos; a marvelous harbor mole that turned the port of Samos into one of the largest and best protected in the Aegean; and the famous tunnel of Eupalinos that brought a plentiful water supply to the city of Samos directly through the mountain overlooking the town. He developed alliances: realizing the Persian threat to his independence, he allied himself with king Amasis of Egypt, who was also concerned about Persian expansion. However, when Cambyses decided to attack and conquer Egypt, Polykrates abandoned this now-dangerous alliance and cultivated Persian good will by sending a naval force to help Cambyses.

His good fortune was legend. Herodotos tells the tale of how Polykrates, in order to avoid divine jealousy at his continued prosperity, threw his most prized possession, a beautiful emerald and gold ring, into the sea. A few days later a fisherman caught a huge fish and brought it to Polykrates as a gift: when the fish was cut open, there was Polykrates' ring returned to him. Yet about 522 the Persian satrap Oroites began the further westward expansion of Persian power by enticing Polykrates into a trap, arresting him, and crucifying him.

Polykrates was succeeded in power by his secretary Maiandrios, but the days of the Samian tyranny were now numbered. A year or two later the new king Darius sent the Persian grandee Otanes to become satrap of western Asia Minor, and Otanes quickly conquered Samos, and brought Chios and Lesbos under Persian control too. For when Darius decided to extend Persian power across the Hellespont and Bosporos to Thrace (Bulgaria) in about 512, he was able to summon naval contingents from all three islands. This Thracian expedition of Darius represented the first major westward expansion of the Persians beyond the Asian mainland, and also likely the first time Darius would have interested himself seriously in the Greeks. It was, as we have seen, a Greek engineer—Mandrokles of Samos—who bridged the Bosporos for Darius, enabling his army to cross to the European side safely and with ease. And it was Greek ships from the Ionian cities and islands that provided the fleet which bridged the Danube River for him to cross into modern Romania to harry the Scythians. In conquering Thrace and adding it to his empire, Darius had also—though he may not have been aware of it—made his first contacts with the Athenians. For the Thracian Chersonnese, the peninsula on the northern side of the Hellespont, was settled by Athenian colonists and ruled by the Athenian aristocrat Miltiades son of Kimon. Athenian interest in this region went back to the time of Peisistratos, as we have seen, and it was originally Miltiades' uncle of the same name who had governed the Athenian outposts and native Dolonkians of the Chersonnese. Lacking the power to resist Darius's army, the younger Miltiades became, willy-nilly, a Persian subject, and was obliged to lead an allied contingent to march with Darius to the conquest of the rest of Thrace. This gave him an up-close experience of the Persian army in action, and a chance to evaluate its worth. For all the excellence and discipline of the Persian infantry and Median cavalry, Miltiades' conclusion was that the Persian army was by no means unbeatable.

Though Darius's European campaign has often been considered rather a disaster by readers of Greek history, following Herodotos to be sure, it was in fact quite successful. He added Thrace up to the river Danube to the empire, including a number of Greek cities on the Aegean and Black Sea coasts of Thrace; and even his excursion across the Danube against the Skythians—though he failed to bring the Skythians to battle and was glad, in the end, to get back across the Danube unscathed—should be considered unsuccessful rather than disastrous. The main outcome of the campaign was the advancement of Persian power much closer to the main Greek lands, and the incorporation of many more Greeks into the empire. It was clear by now to Darius that the western frontier could only be satisfactorily settled by incorporating all of Greece. When he crossed from Thrace back to Asia, therefore, Darius left behind in Thrace a substantial army under the command of a senior Persian general and governor, Megabazos, with orders to finish the pacification of Thrace and extend Persian power further westwards into Greek lands.

Megabazos managed to pacify all the lands up to the river Strymon. He also sent representatives to seek the submission of the Macedonian kingdom, ruled at this time by king Amyntas. Herodotos later heard a story about how the king's son, Alexandros, had these arrogant Persians done to death, but the truth is that Macedonia did in fact submit to Persian suzerainty, bringing Persian authority all the way to northern Greece. Meanwhile Persian power was also advancing across the Aegean, and had the Cycladic islands just off the south east coast of the Greek mainland in its sights. Here again, Herodotos had a characteristically Greek-centric story to tell.

The strongest island in the Cyclades was Naxos, which was at this time (500 B.C.E.) prosperous and had a strong middle class which provided the state with a powerful army of 8,000 hoplites. This hoplite middle class ruled Naxos, and had exiled an aristocratic party known as "the Fat," a testimony to their wealth rather than their corpulence. These exiles appeared in Miletos and appealed to the Milesian tyrant Aristagoras for help in recovering their homeland; and Aristagoras on their behalf persuaded the new satrap at Sardis, Artaphernes, that an expeditionary force to restore these men to Naxos could easily add the Cyclades islanders to the king's subjects. The story ignores the general tendency of Persian power to creep westwards in this era, and sees this Persian expedition—for Artaphernes, with the king's go ahead, of course went along with it—as motivated by Greek initiatives and interests. Whatever the exact occasion for the expedition, however, an expedition did sail to Naxos: a substantial Persian force commanded by an Achaemenid named Megabates, on Ionian ships commanded by Aristagoras himself.

The expedition was not a success. Megabates and Aristagoras quarreled, and the Naxians proved an unexpectedly tough nut to crack. They had gotten wind of the coming attack, and had brought all their movable property out of the open country into their fortified city, reinforced the city walls, and laid in plentiful stocks of food and water ready to stand a siege. Evidently the Persian force lacked the manpower to build one of their patented siege ramps: the siege dragged on for four months, until the Persian force ran short of money and supplies. According to Herodotos, Aristagoras even found himself spending much of his personal fortune to keep the siege going, but to no avail. In the end, the expedition was forced to return to Asia having failed to take Naxos, and this failure was to be the source of major events.

Once again, Herodotos characteristically paints events in terms of the personal intrigues and wishes of a couple of Greek leaders: Aristagoras of Miletos fearful of losing his position due to his role in the Naxian debacle, and Histiaios of Miletos, angry at been carried off to Susa in the king's entourage and eager to get back to the Aegean. What was perhaps more to the point was the impression of the Persian failure. The Naxians had successfully stood up to a Persian force, withstood their siege, and seen them off in failure. What the Naxians could do, surely others could do, too. Perhaps Persian power was not so inevitable, perhaps Persian troops were not so invincible.

THE IONIAN REVOLT

The Ionian Greeks had long resented their subjection to Persia while other Greeks were free, and they resented being ruled by Persian backed tyrants while elsewhere in the Greek world tyrants were becoming a thing of the past, replaced by collective forms of governance. At any rate, Ionia rose up in rebellion in 499, overthrowing the pro-Persian tyrants and striking out for freedom, and Aristagoras—who really was afraid of being punished for his failure at Naxos—took the lead in this rebellion. So began the Ionian Revolt that was to be, in Herodotos's words, the source of great troubles for Greeks and Barbarians alike. One should just bear in mind that to the Greeks of Herodotos's time and earlier, the term *Barbaroi*—the origin of the English word barbarian —didn't carry the negative meaning it acquired after the fifth century and still has today. *Barbaroi* were simply people who spoke languages other than Greek—*barbar* being the Greek equivalent of "blah blah" in English—so that *Barbaroi* were people whose speech was unintelligible, non Greek foreigners whether civilized and friendly or not.

That the Greek cities had been chafing under Persian rule is evident from the speed with which the revolt spread. Beginning at Miletos, it quickly encompassed the Ionian fleet that had just returned from Naxos and was anchored in the Latmian Gulf near Myous, and from there spread with lightning rapidity up and down the Ionian coast. All of the Ionian cities joined up, including the offshore islands of Samos and Chios, and from there the seed of rebellion spread further: to the Aiolic cities around Kyme to the north of Ionia, and on to the Troad and the Hellespont; across the Hellespont to the Greek cities on the northern (European) side, where Miltiades eagerly threw in his lot with the revolt; also south to the Hellenized cities of Karia and Lydia; and even as far as the Greek cities of Cyprus. In the initial stages of the rebellion relatively little happened, as the cities were busy organizing new forms of government after expelling their tyrants, seeing to their defenses, and messaging to and fro in order to try to coordinate common plans and policies. But the Persians were soon to learn a sharp lesson that they had a very serious revolt on their hands.

One of the first decisions the Ionians took was the very natural one of seeking aid from their fellow Greeks across the Aegean. Aristagoras himself was dispatched as ambassador to the mainland Greek states, and made his way first to Sparta: for if the Spartans agreed to send help, their Peloponnesian allies would inevitably follow suit. At Sparta, Aristagoras was received and interviewed by, inevitably, king Kleomenes, who was without doubt the directing mind behind Spartan policy in this era. Kleomenes was, as Aristagoras found out, no pushover.

Aristagoras put on a good show, evidently, talking up the wealth of the Persians, the power and reputation the Spartans could gain by taking them on in the cause of Greek freedom, and the ease of defeating men who fought with bows and short spears and wore *trousers* into battle. Clearly these men must be easy to beat, and to illustrate his point Aristagoras had brought with him a "show and tell" device, the latest product of Ionian rationalism. It was a map of the world, engraved on bronze, showing all the major rivers and peoples, with which Aristagoras illustrated the wealth of the Persian Empire and the ease of communications. All the Spartans had to do was march inland, fighting a battle or two on the way, and capture Susa, to become the wealthiest and most powerful people on earth. He seemed to be taking Kleomenes in just fine, until the moment came when the Spartan king asked just how long the journey was from the Aegean coast to Susa. Unwarily, Aristagoras told the truth: that it was a three-month march. At once, Kleomenes ordered him to leave Sparta for daring to suggest that the Spartans should march three whole months away from the sea.

Rather than leaving, Aristagoras took up the olive branch of the suppliant, and came to Kleomenes' home to try to persuade him to change his mind. The persuasion now took the form of bribery, which Kleomenes refused, causing Aristagoras to keep upping the sum he was willing to pay for Kleomenes' support until the king's eight-year-old daughter, Gorgo, who was present, piped up: "Daddy, if you don't leave the room this visitor is going to corrupt you!" At that Kleomenes walked out, and Aristagoras had to leave without Spartan or Peloponnesian support: for without Sparta's say-so, no other Peloponnesian state would send help, of course.

All that makes another amusing story, but once again the truth is less concerned with personal whims. The Spartans, always in fear of a rebellion by their exploited Helot class, were at all times very reluctant to commit major forces outside the Peloponnesos. Aristagoras' attempt to gain Spartan support was doomed from the start by Sparta's long-time policy, met with over and over again in this era, of

A view from the theatre of Miletos towards the harbor area, with at top the alluvial plain—formerly the Gulf of Latmos—created by the silting of the River Maiandros.

keeping their forces close to home, preferably within the Peloponnesos but certainly not far from it. The Spartans had gone their limit when they sent their embassy to warn off Cyrus long ago: the idea that the Spartiate hoplite phalanx might fight on the eastern side of the Aegean, let alone deep inside Asia, was always a non-starter.

Aristagoras made his way to Athens, where he could hope for a more accommodating reception in that the Athenians were fellow Ionian Greeks with long-standing ties to their eastern Aegean compatriots. And in the event he did indeed persuade the Athenians: they voted to send twenty warships. Herodotos comments that it was easier to fool 30,000 Athenians than one Spartan, but we have seen the reasons why the Spartans would not help and the Athenians would, and can take this comment with a grain of salt. Along with the twenty ships sent by the Athenians, their friends the Eretrians of Euboia also sent five ships: like the Athenians, the Eretrians too were Ionian Greeks with traditional ties to the Greeks of Asia Minor, and in particular to the Milesians. The Athenians have at times been criticized for the paltriness of their aid to the Ionians: only twenty warships. We should bear in mind, however, that we are not here talking of the Athens of the 470s and later, which could mobilize fleets of hundreds of triremes. A little after 490, in fact, the Athenians were able to raise a fleet of seventy warships to match Aigina's fleet only by borrowing twenty from the Corinthians, indicating that the Athenians at that time had no more than fifty warships of their own. Sending twenty warships in 499 thus meant that the Athenians committed nearly half of their total fleet, which shows that they really were making an effort.

Strengthened by the Athenian and Eretrian contingents, then, the Ionian Greeks gathered a substantial force and sailed to Kore-

The acropolis at Sardis, much eroded now but showing how steep and seeming impregnable it was.

185

sos, the harbor of Ephesos where, having landed the troops, they left the fleet and marched inland to Sardis, the capital of Persian power in western Anatolia. They evidently took the Persians by surprise since they met no opposition on the way, and captured Sardis without having to fight. The satrap Artaphernes with the Persian garrison forces took refuge on the virtually unassailable acropolis of Sardis; the town of Sardis itself caught fire and burned to the ground. Finding themselves in a burned out town, with a strongly held acropolis they saw no way to capture, and hearing that Persian forces were being mobilized from the rest of Anatolia to come to Artaphernes' aid, the Ionians decided to retreat to the coast. However, Persian forces hurrying to the rescue of Sardis pursued the retreating Greeks and caught up with them just outside Ephesos. There a battle was fought in which the Greeks were badly defeated, the superior discipline and training of the Persians evidently being decisive. With their archers, javelineers, and cavalry they inflicted heavy losses on the defeated Greeks, and in the aftermath the Ionian army broke up as each contingent made its way home. The Athenians and Eretrians too returned home: they probably felt that in capturing and burning Sardis, the center of Persian power in the region, they had done all the Ionians could expect of them, and that securing the freedom the Athenians and Eretrians had now helped them gain was the Ionians' own business. At any rate, despite further Ionian pleas, no more help came to the revolt from the Greek mainland.

The capture and burning of Sardis was a sensation, however. Many previously uncommitted eastern Greeks now joined the revolt: in the Hellespontine and Bosporos regions, for example, and it was also at this time that the Cypriote Greeks openly rebelled. The sack of the regional Persian capital made it seem genuinely possible to throw off the Persian yoke. The Persians, for their part, had now learned that the revolt was a very serious matter, and that it was going to take the mobilization of major forces to bring the Greeks to heel. King Darius himself was enraged at the sack of Sardis, and determined that whatever the cost Ionia would be reconquered, and that the Athenians and Eretrians would then be punished for their part in Sardis' destruction. If he was not convinced of it before, this event confirmed him in the belief that only the full subjugation of mainland Greece could secure a satisfactory and peaceful western border for the Persian Empire. It was above all the burning of Sardis, then, that brought about the great Persian campaigns to conquer mainland Greece. This is of course why Herodotos saw in the Ionian Revolt the beginning of great misfortunes for both Greeks and Barbarians, as I mentioned above.

After the Ionian defeat at Ephesos, and the Athenian withdrawal, the scene of the warfare shifted to Cyprus. The rebellion there was a key to the further course of the war, because the Persians knew they would need a fleet to effectively subdue the Ionians—especially of course the Ionians of the offshore islands—and the Persian fleet came from Phoenicia, Kilikia, and Cyprus. With the fleets of the Cypriot cities on the Greek side, the Phoenician and Kilikian fleets had necessarily to remain to defend their home waters and ports. The Persians were, therefore, quick to move to restore their control of Cyprus, helped by the fact that not all Cypriot cities had in fact rebelled: the non-Greek city of Amathous did not join in the rebellion. A substantial Persian force landed on Cyprus, led by a general named Artybios, and supported by a Phoenician fleet. The Ionians too recognized the strategic value to them of the Cypriot revolt, and sent a substantial fleet to the Cypriot Greeks' aid. The Cypriot Greeks confronted the Persian force on land, while the Ionians engaged to deal with the Phoenicians at sea. Here the Ionians showed their maritime skill and fighting mettle by defeating the Phoenician fleet.

But on land things did not go so well. Although at first the battle was evenly poised, and the Cypriot commander Onesilos even succeeded in killing the Persian general Artybios, in the end the Greeks were undone by a failing that bedeviled them throughout their history: disunity. At the height of the battle, the contingent from the city of Kourion, led by Stasanor, switched sides, followed by many of the troops from Salamis. This treachery unhinged the Greek line and led to total victory for the Persians. Casualties among the defeated Cypriot Greeks were high, including the deaths of Onesilos and several other key leaders, and the Persians followed up their success by besieging the Greek cities. Only Soloi held out for long, and even that city was captured by tunneling after a five-month siege. The victorious Ionian fleet had no option but to return to Ionia and prepare to defend their homeland. By early 496 the Persians were ready to unleash a large scale campaign of reconquest against Ionia.

Darius had sent large reinforcements to Asia Minor, and operations there were commanded by three of his sons-in-law: Daurises, Hymaios, and Otanes. Daurises first recaptured many of the Greek settlements along the Asian shore of the Hellespont, and then marched south to invade Karia. There he inflicted a crushing defeat on the Karians, and when Milesian reinforcements arrived and emboldened the Karians to try the luck of battle once more, Daurises inflicted another stinging defeat. The Milesians suffered heavy losses in this battle, we are told. But the reconquest of Karia was far from complete. Apparently made overconfident by his victories, Daurises allowed himself to be led into a trap in which he was himself killed and his army largely wiped out.

The second commander, Hymaios, operated against the Greek cities along the Propontis (Sea of Marmara), capturing Kios among other places. Then he moved into the Hellespontine region vacated by Daurises, and completed the reconquest of that region before dying of a sudden illness. The third commander, Otanes, linked up with the satrap Artaphernes at Sardis, and together they marched down to the coast and captured the cities of Klazomenai and Kymai, and most probably Ephesos too since the Ephesians no longer played any part on the Greek side after this. Though the Persians were by no means having things entirely their way, therefore, on the whole they were steadily reasserting their control over the outlying regions of the revolt, and confining it more and more to its

Ionian heartland. The odds on the Ionians successfully establishing their freedom were certainly narrowing. Into this situation came the renegade Milesian Histiaios, released by Darius from his enforced stay in Susa on the promise that he would bring the Ionian revolt to an end.

Unfortunately, Herodotos concentrated his narrative after Histiaios's arrival on that colorful character's doings, so that we cannot any longer reconstruct the details of the fighting between Persians and Greeks. What we do see from Herodotos's account of Histiaios is that the operations had become rather disjointed, not to say chaotic. Apparently Histiaios, who seems to have been entirely out for himself, managed to persuade a number of Persian officers who were disaffected towards Darius to conspire with him—but to do what exactly does not emerge. Artaphernes learned of the conspiracy and had these Persians arrested and killed, sowing turmoil in the Persian camp. Histiaios could no longer show his face in the Persian-controlled regions, but spent his time moving among the offshore islands of Ionia trying to gather forces. When he managed to get control of some ships, his operations with them amounted to little better than piracy, and were a source more of confusion and trouble than of help to the Greek cause. He managed to keep this up for some time, but after the final Ionian defeat he was captured by soldiers of Artaphernes, and the satrap summarily put him to death: a death by no means undeserved if half of what Herodotos tells about him was true, though Herodotos seems to have had considerable sympathy with this arch-troublemaker.

At the beginning of 495, with Artaphernes apparently reasserting his authority and taking control of Persian operations, a new strategy was implemented. Artaphernes had decided that the heart of the revolt and key to ending it was the great city of Miletos, the largest and most prosperous of the Ionian cities. He concentrated all the Persian land forces for a great thrust against Miletos, and at the same time brought up a powerful fleet of Phoenician, Kilikian, and Cypriot ships to attack Miletos by sea.

189

This fleet may have been commanded by the Mede Datis, who was later to command another great Persian expedition: he is attested as operating at Rhodes at this time, which would be on the fleet's route from the Mediterranean up to Miletos.

In the face of this threat, the Ionians, who lacked the resources to fight both on land and at sea at the same time, decided to rely on their strong fortification walls to protect their people from the Persian land forces, and to concentrate all the strength they could muster for a great sea battle. The Ionian fleet concentrated at the island of Lade, just outside the harbor of Miletos—an island that is now, ironically, a smallish hill in a vastly expanded alluvial plain created by the silting of the river Maiandros.

The fleet mustered there was an impressive one: 353 triremes, according to Herodotos's count, the bulk of it coming from four great sea powers: the Milesians themselves contributed 80 ships, the Chians 100, the Samians 60, and the people of Lesbos 70. The remaining 43 came from Phokaia (3), Teos (17), Erythrai (8), Priene (12), and Myous (3). This was a fleet very capable of meeting the Persian fleet in battle with a good chance of winning, if all contingents fought hard. The Persian fleet was supposedly 600 ships strong, but since that seems to be a conventional number for Persian fleets in this era, we may guess that in fact it was considerably smaller, not much more than 400 if so strong. For it seems unlikely that the Kilikians and Cypriots contributed more than one hundred ships each, nor that the Phoenicians could have sent more than 200, if even so many; and any other contingents (the Egyptians may have sent some ships, for example) are likely to have been much smaller.

In sum, the fleets were fairly evenly matched, and the Persian commanders were far from certain about the outcome of a battle at sea. They resorted to seeking to exploit the Greeks' well known Achilles heel: lack of unity. Serving as advisers with the Persian commanders were many of the former tyrants of the Ionian cities, who had been exiled at the start of the revolt, as well as other political exiles. These men were now instructed to get in touch with their fellow citizens and promise that any contingent that should change sides or refuse to fight, returning to allegiance to the king, would be spared punishment for the rebellion and treated well. Initially, Herodotos says, these overtures were rejected by all; but eventually one contingent did decide that safety was the better part of valor. Ostensibly, however, preparations for battle went on as normal, though there was apparently dissension in the Ionian ranks about training methods. Herodotos makes much of this, but in truth the course of the battle was not decided by the Ionians' training, adequate or otherwise. The issue seems largely to have been an excuse for the contingent that decided not to fight, and an opening for Herodotos to tell one of his characteristic stories: this one about the Phokaian general Dionysios, who would have led the Ionians to victory if only they had followed his training regime faithfully.

At any rate, once the Persians had the assurance they wanted, that a key Ionian contingent would not fight, they led their fleet out to battle, and the Ionian ships came out to face them. The Ionian position was to the north of the Persians, and their fleet was anchored by the Milesian contingent on the far left, nearest their

A reconstruction of what a fifth century B.C.E. trireme would have looked like: these are depicted beached at Marathon.

191

home city. The huge Chian contingent manned the center of the line, with the Samians to their right and the Lesbian contingent on the far right wing, the smaller contingents interspersed between the large ones. As the Ionians rowed forward to engage the Persian fleet, however, the Samian contingent, all but eleven ships, raised sail and turned away from battle and back to Samos. Seeing the huge gap in the line beside them, the contingent from Lesbos realized that there was now no hope of victory, and followed suit, as did most of the smaller contingents.

The battle was thus lost before a blow was struck, and not because Ionian Greek ships could not defeat Persian-led Phoenician and Kilikian ships, but because Greek city-states characteristically tended to put their own narrow self-interest above the common good. The eleven Samian captains who kept their ships in line and fought were later honored for their loyalty and bravery, but it was a futile gesture when most of their countrymen had fled for home. The Chian ships in the center of the Greek line reportedly fought heroically, perhaps more due to circumstances than anything else: they had no easy way to get away, hemmed in on both sides, and found that their best escape lay in breaking right through the enemy line. They succeeded in doing so, but only after suffering huge losses. Those who did break through were hotly pursued, and obliged to beach their ships on Cape Mykale and make a run for it on land. There they suffered the misfortune of being taken for brigands as they passed through Ephesian territory at night. Attacked by the Ephesians in supposed self-defense, the wretched Chians were slaughtered by their own fellow Ionians.

The Milesian ships had no option but to fight, since they were right outside their home city, which would be attacked as soon as they gave way. Hopelessly outnumbered, they put up a desperate fight, but the outcome was never in doubt. Miletos was blockaded and besieged by the Persians from both land and sea, and inevitably captured. Many Milesians were killed during a terrible sack. The remnants were rounded up and set marching towards Susa, to be judged and punished by the great king himself. In the event, Darius did not punish them further: they were resettled at a new home on the Persian Gulf. Miletos was before long re-peopled with new settlers, but the city never attained more than a shadow of its former wealth and glory. Over subsequent centuries the silting of the Maiandros gradually filled in its harbor and made the city landlocked, after which it was abandoned.

The sack of Miletos decided the outcome of the revolt: there was much in the way of "mopping up" operations still ahead of the Persians, but the destruction of Ionia's greatest city and the dispersal (and in large part destruction too) of the Ionian fleet effectively ended hope of a free Ionia. After wintering at Miletos, the Persian fleet set out in the spring of 494 and easily reconquered the offshore Ionian islands, the inhabitants realizing they had no choice but to submit. The mainland Ionian cities that had still been holding out also submitted, as did the Karians.

Initially the Persian punishment was harsh: destruction of sanctuaries, and selection of the handsomest boys for castration, and the most beautiful girls for enslavement. These boys and girls were evidently destined for the royal harem. Soon, however, Artaphernes switched to a more conciliatory policy, seeking to bring the Ionians to terms with their re-subjection, and to rebuild the region after the devastations of the revolt. The fleet, meanwhile, proceeded to the Hellespont to reassert control on the northern side of the straits, the southern side having already been reconquered. They sailed up the Hellespont and through the Propontis to the Bosporos, subduing and in some cases destroying cities as they went, and then sailed back again along the European shore, finalizing the reconquest.

It will be recalled that the Athenian Miltiades was ruling most of the Thracian Chersonnese at this time. He had withdrawn into the strong city of Kardia at the neck of the Chersonnese, with all his property and dependents, which he had placed on five ships. When he heard that the Phoenicians were approaching, he set sail in the Black Gulf, on the northern side of the Chersonnese, and ran down the coast under the peninsula's shelter to then make the run across the open sea south-westwards towards mainland Greece and, ultimately, Attica. As he emerged from the shelter of the Chersonnese, however, his five ships were spotted by a detachment of Phoenician vessels off the island of Tenedos, which gave chase. Miltiades headed for the island of Imbros, and managed to reach there safely, but with the loss of one ship, which happened to be carrying his oldest son, Metiochos. The rest of his family, including his son Kimon, escaped with Miltiades, and they made their way safely to Athens, where Militiades became very quickly a leader of those hostile to the Persians. He was at first prosecuted by political rivals under the anti-tyranny law, as having ruled as a tyrant over the Athenian settlers in the Chersonnese, but was acquitted by the assembly of Athenian citizens. They seem to have realized that his close familiarity with the Persians, their methods and fighting tactics, could likely be of value to them in the future. For the Athenians can hardly have supposed that Persian power would now end its westward expansion, or that the king would forget the role they had played at the start of the Ionian revolt, particularly in the sack of Sardis.

MARDONIOS AND THE PERSIANS' FIRST ATTACK TO THE WEST

In 493, Artaphernes concentrated on settling Ionia peacefully after the revolt. To the Greeks' surprise, he summoned a meeting of representatives from all the cities, and obliged them to agree to peaceful means of settling future differences and conflicts among themselves, forbidding the traditional practices of raiding and plundering. He had an accurate measure of the territories of each of the cities made, and set their tribute according to their territories and resources: an assessment that was widely considered reasonably fair (if unwelcome), and that seems in fact to have been used later by the Athenians as the basis for their own assessment of the "contribution" each east Greek state could make to the joint funds of the so-called "Delian League." In 492, a new commander for all Greek matters was sent down to the coast by Darius. This was Mardonios, son-in-law of the king, who brought with him a great army and fleet for further campaigning.

Mardonios ordered the army to march straight from Kilikia to the Hellespont, but himself came to Ionia with his fleet and there pleased the cowed Ionians enormously by deposing all the city tyrants and permitting the cities to establish systems of collective self-governance, apparently mostly moderately democratic in nature. The aim was clearly to reconcile the Ionians to Persian rule, and to avoid any more trouble from them in the future by showing that the Persian government could be sensitive to their particular culture and wants. Ionia was, however, just a brief stopover for Mardonios: his brief was to carry Persian power into the Greek mainland by marching across the north shore of the Aegean and down into Greece from the north, while the fleet accompanied the army along the coast and provided naval support and supplies. The push to create a workable western frontier for the empire by rounding off the conquest of the Greeks was on.

Mardonios sailed up to the Hellespont with his fleet to rendezvous with the army, which the fleet then ferried across to the European shore. The army then marched westward along the northern Aegean shore, with the fleet sailing alongside it. This region had, of course, already been subdued by Darius and his general Megabazos twenty years earlier, so it was essentially a matter of reasserting Persian authority. The expedition's first real action was at the wealthy island of Thasos, which was overawed by superior force into submission. The army then proceeded to Macedonia, which renewed its acceptance of Persian over-lordship.

The fleet, meanwhile, set out to sail around the Chalkidike peninsula, but here disaster struck. The long coast of the Athos peninsula—the easternmost of the three peninsulas jutting southwards from the Chalkidike—is rocky, harborless, and devoid for the most part even of beaches or sheltered bays. During the sailing season it was usually not difficult to circumnavigate, but local mariners were aware that care must be had: the prevailing summer wind from the north-east—today called the *meltemi*—could quickly change from a pleasant breeze to a near gale, and if that were to happen, ships on the east coast of the Athos peninsula were doomed, as the wind would blow them straight onto the rocks and cliffs. This is what in fact happened to the Persian fleet, which had either not thought to acquire navigators with knowledge of local conditions, or not heeded their advice. Many of the ships were wrecked, and most of their crews either drowned, were smashed onto the rocks of the coast, or were attacked and killed by sharks which infested those waters, as Herodotos tells us. With that, the Persian strategy of an amphibious attack on Greece was ruined, but there was worse to come for Mardonios's expedition. The army was encamped in eastern Macedonia and apparently—perhaps relying on the Macedonians' submission—failed to keep an adequate watch. At any rate, a local tribe called the Brygoi launched a night attack and took the Persians by surprise. Heavy casualties were inflicted, and Mardonios himself received a bad wound in the thigh, before the Brygoi were finally driven off.

Mardonios somewhat restored his prestige by staying in the area and fighting relentlessly against the Brygoi until they surrendered, but he was then obliged to call off his campaign. The fleet could no longer fulfill its role, the army was severely weakened, and Mardonios himself needed time to recuperate. So this first attempt to conquer Greece ended ingloriously with nothing really achieved: the Persian frontier had been pushed no further westward than it had reached twenty years earlier at the time of Darius's Thracian campaign. The king, however, was not disheartened by this, nor deterred from his determination to conquer Greece.

In 491, as a preliminary to further campaigning, Darius sent emissaries throughout mainland Greece to demand earth and water for the king: the formal tokens of submission. The aim was no doubt to gauge the likely strength and determination of opposition, and tailor future strategy for conquest accordingly. Overawed and fearful after what they had seen happen to the Ionians, all the Greeks of the Aegean islands sent the tokens of submission, and so did many on the mainland in central and northern Greece. The Athenians and Spartans refused, however, and in a very marked way: in both places the Persian heralds were killed by being cast into a pit or well. This was a violation of the acknowledged international law that heralds were sacred and inviolable, so that even peoples at war could still safely communicate with each other through heralds, which shows the very strong feeling on the matter shared by the Spartans and Athenians. In the face of the Persian threat, the Spartans and Athenians now settled their differences and became allies. Even king Kleomenes gave up his past hostility to the Athenians. When the Athenians reported that the Aiginetans, allies of the Spartans, had sent earth and water to the king and so threatened Athens' ability to resist the Persians, Kleomenes in fact forced the Aiginetans to retract that submission and to send hostages for their future good behavior to Athens. Given that, in order to achieve this, Kleomenes had to find a way first to depose his own co-king (and personal rival) Demaratos, who was obstructing him on behalf of the Aiginetans, we can see how committed Kleomenes was to this Athenian alliance against Persia. Demaratos showed, for his part, where his sympathies lay by secretly fleeing Sparta and taking service with the Persian king, a traitor to his home city and to Greece.

THE CAMPAIGN LEADING TO MARATHON

The scene was now set for Darius's second attempt to conquer Greece and punish those who had supported the Ionian Revolt. Since the Greek islanders and most of the mainland Greeks north of Attica had offered submission, Darius and his advisers calculated that it would not be necessary to mount another expedition on the scale of that of Mardonios. A new strategy was devised. A smaller amphibious expedition could strike directly across the southern Aegean at the Cyclades, Eretria, and Athens. This would have a number of advantages. Less manpower and resources would need to be mobilized. The fleet could avoid the dangerous Athos peninsula and a repeat of the disaster there. The three states that had fought against and humiliated Persian power—the Naxians, the Eretrians, and the Athenians—could be punished as a lesson to all Greeks. And from an occupied Attica, the conquest of the rest of Greece could be organized and undertaken at leisure from a base in the heart of Greece. In effect, since Greece north of Attica had already offered submission and would be hardly likely to retract that in the face of the punishment to be meted out to the Athenians, only the Peloponnesians, led by the Spartans, would remain to be dealt with. During the second half of 491 and early 490 work was carried out to build a large number of special transport vessels for the cavalry that was to form part of the expedition. Datis the Mede and Artaphernes, son of the Artaphernes who was satrap at Sardis, were placed in command of the expedition. And in spring of 490 a large army, fleet, and squadron of transport vessels gathered in Kilikia to put into effect this new strategy of conquest.

The numbers of the various parts of this expeditionary force are, unfortunately, impossible to establish due to the standard Greek habit of grossly exaggerating Persian forces in this era. Herodotos speaks of the standard "600 triremes" for a Persian fleet of this period; he does not give a number for the soldiers, but other sources speak of hundreds of thousands. Basic practicalities of cost, logistics, and need suggest very much smaller numbers. There were no very large fleets in mainland Greece at this time; even ten years later, after the Athenians had built 200 new warships, the mainland Greeks combined could muster only fewer than 400 triremes, and at this time those 200 Athenian triremes did not exist, the Athenians having barely fifty ships, as discussed above. Many of those fifty were probably old fashioned *pentekonters* (fifty-oared galleys). A Persian fleet of 600 triremes would thus have been some three times the size of any fleet it was likely to encounter under even the most pessimistic of projections; in fact it was never likely to be opposed by more than a few dozen Greek warships. A much more plausible number for the Persian fleet, then, adapted to the actual scale of operations, would be 200 or fewer.

Some of our ancient sources speak of hundreds of thousands of soldiers in this expedition. In sober reality, the size of ancient field armies was limited by ancient conditions of transport, which made feeding huge numbers of people abruptly gathered together in one spot simply not feasible. Even finding supplies for armies numbering in the tens of thousands was often very difficult; to have fed and supplied armies numbering in the hundreds of thousands would have presented insurmountable logistical difficulties: many of the men would simply have starved to death. Since the strategy being pursued was one of relatively low cost and moderate mobilization of resources, it can be regarded as certain that the Persian army numbered far fewer than 100,000 men. Probably it had no more than about 25,000 infantry and several thousand cavalry, which would be two or three times the size of the forces any of the three main targets—Naxos, Eretria, and Athens—could mobilize, and substantially larger than their armies even if they could somehow bring in significant reinforcements of allies.

This force, then, set sail along the southern Anatolian coast, up the east Aegean coast to Samos, and then crossed in the lee of the long island of Ikaria to the Cyclades in the south west Aegean. They landed on Naxos. Unlike in 500, the Naxians did not make a fight of it and defend their city; instead they took to the hills. The Persians made an example of the place by burning the town and the sanctuaries, captured and enslaved a few stray Naxians, and then moved on to Delos. By way of contrast, Datis treated the island of Apollo with respect: the Delians were assured that no harm would come to them, and a huge offering of frankincense was made to the god Apollo. The rest of the Cyclades islands surrendered, offering auxiliary troops and hostages: the contrast between Naxos and

Delos was clear to them. Reaching the southern end of Euboia, the Persians summoned the Karystians too to surrender. After their land had been devastated and their city besieged for a few days, the Karystians submitted, and the Persians moved on to the second of their main objectives: Eretria.

By now, the middle of July, the Eretrians had had ample time to bring their city into a state of defense, and debate their best course of action. They had sent to the Athenians for help, and the Athenians had instructed their 4,000 settlers at Chalkis to help the Eretrians. But the Eretrians were themselves divided as to what to do: some wanted to abandon the city and take to the hills of central Euboia, some wanted to man the city walls and defend them, and some argued for outright surrender. In the midst of this dissension, and following the advice of a leading Eretrian named Aischines—who told them to save themselves as Eretria was doomed—the 4,000 Athenians crossed the Euboian channel and made their way back to Athens. The Persian armada then landed in Euboian territory and drew up their forces, cavalry to the fore, but found no-one to fight. The Eretrians had finally decided to withdraw behind their fortified walls and defend their city.

So the Persians set about to besiege Eretria. For six days the city walls came under attack, and there was fierce fighting with losses on both sides. But, as we have seen, the Greeks always tended to be bedeviled by one characteristic weakness: disunity. On the sixth night, two prominent Eretrians put their own and their families' safety before their community and opened a city gate to the Persians. Herodotos named them as Euphorbos son of Alkimachos and Philagros son of Kyneas. Once inside the city, the Persians rounded up the population and moved them out, burning down the empty city and its sanctuaries. So, around the end of July, the Eretrian people were loaded onto ships to be carried back to Asia, where they were to be brought inland to Susa to face the king. Since the Persians still had one main objective to attack—the Athenians—they "parked" the Eretrians on some islets in the Euboian sound for the duration of the operations in Attica. Eventually the Eretrians were indeed brought to Susa where, as with the Milesians, King Darius had no interest in punishing them further but settled them in a new home not far from the Persian Gulf. Herodotos states that they (that is, no doubt, mostly their children) were still living there in his day.

Thus far the Persian expedition had been a total success. The Cycladic Islands and the southern end of Euboia belonged to the Persians, and two of the three main objectives had been achieved, and all this with little fighting as the Greeks were either too over-awed or too disunited to put up any serious resistance. As the Persian commanders, Datis and Artaphernes, rested their army for a few days after the sack of Eretria and discussed their exact plans for the invasion of Attica with their Greek advisers—who included the former Athenian tyrant Hippias—they must have been in a confident mood. They can have had no reason to suppose that the last part of their campaign would go any differently than the rest, and were no doubt being advised by their Athenian informants that Athens was no more united in purpose and determination than Eretria had been. Part, at least, of the Athenian aristocracy remained unhappy with the democratic constitution whose creation by Kleisthenes was still so recent—only fifteen years or so ago. And there seemed no reason to believe that there would not be, among the Athenians as in other Greek communities, some people who would place calculations of personal advantage over loyalty to the community.

The Persians had a long history, by now, of successfully exploiting Greek disunity, and had reason to believe that if the Athenians, as seemed most likely, defended their walls, either dis-unity or Persian siegecraft would beat them. And even if the Athenians were to come out and fight, the Persians outnumbered them significantly, they trusted in the training and discipline of their forces, who had a long history of imperial success behind them by this time, and in particular they believed that their cavalry and archery gave them a huge advantage against the slow moving and ponderous hoplite force that the Athenians would oppose them with. So it was likely in a buoyant mood of optimism that the job would soon be completed that the Persians reboarded their warships and transports for the short crossing from Euboia to Attica.

CHAPTER 5

THE BATTLE OF MARATHON

AT THE BEGINNING OF AUGUST, THE PERSIAN SHIPS MADE THE short crossing of the Euboian Channel from Eretria to the Attic coast, and landed at the northern edge of the broad bay of Marathon. The site was well chosen: Athens was at least six or seven hours away by foot, and Athenian forces could not therefore be mobilized in time to interfere with the Persian landing; and the long peninsula called Kynosoura (the Dog's Tail) protected the beached ships from the normal north-easterly winds of that time of year (see map 5). In addition, the plain of Marathon was broad and well suited to the deployment of the Persians' superior numbers, giving room for their cavalry to maneuver.

THE PERSIANS AT MARATHON: PRELIMINARIES

Established at Marathon, the Persians could either fight a battle under favorable conditions, if the Athenians dared to come out to offer battle; march on Athens by a convenient road of some twenty-six miles to invest the city if the Athenians chose to defend their city walls; or, if the Athenians should come to Marathon but avoid battle, Athens itself would be left vulnerable to a sea-borne attack

The plain of Marathon, where the battle was fought. The Athenian camp was in the hills at the upper right; the great marsh is in the foreground.

around the Attic peninsula. The choice by Datis and Artaphernes of this landing site was very well thought out and offered a degree of convenience and strategic flexibility no other landing site in Attica could match. They deserve credit for this, though the credit for the choice of landing site is usually, following Herodotos, given to the aged ex-tyrant of Athens, Hippias, who accompanied the Persians as an adviser.

Hippias had himself landed at Marathon with an army nearly sixty years earlier, when his father, Peisistratos, returned from exile and successfully attacked and won control of Athens from this landing site. It is natural to think that Hippias will have recommended following the same strategy that had been successful for his father, but the decision was not his. Herodotos and other Greek sources habitually overrate the influence of various Greek exiles and advisers on Persian decision-making, no doubt following what those Greeks themselves claimed about their influence: for they (or in many cases their descendants) were of course Herodotos's

sources. In reality, one imagines that the experienced Median commander Datis scarcely would have needed to have the advantages
of Marathon as a landing site pointed out to him: he needed information, but we can safely attribute the decision-making to him and
his colleague Artaphernes.

Hippias was now a very old man. Since he had apparently
been grown up already in 558, when his father's marriage to the
daughter of Megakles was ruined by Peisistratos's unwillingness to
raise sons by her to rival the grown-up sons he already had—i.e.
Hippias and his brother Hipparchos—Hippias must have been
nearly ninety at the time of the Marathon campaign. He wanted to
regain his power in Athens before he died, and be buried in his
home country. Herodotos reports that Hippias had a dream at this
time that encouraged his hopes. He dreamed that he was sleeping
with his mother and took this to mean that he really would win
back Athens and be buried there. But when he landed at Marathon,
he was overcome by a fit of sneezing that dislodged one of his teeth,
which were loose with old age. He searched for the tooth at length
but couldn't find it and concluded sadly that only that lost tooth
was destined to achieve burial in Attic soil.

The story is obviously more symbolic than real, no doubt
made up after the event by the Athenians or by Hippias's descendants. At the time, Hippias's hopes were, despite his great age, not
at all unrealistic. He had relatives and associates still in Athens—his
cousin Hipparchos son of Charmos, for example—who might well
decide to put personal advantage over patriotism and betray Athens
to Hippias and the Persians, as men had done at Eretria.

And the Persian force seemed irresistible. When news reached
Athens, presumably some hours later on the day of the Persian landing, the Athenians at once sent a runner to Sparta with the news and
to ask for Spartan help and, meanwhile, debated what to do in the
face of the Persian threat. There were two options: to bring all available forces into Athens and man the city walls for defense, while
waiting for the hoped-for Spartan aid; or to march out with all avail-

able forces to Marathon to confront the Persians at their landing site. The first option was understandably popular: it seemed a safer option, and this is what the fortification walls Greeks surrounded their cities with were for. But Miltiades came forward as the proponent of the attacking strategy. He could point out the many Greek cities that had failed to successfully withstand a Persian siege and, particularly, that staying behind the city walls opened up the possibility of a betrayal such as the one at Eretria. All Athenians knew that there were citizens who were not 100 percent loyal. In addition, Miltiades argued, if they would only fight with proper commitment, Greek heavily armored hoplites were easily a match for the lightly armored Persians. His long experience of Persian warfare gave him credibility. So Miltiades' suggestion won the day, and the Athenians ordered all able-bodied citizens of hoplite status to take up their arms and several days' provisions and march to Marathon.

Meanwhile, the Athenian runner Philippides (or in some sources, Pheidippides) was on his way to Sparta. In a remarkable feat of running, he covered the 140 miles from Athens to Sparta, which went over several quite demanding mountain passes, in two days, arriving at Sparta on the day after he had set out. There he announced the Persian landing and asked for Spartan aid as ordered, urging the Spartans not to allow Greece to lose another of her great and ancient cities.

The Spartan response, however, was not the one Philippides and the Athenians must have hoped for. The Spartan authorities stated it was not Spartan custom to march out to war during the second week of the Karneian moon (that is, the second new moon of the year), and they would not march to the Athenians' aid, therefore, until the moon was full in six days' time—it was the ninth day of the moon when Philippides arrived in Sparta, and the moon would be full on the night of the fifteenth (that is, the eleventh of August in modern reckoning). The Spartans were, admittedly, a people given to religious scrupulosity, and this reason for delaying deserves some respect. But at the same time, the situation was an emergency that called for immediate action: in six days' time Athens might already be in Persian hands, as the example of Eretria showed. In truth, the Spartans were always reluctant to commit their forces outside the Peloponnesos, and they didn't seem to have had difficulty overcoming religious scruples when their own vital interests were at stake. After all, the Spartans were risking Athens' existence by their delay.

Philippides, after a night's rest, set out back to Athens to bring the news that the Athenians would have to hold out alone for at least a week. As he ran over the mountain pass between Sparta and Tegea, he claimed to have had a remarkable experience: the god Pan appeared to him, announced his friendship towards the Athenians, and upbraided the Athenians for not worshiping him properly. After Marathon, the Athenians did in fact set up a new cult of Pan in a cave below the Akropolis. We are naturally inclined to think of Philippides' vision as a hallucination caused by exhaustion and the endorphins and adrenaline running through his bloodstream, but to him and the Athenians the experience was a very real religious revelation. The Athenians came to believe that Pan really did help them: they attributed the Persian flight in the battle to an attack of "panic" fear brought on by the god Pan.

Since Philippides had left for Sparta before the Athenians decided what their strategy was going to be, he presumably returned to Athens and learned there that the army was at Marathon. He joined them there and reported the news: they would have to look out for themselves for a week, before any Spartan help could be expected.

The Athenian commander was the *polemarchos* (war archon) of the year, Kallimachos of Aphidnai. He was assisted and advised by the ten tribal generals of the Kleisthenic constitution, among whom were Miltiades and two younger leaders who were to become famous later: Themistokles and Aristides the Just (per Plutarch in his *Life of Aristedes 5,* though Themistokles' post as general is only strongly implied there).

The Athenian hoplites, no doubt accompanied by some thousands of light infantry and slaves, had taken up position in the hills at the southern end of the plain of Marathon, astride two roads that lead from Marathon to Athens and covering both. They were encamped by a sanctuary of Herakles, probably near the present-day chapel of St. Demetrius, in a strong position from which they could give or avoid battle as they chose. The usual notion is that they marched there in a united force, nearly ten thousand strong, but that is hardly likely. No doubt in fact the *hippeis*, wealthy Athenians who could afford to own horses, arrived first, some hundreds in number. Though they did at times function as cavalry, more often they were mounted infantry, leaving their horses and taking places in the phalanx when a battle was to be fought. They likely secured the position in the southern foothills of the plain as an advance force, to be joined a few hours later by some thousands of hoplites marching from Athens. But only about half of the Athenians actually lived at Athens: the rest lived in the towns and villages dotting the rest of Attica, and contingents from there are likely to have continued joining the Athenian camp over the course of the next day. A force of Plataians also joined the Athenians that day, having marched *pandemei* (in full force) to stand by their Athenian friends in their hour of need. They were about six hundred strong and commanded by Arimnestos.

Once the entire Athenian force was mustered, together with the Plataians, they amounted to about ten thousand hoplites, a remarkable number for so small a state. Athens at this time numbered perhaps 30,000 adult male citizens in all, less than half of whom were sufficiently well off to equip themselves as hoplites. The mobilization of more than nine thousand hoplites to confront the Persians thus represented essentially a full call-up of all able-bodied Athenians of military age and hoplite status, and about one-third of the total citizen body. Including thousands of light infantry who certainly accompanied the hoplites, it seems likely that more than half of the Athenian citizens took the field.

It says a great deal for the commitment and civic pride of the Athenians that such a large proportion of them were ready and willing to lay aside other concerns in their city's hour of danger and risk their lives to protect her. Such an enormous mobilization of national manpower, percentage-wise, is virtually unparalleled in the history of warfare: only the fundamentally democratic and participatory nature of the Greek city-states, and especially of Athens, which made the city-state, in all important respects, the same as the citizen body and thus made the citizen feel the state was *his* state and *his* business, can explain the kinds of mass mobilization of which Greek city-states were routinely capable. This often goes unremarked by historians, as if such mobilizations are natural and normal occurrences.

The size of the Persian army is, as we have seen, impossible to establish accurately. We have to be content to say that our sources agree that the Athenians were significantly outnumbered, and that the Persian advantage in cavalry and archery was especially troubling.

Faced with this Persian superiority, and hoping for Spartan reinforcements, the Athenians were content to hold their position in the foothills of the Pentele mountain range and play a waiting game. They cut down trees and laid them, untrimmed, into a so-called *abattis*: lines of untrimmed trees with their branches towards the enemy forming an anti-cavalry obstacle on each flank, preparing a secure advance into the plain for battle when their Spartan reinforcements should have arrived.

The Persians too played a waiting game: Datis and Artaphernes saw no reason to risk an attack uphill against the heavily armored Athenians. If the Athenians would not come into the plain to fight, the war might be won by other means. They were probably hoping for a movement among some of Hippias's former supporters to betray Athens to them; and if that failed to happen, there was always the option of dividing their forces and launching a sea-borne attack on the city of Athens while the Athenians were at Marathon. It is very likely that they were receiving information from the Athenian camp, knew of the divided views on whether and how to fight among the Athenians, and knew when, at the earliest, Spartan troops could be expected to arrive. For it can hardly be a coincidence that, after days of inactivity, Datis and Artaphernes made a decisive move on the night before the full moon, when the Spartan delay would end. But granted that information was passing from the Athenians to the Persian camp, it was not a one-way traffic.

In the middle of the night of August 10–11 by the modern calendar, the Athenian *polemarchos* Kallimachos was awakened by a messenger from the Athenian outposts. Some Ionian Greeks from the Persian force had crossed no-man's land and contacted the Athenians on guard duty with vital news. Messengers were sent to rouse the ten tribal generals and, no doubt, the Plataian commander, and summon them to a meeting in Kallimachos's tent, where the Ionians were interviewed. They reported the Persians were busy embarking a substantial part of their army, importantly including most of their cavalry force, back onto their ships with the aim of sailing around Cape Sounion and up to the bay of Phaleron, to attack the undefended city of Athens while the Athenian army was absent at Marathon. One can imagine what a sensation this news caused among the Athenian commanders, and the result was a heated debate as to what was to be done, a debate which revolved around two possible courses of action.

It was immediately clear that the Athenians could not simply continue to occupy the position they currently held and wait for the Spartans to arrive. Landing at the broad bay of Phaleron, the Persian cavalry would be able to overrun the Athenian plain and advance along the road to Marathon, taking the Athenian army there in the rear at the same time as the main Persian force moved forward to attack from the Marathonian plain below.

Meanwhile, Persian infantry likewise disembarking at Phaleron would be able to attack the city of Athens, defended only by the old, the very young, and some of the unarmed poor. Even if

A view north from Cape Sounion towards Phaleron, the goal of the Persian fleet.

the city was not betrayed as had happened at Eretria, it was all too likely that the experienced Persian infantry would be able to break in and capture the city. For the Athenians to remain where they were thus courted almost certain disaster.

In view of the great danger to the city, with the women and children and much of the movable property of the Athenians held there, some of the generals argued that the only sensible course was to leave Marathon and march back to the city, taking shelter behind its fortified walls and defending them against Persian attack. This was, of course, the policy that many Athenians had favored from the start, and it is understandable that it should have been revived under the present circumstances. But the same objection that had prevented adoption of this policy from the start still held, to an even greater degree. As leader of the group who had urged making a stand at Marathon, Miltiades will likely have been the key voice in putting this objection.

For the Athenian army to retreat from its position at Marathon would be demoralizing. Many of the nine thousand or more Athenian hoplites did not live in the city of Athens and would be tempted to peel away from the march from Marathon to Athens to head for their own home towns and villages in Attica, to secure their families and homes. The Plataians would be even more strongly tempted to leave their Athenian allies and march home. Those who did occupy the city and man the walls would be conscious of the failure of the initial strategy, and the temptation for someone to place his and his family's interest above that of the community and make a deal with the Persians, opening a city gate to them—as had happened at Eretria just a few days before—would be all the stronger. And again, it will have been noted that the old tyrant Hippias, who was with the Persian army, still had relatives and former associates living at Athens, not all of whom could be considered entirely reliable in their loyalty to the new, post-Kleisthenes Athens.

Miltiades argued that, as great as was the threat posed by this Persian move, it offered at the same time an opportunity that the Athenians must seize as their only good hope for survival and freedom: an opportunity to fight the Persians in battle on the plain of Marathon under more equal conditions than they could have reasonably anticipated. The main factor that had made the Athenians fear advancing into the open plain of Marathon had been the great Persian superiority in numbers, and especially in cavalry. It was the risk of Persian cavalry out-flanking the Athenian phalanx and attacking it in the rear at the same time as the more numerous Persian infantry drove against it from the front, which had kept the Athenians up in the hills astride the roads to Athens, waiting for a Spartan army to reinforce them. That risk was now greatly reduced: most of the Persian cavalry were on ship and would not be able to be disembarked again in time to fight, if the Athenians were to advance into the plain early in the morning. Indeed, once the Persian ships had sailed, the Athenians had a window of opportunity: it would take some twelve hours for ships to make the voyage from Marathon, round Cape Sounion, to the bay of Phaleron; but the march by land was only around six or seven hours long, giving some four or five hours' time in which to fight the diminished Persian force at Marathon. Miltiades argued that the prospects for a successful battle had never been as bright as they were now, and that the Athenians should arm at dawn and march down to draw up their phalanx in the plain, forcing the Persians to come out and fight them without their cavalry, and with their infantry superiority also reduced by the numbers of men embarked on ship for the attack on Athens.

The debate was apparently lengthy and fierce, with the ten generals fairly evenly divided between retreat and advance. In the end, the decision lay with the war archon Kallimachos and—fortunately for the Athenian people and their (and our) subsequent history—he agreed with Miltiades that it would be best to fight. So the decision to advance into the plain and offer battle was taken, and Kallimachos apparently gave the experienced Miltiades, whose strategy this decision was, the task of determining and organizing the battle strategy and tactics. At any rate, all sources agree on giving Miltiades the credit.

THE BATTLE

We can imagine that news of the meeting of the generals, and of the fierce debate among them, will have spread through the Athenian camp during the night, so that it will have come as less of a surprise when heralds began to spread out through the encampment in the pre-dawn dark calling the men to awake, prepare and eat an early breakfast, and see to their arms. Campfires that had dwindled to embers during the night will have been stoked up again, servants will have bustled about preparing the standard military barley stew with vegetables and watered down wine for their masters' breakfasts, and the hoplite warriors will have been inspecting their armor and weapons, making sure that they were ready for action. The officers of the sections of the Athenian phalanx will have been summoned to meet with the generals to be instructed in the battle plan they were to follow once the sun was up.

For in the face of the still considerable Persian superiority in numbers, Miltiades had developed a uniquely innovative and complex plan of battle. The normal battle tactics of the Greek hoplite phalanx were simple and uniform: the men formed a rectangle made up of eight or more lines of men, each line establishing an unbroken shield wall, and marched forward at a steady pace, so as not to disrupt the neat lines, to confront the enemy. But this simple and standard system was to be changed in several crucial ways to cope with the specific threat posed by the Persians, in an example of tactical ingenuity that had no known parallel in earlier Greek warfare and was not to be matched again for another 120 years, until the famous Battle of Leuktra in 371 at which the Thebans finally defeated the Spartans in battle.

Miltiades was concerned with two specific dangers posed by the Persian army: that it significantly outnumbered the Athenians and Plataians and it was likely to be drawn up in a much longer line of battle, thus outflanking the Greeks on one or both sides and thereby creating the risk that the Athenian phalanx might be enveloped on either or both flank(s) and so defeated; and that the large number and high quality of the Persian archers would expose a phalanx marching forward at a standard sedate pace to a long and possibly withering fusillade of arrows that could demoralize the Athenian hoplites, or potentially even drive them back in flight before they properly had come to grips with the Persians. Miltiades had to come up with measures to counter both threats. In order to avoid the danger of outflanking, it would be necessary to extend the length of his phalanx. Around ten thousand men drawn up in a standard eight-line phalanx would create a front of some 1,200 men. Granted that each man occupied on average around one meter of space, or perhaps a shade more, the front line would thus extend for around 1,300 meters, give or take. That front line could be significantly extended if one adopted a phalanx of six lines, or even fewer; but the thinner the phalanx, the less weight its charge into the enemy formation had, the more likely it was to be pushed back and broken open.

Miltiades decided to take the risk of thinning out his phalanx, but only in part of the formation. He separated the army into three parts: a right wing, a left wing, and a center. The two wings were to be drawn up in the standard eight-line formation; only the center was to be thinned out to extend the line, being drawn up only four lines deep. The hope was that the two strong wings would be able to defeat the two wings of the Persian army opposing them, drive those Persian wings backward into flight, and then turn inward to envelope the Persian center. The thinly manned Athenian center would, as a result, come under enormous pressure from the Persian center, and it was crucial that it succeed in holding formation unbroken, not giving up too much ground, until the Athenian wings could outflank the Persian center and relieve the pressure on the Athenian center. This battle strategy was risky: if the Athenian center were to be broken and penetrated by the Persians before the Persian wings were driven back in flight, it would be the Athenian wings that would be outflanked from the inside out, and enveloped, not the Persian center. It was crucial, obviously, that the officers and hoplites of the Athenian army understood this plan of battle and the respective roles of the two wings and the center.

Further, to counter the threat of the Persian archers, Miltiades had decided that, as soon as the phalanx came within bow-shot of the Persians, it was to give up its steady pace and advance to meet the Persians at a run, reducing as much as possible the amount of time it would be exposed to the Persian archers. Herodotos tells us that the Athenians at Marathon were the first Greek hoplites to charge the enemy at a run. The reason is obvious: it was almost impossible for thousands of men running forward to maintain formation properly. Even on a parade ground, differences in stamina and running ability would tend to make lines ragged; and the plain of Marathon was no parade ground. But Miltiades calculated that the inevitable disruption of the lines of his phalanx was a preferable risk to long exposure to Persian archery.

In hindsight, this plan of battle developed by Miltiades seems simple and obvious, so it needs to be emphasized just how unusual and remarkable it was at the time. Greek generals were not really expected to think much, or to create plans of battle. Greek warfare had not developed to highlight the inventiveness or ingenuity of generals; it was based on a simple and uniformly accepted system that depended on the discipline, uniform equipment, and steadfastness of the hoplite warriors. Every man understood the standard formation and the importance of maintaining his particular place in the formation, so that the phalanx should remain intact and hence undefeated.

This uniformity and standardization of warfare, emphasizing the collective discipline of the mass of warriors rather than the abilities of leaders, underlay the collective and egalitarian nature of Greek, and especially Athenian, political life. This is probably why the usually so inventive Greeks gave no serious thought to military innovation for several centuries (between the early sixth and the early fourth centuries B.C.E.) when their city-state civilization was at its peak, and it is all the more remarkable that the great exception to that rule should have occurred at democratic Athens, allowing the great aristocrat Miltiades to impose his special ideas on the democratic phalanx. Miltiades deserves to receive more credit as a brilliant general and leader than he generally gets: his tactics were more than a hundred years ahead of their time. In the end though, Miltiades' reliance was on the superior armor and collective discipline and morale of the Greek hoplite to overcome the experience, training, and numbers of the Persians.

The Athenian army must have broken camp and marched down from the hills into the open plain as soon as dawn's light made the move practicable. They could not afford to delay, since they had to make their move as soon as the Persian ships had set out for the voyage around Attica: the window of opportunity for battle was a narrow one, not more than five hours at most. As each of the Athenian tribal regiments came down into the plain, it deployed from column of march into line of battle. It is most likely that the right wing regiments will have marched first, led by the war archon Kallimachos at the head of his *Aiantis* tribe, which took the position of honor on the far right.

We know that the Athenian center was held by only two tribal regiments: the *Leontis* led probably by the great Themistokles, who was to win fame as the architect of Athenian naval power in the decade after Marathon, and the *Antiochis* tribe led by Aristides the Just. That would mean that each wing had four tribal regiments, with the left wing also being further strengthened by the 600 Plataians on the far left. Assuming that each tribal regiment was roughly equal in numbers, the two regiments of the center should have numbered about 1800 men; and drawn up only four ranks deep, they will have occupied a front of some 500 meters or so. The two wings, each twice as numerous but drawn up twice as deep, will each have occupied about the same space, so that, including 100 meters or so for the 600 Plataians, the total front line of the Athenian army will have been around 1600 meters long, or about one mile. It must have taken an hour or two for the Athenians to deploy into this line and begin to advance forwards, and it will have taken at least as long for the Persians to bring their army out of camp and draw it up facing the Athenians.

The initial distance between the two armies, Herodotos tells us, was about eight *stades*, which is also about one mile. Apparently, therefore, the Persian forces that remained at Marathon had advanced into the open southern part of the plain at dawn, no doubt to cover the departure of the ships and counter any Athenian move. The Persian center, which was considered the place of honor in their army, was manned by the elite infantry of the expedition: Persians and related Iranian Saka infantry, with units drawn from subject peoples making up the two wings. Virtually all of the Persian cavalry were apparently aboard the ships, since no cavalry appear in accounts of the fighting; though the frieze of the Nike temple on the Akropolis may indicate that a few Persian cavalry did remain and fight in the battle.

Herodotos gives the impression that the Athenians covered the entire eight *stades* distance between the armies at a run, but this cannot have been correct. Though scholars have argued over whether it would have been possible for fully armored hoplites to run a mile to give battle, possibility is really beside the point: it would have made no sense to do it. Why should the Athenians exhaust themselves running hundreds of meters in full armor (and in heat of August!) and risking total disruption of their phalanx formation, when Persian bows were only effective at around 150 meters? Even historians who argue that the Athenians ran the last 200 meters, therefore, exaggerate: it is only the final 150 meters or so that will have exposed the Athenian and Plataian hoplites to seriously dangerous bow fire, and only the most necessary distance will have been run.

Assuming that the Athenian army began to leave camp and deploy into the plain at or very shortly after dawn—which will have occurred around 6:30 A.M. on August 11—the battle will likely have begun between eight and nine o'clock in the morning. The Athenian *polemarchos* Kallimachos will have ordered his *salpinktes* (trumpeter) to sound the signal to advance, and that signal will have been taken up successively by trumpeters along the line until it reached the left wing. Starting from the right, then, the entire mile-long line will have begun to march forward at a steady pace, line by line, the men doing their best to maintain the cohesion of the lines as they walked over unevennesses in the ground and negotiated minor obstacles.

As they walked forward, the entire army will have begun to chant the simple hymn in honor of Apollo as protector and bringer of victory called the *paian*. Every Greek state had its particular version of the *paian*. The effect was to foster among the men, as they

BATTLE OF MARATHON PHASE I

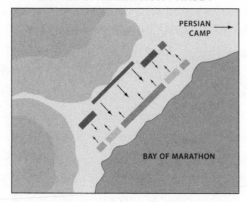

BATTLE OF MARATHON PHASE II

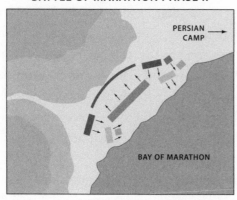

BATTLE OF MARATHON PHASE III

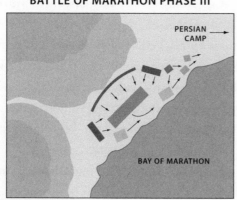

advanced into the fearful act of battle, a sense of cohesion and common purpose, to still the fears and settle the nerves. One can imagine the sound of 10,000 men walking steadily forward chanting the *paian* by listening to a British football or rugby crowd singing together to urge on their teams—the fans of Liverpool F.C. singing "You'll Never Walk Alone" for example, or the Welsh rugby fans at Cardiff singing "Land of my Fathers"—or in an American context, the fight songs sung by thousands of students at their universities' football games.

As they drew closer to the enemy, the singing of the *paian* ceased and men took up the yelling of war cries—typically a wordless cry of *"Eleleu! Eleleu!"* for example—the purpose of which was to screw up one's courage and strike fear in the enemy. As they yelled in this way, and as the first Persian arrows began to rattle down among them, Kallimachos will have ordered his trumpeter to sound the signal to run, and as the trumpeters down the line repeated that signal, the Athenians and Plataians increased their pace from a steady walk to a brisk run, shields held up and out to avoid banging against their legs and (hopefully) to protect against arrows, spears held high at the ready to thrust down at the Persian front rank as soon as they came within reach.

From the Persian perspective, the sight must have been fearful: a vast mass of bronze-clad men, made seemingly taller and more fearsome by the tall crests waving above their helmets, their heads entirely covered by those gleaming bronze helmets, their bodies hidden by huge bronze-faced shields, charging towards them at a run, yelling at the tops of their voices. Arriving at the Persian front line at such speed, the Greeks must have literally crashed into the lightly armored and wicker-shielded Persians with a terrible impact, and the initial harm to the Persians, in men knocked over and/or wounded or killed by spear thrusts, must have been great—especially on the wings. It seems likely, in fact, that the Athenian center, only half the depth of the wings, was held back somewhat: the Athenian strategy, after all, was for the wings to defeat the Persians in their parts of the battle first, while the Athenian center tried to hold its ground against severe odds. In the center, therefore, the fight likely began a little later than on the wings, and there it was the Persians who piled pressure on the Athenians.

It's certain that the Persians fought well, in spite of the initial shock of the Athenian charge. The Persians were a proud military people who had conquered a great empire and rightly enjoyed a reputation for valor and invincibility. They stood their ground in spite of heavy initial losses and fought back hard. In the center, indeed, the battle seemed to be going their way, as their superior numbers told, and they began to push back the thin line of Athenians. The two tribal regiments in the Athenian center had a terrible time of it, in fact, giving ground and, according to our sources, very nearly breaking. Legends arose around this desperate fight in the center: according to one, a huge warrior in archaic equipment appeared out of nowhere right where the pressure on the Athenians was greatest, wielding a club rather than a spear, and rallying the Athenians to stand and hold their line. This was supposed to have been the great Athenian hero Theseus, rising from his grave to defend his people at their hour of greatest need. This legend indicates to us how desperate the fight was for the thin ranks in the Athenian center.

But telling the story of the battle in this way, the armchair historian's way of calm, rational, bloodless, almost antiseptic narrative, can't possibly give a full and fair sense of what the battle was really like. We should try to imagine how it will have seemed to an Athenian hoplite as it happened. Awakened in the hour before dawn with news he must prepare for battle—if indeed he hadn't awakened even earlier from the buzz around the camp of important news come in and the generals debating what to do—he had to take an early breakfast and check and strap on his armor. Many men must have found it hard to choke down their food, nerves unsettling their stomachs in anticipation of risking their lives, but the older men and officers will have been encouraging everyone to eat and drink properly. Strapping on his cuirass; snapping on his greaves; slinging the strap of the short sword across his torso, the sword hanging neatly against his left hip; placing the helmet on the crown of his head, ready to be pulled down over his face once the march towards the enemy began; hefting up the huge shield to slide his left arm through the central grip, grasp the hand grip, and settle the rim of the shield on his left shoulder; and finally taking up the eight-foot-long spear and settling his grip in just the right spot to hold it nicely balanced; his nerves must have been jangling the entire time as his imagination worked on the thought of facing the dreaded Mede. Around him was the bustle and hubbub of nearly 10,000 fellow Athenians preparing in the same way. Then he had to find his place in his line and file of his tribal regiment, and as the pre-dawn dark and chill gave way to the light and warmth of an early August morning, he marched down into the plain.

The mass of men around him, marching in the same rhythm, wearing the same equipment, ready to fight for the same cause must have been a comfort, and no doubt the sheer act of marching in unison, of *moving,* will have settled his nerves a bit. Then came the trumpeting and shouting of orders as the regiments wheeled from column of march into line of battle, and with it the front-rank hoplite will have gotten his first clear sight, through the eye-holes of his now pulled-down helmet, of the massed Persian ranks. Thousands upon thousands of strange-looking men, wearing trousers rather than tunics, and other exotic gear, must have started up the nerves again.

A crowd, especially a hostile crowd, is apt to seem bigger, more numerous than it really is; and in this case the Persians undoubtedly outnumbered the Greeks, perhaps by as much as two to one. The steadying influence of the *paian,* the uplifting sense of thousands of fellows around one, moving with one, united in purpose, and of a god being called on who would stand by one if one showed oneself worthy: all this must have played its part in keeping our hoplite calm enough and focused enough to march steadily

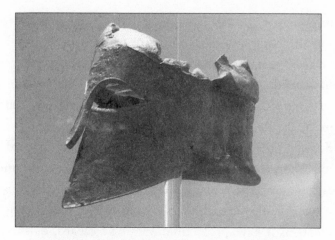

The famous helmet of Miltiades, one of the Athenian generals at Marathon. Per the inscription, Miltiades dedicated the helmet to Zeus, at Olympia.

forward towards the danger in front of him. Then came the rattling of arrows dropping from the skies amongst his ranks, the occasional grunts or cries of a man being hit, the trumpet signal to start the run, and the lung-searing run itself with sixty or more pounds of equipment strapped to the body or held in the hands to make it more difficult. That run forward, likely a clumsy, at times stumbling run, over less than even terrain, must have started the adrenaline pumping, and it may have been with surprise that our hoplite would have noticed that he was yelling at the top of his voice as he charged.

The crash into the Persian ranks began the battle proper, and the concern amidst the panting, the din, the commotion, was to stab at and into any Persians one glimpsed, while keeping the shield well up and in front to ward off enemy blows. It's hard for modern Western man to imagine what battle in the days of thrusting and cutting weapons, of hand-to-hand combat in massed formations, will have been like. It involved all the senses—sight, hearing, smell, touch—and those senses were sharpened by fear, by exhilaration, by adrenaline. The nearest modern man may get to that experience is not modern battle, with its small units, dispersed formations, and firearm weapons causing death or injury to come unseen from almost any direction and often from great distances. It is rather the experience of being in a huge crowd that gives way to commotion: a demonstration crowd, perhaps, confronting a formation of police and surging to and fro under police baton charges, or the water cannon, or charges of mounted police.

For the Greek hoplite the sense of losing control of one's movement and choices was increased by the helmet that muffled the hearing and restricted sight to what was directly in front, and by the weight and unwieldiness of the shield, hampering one's movements as it gave protection. Surging forward, or—frighteningly—being pressed backwards, one heard the yells of men fighting, the grunts and cries of men wounded and dying, the thudding of weapons against armor and into flesh. One saw an indistinct surging of glimpsed figures, to be thrust at if wearing robes and trousers and felt caps with flaps, to be supported if wearing bronze armor and short kilts. The muscles ached from running, from the weight of the equipment, from the jarring of thrusting spear into enemy bodies, or receiving enemy thrusts on one's shield. And the nose was assaulted by a pungent array of smells: the sweat of struggling men, the sweetish coppery smell of blood, and above all, no doubt, the acrid scent of piss and dank stink of shit as fear, trauma, and death caused men's bladders and bowels to be loosened.

The point of all this is that battle was a confusing, terrifying experience for the individual soldiers engaged in it. This was true even when—as was the case with the Athenians at Marathon—the plans made before the battle worked almost perfectly, and the battle went well. For the soldiers on the Persian side, this battle must have been even more terrible. Swathed from head to toe in cloth, but wearing little or no armor and carrying only a light wickerwork shield which, though a useful protection from the arrows and javelins of their native warfare, offered little resistance to the firm thrusts of the heavy Greek spears, they found themselves at a huge disadvantage in this battle against heavily armored Greek hoplites. Their own weapons had little impact against the heavy shields and bronze body armor of the Greeks, while the heavy Greek spears inflicted all too much damage.

Miltiades proved to be right in his estimation of the relative fighting value of heavily armed Greek hoplites and Iranian light infantry, no matter how well trained and disciplined, and the battle went exactly according to his plan. The two Athenian wings, the left reinforced by the allied Plataians, relentlessly drove back the forces opposed to them, and before too long the Persian wings broke, the soldiers turning to flight along the narrow path between the marsh and the sea, leading to where the Persian ships were drawn up close to shore offering safety. This was the crucial stage of the battle: the natural instinct of masses of soldiers driving back enemy forces into flight is to pursue and kill. Would they be able to restrain that impulse and remember to carry out their instructions, driving around the rear of the Persian center and turning inwards to outflank it and attack it from behind?

If they failed to do so the consequences could be disastrous. The Athenian center was being driven steadily back, and though the hoplites there, knowing their role, had remained steadfast and refused to break and flee, they could not withstand indefinitely the immense pressure being applied to them. If the Athenian center were to be driven to flight, the risk was that the battle could still be lost by the Athenians or, at best, turn into a stalemate that would have offered the Persians the chance to gain success through their force that was sailing around Attica to capture Athens.

When the Athenian wings did turn inward and outflank the Persian center, however, the outcome of the battle was sealed. As soldiers in the rear ranks of the Persian center came under attack, or became aware that they were about to be surrounded, they turned and fled towards the ships, like the soldiers from their wings. As more and more soldiers from the Persian center peeled away into flight, the pressure on the Athenian center eased and, sensing the victory, they were able to fight back and drive the Persians oppos-

The Soros, *or burial mound, in which the Athenians who fell at Marathon were interred. It marks the site of the actual battle.*

ing them backwards into the enveloping forces of the Athenian flanks. There was still hard fighting to do, as the Persians and Saka of the center certainly did not sell their lives cheaply, but the inevitable outcome was total Athenian victory.

After the collapse of the Persian center, the Athenians pursued the fleeing Persian forces towards the Persian camp and their ships. Even more than their casualties in the fighting, we are told, Persians suffered heavy losses during this flight, as the narrow path became too crowded and numerous Persians were pushed into the marsh on one side or the sea on the other, while the pursuing Athenians constantly cut down Persians in the rear of the flight. All the same, most of the Persian army did manage to reach the ships and begin to board them. Here the last phase of the battle took place, as Athenians tried to prevent Persians from getting onto their ships, and even fought to capture some of the ships.

The brother of the famous Athenian tragedian Aischylos, Kynegeiros, died in this struggle, fighting hard to capture a Persian ship. Here died too the Athenian war archon Kallimachos and Stesilaos, one of the ten tribal generals. In the end, the Athenians did

226

manage to capture some seven Persian ships, but the overwhelming majority, having picked up as many survivors of the battle as they could, successfully fought off the Athenian attack and stood out to sea. The battle was over, and the Athenians—quite likely to their own great surprise—found themselves the clear winners. Rounding up the wounded and dead, they found that, thanks to their excellent defensive armor and shields, their losses in men killed were slight: only 192 Athenians and eleven Plataians died, most apparently in the final struggle at the ships. By contrast, the Athenians found 6,400 enemy dead: they made a careful count, since they had made a vow to the goddess Artemis, if she helped bring them victory, to sacrifice to her one goat for every enemy warrior slain. In the event, the number of enemy dead was so huge that the Athenians could not discharge the vow at once: they were obliged to fulfill their promise on the installment plan, sacrificing to Artemis 500 goats per year.

We can surmise that, having begun between about eight and nine o'clock in the morning, the battle would have been over and the Persian ships away to sea not long after 11 A.M. The day was still young, eventful as it had been, and there was much work to do in gathering the dead and caring for the wounded. Both of these tasks would have been seen as crucial. The importance of caring for the wounded is obvious; but ancient Greeks placed almost as much emphasis on care for the dead. In Greek religious belief regarding death, proper burial was crucially important for the fate of the shade (or as we might say, spirit) of the deceased. Only when properly buried could the shade of the deceased be ferried across the river Styx by the ferryman Charon and reach a peaceful rest in Hades, the underworld. The shades of men not so buried were doomed to an eternity of restless wandering on the wrong shore of the Styx, never to find peace. At Marathon, as a unique tribute to the heroic dead of the great battle, the corpses were collected to be buried in a communal grave surmounted by a great burial mound, called the Soros, which can still be seen today.

THE DASH TO ATHENS

But, though the battle had been won, Athenian victory in the campaign of Marathon was not yet secure. As the Athenian leaders watched the Persian ships making their way southwards from Marathon, they were filled with anxiety about the Persian force that had sailed for Athens that morning. If this force succeeded in capturing Athens while it was undefended, they could still turn defeat into victory. The question facing the Athenian leaders, then, was whether Athens could be provided with an adequate defense force before the Persian ships arrived there. According to Herodotos, their fear that the Persians would capture the city of Athens was strengthened by a report that someone had "raised a shield" to signal the Persians that the city was vulnerable.

This report is puzzling: there were thousands of shields being raised and lowered around the plain of Marathon that day: what does Herodotos mean by this "raising" of a shield? Some historians speculate that it was high on the slopes of Mt. Pentele, overlooking the plain, that the shield was used to signal the Persians by flashing sunlight from the polished surface. That is only speculation, however, as Herodotos doesn't say anything like that. The entire shield episode seems dubious, especially as this supposed signal was reported to Herodotos in the context of alleging treason by the powerful and controversial Alkmaionid family. The whole story of the shield may be a fabrication by enemies of the Alkmaionids.

At any rate, the Athenian generals knew that forces had to reach the city of Athens as soon as humanly possible, to protect it from Persian attack. The Persian ships had a long way to go, all around Attica, to reach the bay of Phaleron: rowing as directly as possible, the distance to be covered was a good seventy miles. Presumably the triremes rowed at the best speed of which they were capable, leaving the slower transport ships to make what speed they could by sail. We know that ancient triremes were capable of achieving speeds of six to eight knots, which is to say about seven to nine miles per hour, for short sprints; and we can assume that the Persians will have pressed their rowers to make an extreme effort. All the same, the fastest of the Persian triremes could hardly have averaged better than six miles per hour over such a distance, nor have reached the bay of Phaleron in under twelve hours, which is to say that Persian ships might have begun to appear in the bay of Phaleron opposite Athens in the hours just before dusk (which will have occurred at about 8:30 P.M.), between about 6 and 7 P.M. assuming an all out effort. Athenian soldiers traveling from Marathon to Attica by land had a much shorter route: either some twenty-two miles by the shorter route across the northern shoulder of Pentele, or twenty-five to twenty-six miles taking the coast road south and then cutting over the southern slopes of Pentele and through the pass between Pentele and Hymettos, dropping into the Athenian plain from Pallene. This latter was the flatter, less demanding route, and the route taken by the army of Peisistratos and his sons when they conquered Athens in 548/7. The northern route, though significantly shorter, involved a steep climb of some three or four miles at the beginning along a narrow trail through rough wooded terrain; but it had the advantage of then offering a fairly direct and downhill path of some eighteen miles into the city.

Historians have debated which of these routes the Athenians are likely to have taken in this crisis. But any choice between them seems to me a false one. The situation required above all speed, as Herodotos emphasized in his narrative, and stringing thousands of men out along one narrow route doesn't make for the greatest speed. There is an old principle in warfare: march divided, fight united. I think it's highly probable that the Athenians marched back to Athens via both routes so as to make the best possible speed.

The generals could divide the army for this march according to either of two basic principles: by tribe or by age class. In the former case four of the eight tribes marching (two were designated to stay at Marathon, as we shall see) could have been assigned to each route. In this instance, however, a division by age classes seems more likely: in view of the steep and demanding climb that would be required of the men taking the northern route over the first three to four miles of their journey, it would have made sense to send the younger men by this route, reserving the flatter and therefore physically less taxing southern route for the older troops. At a guess, one could speculate that age classes eighteen to thirty were sent by the northern route, with orders to march steadily up to and through the Pass of Dionysos at the apex of the route, and then to put on all the speed they could manage on the long downhill run into Athens; while the men over thirty would have marched at the fastest pace they could sustain along the southern road. As brutal as the initial climb would be for the younger soldiers, in full armor in the glare of the midday sun and having spent the morning fighting a battle, it could be hoped that as men got over the pass they could pick up their pace on the eighteen miles or so of basically straight downhill road and reach the city in advance of the older men on the southern road.

But of course the most famous legend about the Battle of Marathon tells of the runner Philippides, who was sent by the generals at Marathon to run to the city to announce the battle's result. Reputedly he reached the city having run the entire way, announced to the council there "we have won," and dropped dead of exhaustion. This legend is not found in Herodotos's account: it first surfaces during Roman imperial times, 600 or so years after the event, in stories told by Plutarch and Lucian.

The truth is in this case much more impressive than the legend. Philippides ran, not a paltry twenty-five or so miles from Marathon to Athens, but the roughly 140 miles from Athens to Sparta and then the same distance back again. To this super-fit "all day runner" the run from Marathon to Athens would have been a pleasant little training exercise. But it was in fact the majority of the Athenian army, those who were still fit and able after the battle, who traveled that afternoon of August 11, 490 B.C.E., from Marathon to Athens, after fighting the most desperate battle of their lives in the morning. And they traveled not in running gear, but in full armor, with shields and spears. The two tribal regiments who had fought in the center of the Athenian formation, and who had suffered the most during the battle as we have seen, were told to secure the battle site, care for the wounded, and gather the dead. The remainder of the Athenian army, all who were fit to travel, were instructed to make for Athens as fast as their feet could take them, as Herodotos put it. Leaving two regiments behind, and granting that in addition to the nearly two hundred killed many hundreds of hoplites must have been injured in the battle, it may have been about six thousand or so men who set out on this speed march to save Athens. We should remember that men in ancient times were used to walking everywhere, often for hours at a time and on hilly dirt roads, so that this march will have seemed much less extreme to an ancient Greek than it would to a modern man used to covering long distances in motorized vehicles. All the same, it was an amazing march the Athenians completed that summer afternoon.

Inevitably, given natural differences in fitness, stamina, and running ability, the thousands of Athenian warriors would have become seriously strung out along the roads over the following hours; and naturally they would not have run the entire way. That would hardly have been possible in full armor even at the best of times, let alone in the early afternoon heat after fighting a battle all morning.

The younger troops would have started out on the difficult initial uphill stage over the north slope of Pentele at a brisk walk, and many would have slowed down seriously after the first mile or so. However, once the Pass of Dionysos was reached, the fittest men may well have managed to trot or jog at least part of the rest of the way on the downhill run into Athens.

A good amateur Marathon runner can complete the modern twenty-six-mile distance in about four hours. Many of the Athenians in 490, I have suggested, took the shorter route, by which N.G.L. Hammond reported walking from Athens to

Marathon in six hours, and back again the same day in seven hours. We can assume, then, that the first exhausted Athenian hoplites began to trickle into the city of Athens about six hours after setting out, and it will likely have been at least seven hours before large numbers of Athenian hoplites reached the city. We can guess that the *hippeis,* the wealthy aristocrats who owned horses and included the generals and some of the officers, will have ridden with all speed by the flatter Pallene route to arrive sooner back to the city to prepare the defense. The decision was taken to station the Athenian hoplite force just outside the city on the western side, at the gymnasium of Kynosarges, facing the bay of Phaleron. It seemed a good omen that, just as there had been a sanctuary of Herakles at the Athenian camp at Marathon, so Kynosarges too was sacred to Herakles.

As the weary Athenian hoplites trickled down the dusty roads through the plain of Athens, then, they were met with instructions to make their way straight through the city to Kynosarges and draw up there in military formation. Old men and boys, and in this situation perhaps women, too, probably collected jars of water from the fountain houses of the city to refresh the men exhausted by their exertions, producing scenes not unlike those at watering stages in a modern Marathon run. What we know is that when, in the evening, the first Persian ships hove to in the broad bay in front of Phaleron, they saw waiting for them in front of the city a force of several thousand hoplites already. Since they had left the bay of Marathon in the morning, before the battle, they must have wondered at first who these troops could be. But they must have seen, moving down the dusty roads of the Athenian plain to join the force at Kynosarges, a steady stream of Athenian hoplites that will have given them the clue.

These were no defeated or retreating soldiers being harassed by a pursuing army, and their presence could only be explained on the assumption that the Persian force at Marathon had been put out of action in some way. The Persians anchored in the bay in uncertainty, and waited. We can guess that before too long definite news reached them: it will have been important for the Persians retreating from the bay of Marathon to let the Persian ships at Phaleron know what had happened, and a light reconnaissance vessel could make the voyage around Attica significantly faster than the triremes and transports could. At any rate, after resting in front of Phaleron beach for a time while the leaders discussed what to do, the Persian ships turned away and rowed back towards Asia. No one in the Persian army had any appetite for trying to force a landing in the face of a large, determined, and victorious force of hoplite warriors. Total Athenian victory was confirmed.

A few days later, an advance force of 2,000 Spartiates reached Athens, having left Sparta on August 12, immediately after the night of the full moon, and by hard marching arrived at Athens (remarkably) on the third day. They learned that the battle was over and they were no longer needed. They asked to be allowed to view the battlefield and, having done so, left impressed at the Athenians' achievement, as well they might be. The Athenians themselves, very likely, had not yet fully grasped the scale of what they had achieved. Such events take time to sink in. But it was not many years before the Battle of Marathon was to become recognized as the proudest day in Athenian history, and one of the turning points in Greek and Western history.

CHAPTER 6

THE CONSEQUENCES OF
THE BATTLE OF MARATHON

I N THE IMMEDIATE AFTERMATH OF THE ATHENIANS' UNEXPECTED
victory at Marathon, they must have felt an enormous sense of
relief and even elation. But it's fairly clear that it took time for
them to grasp what they had achieved, and how important the battle's outcome was to be. The praise of the Spartans who had viewed
the battle site must have been a source of pride, given the Spartans'
reputation as unmatched warriors. And when the Athenians counted
the enemy dead in order to fulfill their vow to the goddess Artemis
to sacrifice to her one goat for every enemy soldier slain if she would
help the Athenians to victory, they found that there were some 6,400
of them. This huge number of enemy dead, fully two- thirds of the
total number of Athenian hoplites at the battle, gave the Athenians
a sense of having done something big. The sense of achievement was
to grow over the subsequent decades, until the battle loomed large
in the Athenians' historical sense of themselves. But we may still
wonder how important it really was. After all, the Persian army at
Marathon had been a mere expeditionary force, for the Persians, on
a relatively small scale and unaccompanied by the king. As is well
known, Persian determination to conquer Greece was not affected,
and ten years later a much larger scale invasion of Greece, by both

land and sea and led by the Persian king in person, was mounted. So why should Marathon be seen as a crucial battle, as a turning point? To answer that we must look both at what actually happened, to the Athenians and to the Greeks and Persians more generally, in the decades after the battle, and at what likely would have happened if the Persians had won, as had been very possible, even probable.

ATHENS AND GREECE AFTER VICTORY AT MARATHON

The hero of the hour at Athens in the battle's aftermath was Miltiades: it had been his policy to call out the Athenian hoplite force and make a stand at Marathon, and his strategy and tactics that had brought victory in the battle, as all acknowledged. The death of the *polemarch* Kallimachos in the closing stage of the battle helped Miltiades claim credit for the victory—removing the most obvious rival for that credit—but the universal praise in our sources of Miltiades as the key Athenian general shows that Miltiades' role really was crucial. He was triumphantly re-elected one of the ten generals for the following year and was the dominant voice in Athenian policy, though that was not to last. An ill-advised expedition aimed at extending Athenian power into the Cyclades came to a disastrous halt on Paros, where Miltiades himself received a crippling thigh wound. The great aristocrat's enemies pounced, prosecuting him for deceiving the Athenian people. Too ill with terminal gangrene to defend himself, he lay in the assembly place as the people found him guilty and imposed a huge fine. It was more than he could pay, but he died shortly afterwards anyway, leaving the debt to his son Kimon, who discharged it with the help of relatives. Thus, after the glorious victory, the Athenians showed the dark side of their democracy: the envy and haste to judge and punish that were to bedevil most of the Athenians' successful leaders over the next decades.

On the whole, though, the mood at Athens in the 480s was buoyant. In 487 the Athenians ended the election of the nine archons, realizing that elections would always favor the rich and prominent, and instead enacted an allotment process to appoint these magistrates, making the chance of men from newly wealthy and obscure families every bit as great as those from the older and famous families. The prestige of the archons declined significantly as a result and so, eventually, did the prestige of the Areopagos Council that was made up of ex-archons.

In future, the ten annual *strategoi* established by Kleisthenes' reforms, the only major magistrates at Athens, other than top financial officials, who continued to be elected, became the most prominent and important magistrates in the Athenian state. At this same time, the Athenians began to make use of the system of ostracism Kleisthenes had instituted. Hippias's relative Hipparchos son of Charmos, who had remained at Athens until now despite suspicions regarding his loyalty to the Athenian democracy, was the first to be exiled for ten years. After him, Megakles the Alkmaionid (probably Kleisthenes' nephew), Xanthippos (father of the famous Perikles), and Aristides the Just were each ostracized in turn, as Athenian politicians vied for leadership of the people.

Themistokles was left as the leading politician in Athens, with a policy of pursuing naval power. Already as chief archon in 493/2 he had persuaded the Athenians to begin building a real port for themselves at the Peiraieus, which boasted one of the best protected harbors in the Aegean region. Until that time Athenian shipping had simply anchored off, or been hauled up on, the gently sloping beach of the bay of Phaleron. In 483/2, however, the Athenians received a windfall. In southern Attica, around Laureion, the Athenians had valuable silver mines where rich new veins of the precious metal were now found, bringing vast new revenues to the Athenian state. Themistokles, citing particularly the Athenians' long time unsuccessful naval rivalry with the Aiginetans, persuaded the Athenians to use this revenue for a naval building program: over the next two years 200 brand new triremes were constructed, creating an Athenian fleet which totally dwarfed the Aiginetan fleet of some seventy vessels. Inevitably, one suspects that the Aiginetans were just an excuse for this building program. Any intelligent Greek leader who looked further than the purely local affairs of his state must have been aware that the threat of Persian expansion into Greece was far from over, and ship building on the scale Themistokles persuaded the Athenians to engage in could really only have the Persian threat in mind, since only the Persians could mobilize the sort of naval power that would require such massive ship building.

As it turned out, the new Athenian fleet was made ready just in time. King Darius died in 487/6 and was succeeded by his son Xerxes. Though Xerxes' attention was at first occupied by a rebellion in Egypt, as soon as that rebellion had been put down he turned his thoughts to further conquest: as the successor to the throne of Cyrus, of Cambyses, and of Darius, each of whom had conquered new lands and extended the empire of the Persians, Xerxes too felt it necessary to prove himself worthy to be king of the Persians by extending the Persian power. And since the lesson of the Ionian revolt and the setback at Marathon, there could be no doubt which Persian frontier needed attention and in which direction Persian power should be extended.

Vast plans were set afoot beginning about 484 for a royal expedition to settle the empire's western border and teach the Greeks a lesson once and for all. The lessons of the past were to be learned in full: no half measures, no economies of scale or preparation were to jeopardize Xerxes' success. Strategically, the decision was to launch the assault by both land and sea using the northern route. The army to be mobilized would be too large to be carried by ship and so must march across the northern Aegean shore and invade Greece from the north. In order to avoid a logistically dangerous delay at the crossing of the Hellespont, bridges were to be built across the strait so the army could march rapidly across and on into southern Thrace. Ironically, these bridges, which are described in great detail by Herodotos, were probably designed by Greek engineers: a late source mentions a certain Harpalos, and Herodotos himself informs us that Darius's earlier bridge across the Bosporus had been designed by Mandrokles of Samos. Similar bridges were also prepared at the major rivers the army would have to cross, such as the Strymon; and supplies were gathered at staging posts along the north Aegean coast to make sure the army would not go hungry.

As to the fleet, the great danger for it was the passage around the Athos peninsula, where Mardonios's fleet had been wrecked in 493. Mardonios was acting as Xerxes' second-in-command at this time, and he was well aware of the danger. To avoid it, a canal was dug through the neck of the peninsula, the remains of which (it silted up long ago) can still be seen. Such immense and lengthy preparations couldn't, obviously, be kept secret from the Greek states who were the target of the invasion. All states willing to think of resistance sent envoys to a common council at the Isthmos of Corinth, probably at the summons of the Spartans, who took the lead in resisting the Persians. The aim was to discuss a common defense strategy, but the council revealed the usual divisions among the Greeks.

In the end, the Greeks north of the pass at Thermopylai in central Greece submitted to the Persians without a fight; most of the states and communities in central Greece, north of Attica and Megara, were half-hearted about resisting at best; and even within the Peloponnesos the Argives—out of hostility to the Spartans— were friendly towards the Persians. Nevertheless, an alliance to resist the Persians was created. It essentially had two parts: the Spartan organized and led "Peloponnesian League," which included at this time Megara and Aigina; and the Athenians with their allies the Plataians. The Phokians too joined in resistance but, cut off from the main alliance by the half-hearted Thebans and other Boiotians, they suffered much from the Persians and contributed little or nothing to the Greek resistance effort.

The strategy of the Greeks, after some initial thought of fighting far north in Thessaly, was to make their stand against the Persians, when they eventually invaded Greece in 480, at the narrow pass of Thermopylai, while a fleet of warships would cover the army at the pass from seaborne attack by guarding the narrows between Thessaly and the northern tip of Euboia, based at Cape Artemision. The Greeks knew they would be seriously outnumbered and would thus need to make their stand at a place where physical geography would make it impossible for the Persians to deploy their superior forces. The Spartans would have liked to make this stand at the Isthmos, thus pursuing their longtime policy of not committing their forces outside the Peloponnesos. The problem with that strategy was that Megara and, crucially, Athens lay beyond the Isthmos and would be exposed to Persian occupation by any stand at the Isthmos, and Aigina too would be opened to Persian occupation by a naval stand at the Isthmos.

As events unfolded, it seemed the Spartans would have cared little about that but for one thing: they needed the Athenians' 200 triremes, and the seventy or so the Aiginetans could mobilize, in order to prevent the Persian fleet from landing troops wherever they pleased inside the Peloponnesos—in the territory of friendly Argos for example—and so turning the Spartan defense position at the Isthmos. So, in order to keep the Athenian alliance intact, the Spartans reluctantly agreed to the Thermopylai strategy, but they never in the end committed their forces to it.

In 480 a huge Persian army, led by King Xerxes himself with the experienced Mardonios as second-in-command, crossed the Hellespont and began to march along the north Aegean shore towards Greece. Alongside it sailed a vast fleet of warships and supply vessels. The numbers of army and fleet are impossible to determine, because Herodotos—our main source—gives vastly exaggerated figures: according to him the army numbered several million, and the fleet over 1,200 triremes. It's clear that what Herodotos has done is to estimate the total forces that all provinces of the Persian Empire could have mobilized, and then to assume that they did so. He may have been influenced in that assumption by a well-known war epigram written by the poet Simonides—who was a contemporary of these events—for the men who fought at Thermopylai, to the effect that four thousand

Peloponnesians there fought against three million.

In reality, several million men suddenly concentrated together at one place would have been impossible, with ancient supply mechanisms, to feed, and would have died of starvation. The maximum number of armed men who could be fed and supplied by ancient logistics would not seem to exceed 150,000: at any rate no larger ancient army is reliably attested. We can reasonably guess that the Persian army, so impressive for its vast size, may have numbered in the range of 100,000 to 150,000. As to the fleet, it was large enough to absorb heavy losses from two storms and yet still significantly outnumber a Greek fleet of around 380. Perhaps this fleet numbered about 600 and was the source for this number as a standard figure for a Persian fleet. Most of the Persian army, however, were present more as auxiliaries and for show, than to do any major fighting: it was the core of Persian, Median, and other Iranian troops, making up perhaps a third to a half of the total force, who would decide the outcome of the war. The fleet was built around an elite of Phoenician ships, with additional contingents of Kilikians, Egyptians, Cypriotes, and Ionian Greeks. But though the ships and sailors were of these peoples, each ship carried a contingent of Persian marines, as many as thirty per ship, to do the real fighting.

When news came that this army and fleet had reached northern Greece, a Greek fleet of some 300 triremes, half of them Athenian, sailed to Artemision, and a Greek army led by the Spartan king Leonidas marched to hold the pass at Thermopylai. But Leonidas, as is well known, brought with him a mere 300 Spartiates, along with several thousand Helot servants and a few thousand allied Peloponnesian hoplites, mostly from Arkadia. Together with Theban and other Boiotian forces more or less reluctantly recruited along the way, and 1,000 Phokians who came to join, the total force stationed at Thermopylai didn't exceed 7,000 hoplites. The Spartans explained that this was a mere advance force, and that the main Spartan and Peloponnesian army was delayed by religious commitments and would join Leonidas soon.

They never did. In fact the Spartans were busy working on a fortification wall across the Isthmos of Corinth: their true belief was still in the Isthmian strategy. The Greek fleet at Artemision gave a good account of itself against the numerically superior Persian fleet, helped by the fact that a major storm off the coast of Thessaly had significantly thinned the Persians. As to Leonidas and his army, they fought heroically, and surprisingly—utilizing the narrow space of the pass and their superb defensive armor—managed to hold off the Persians for several days in spite of the grotesque disparity in numbers. The Spartiates showed their usual indomitable fighting spirit: as legend has it, when someone tried to frighten one of the Spartiates named Dienekes by pointing out that the Persians were so numerous that, when they fired their bows, the arrows blocked out the sun, he replied imperturbably: "This is good news: we shall fight in the shade!"

All the same, the outcome of the fight could not be seriously in doubt so long as the Spartans refused to commit their main forces. The pass at Thermopylai had a weakness: a mountain trail, narrow but serviceable, led around it, and the Spartan-led force was too small to be able to commit troops to block this trail effectively. The 1,000 Phokians were stationed there, but when the Persians learned of the path's existence from a local man named Ephialtes, branded ever after as a traitor throughout Greek history, and sent the elite Persian force the Greeks called the "Immortals" to outflank Leonidas and his Spartans, the Phokians could do no more than retreat up the mountain to save themselves, and send a runner down to Leonidas to warn that he was about to be surrounded.

Leonidas ordered his allies to march away at once and save themselves: he would stay with his 300 Spartiates to cover their escape. Distrusting their loyalty, he kept a small Theban contingent with him, and 700 Thespians, realizing that their city was bound to be captured now anyway, volunteered to fight too. It was the suicidal stand of Leonidas and his 300 Spartans that was remembered ever after, however. Many forces throughout history have declared their determination to fight to the last man, but few have ever really done so. Leonidas and his 300 did, and their fight to the death that day probably saved the Greek alliance.

The plain truth is that the Athenians had been badly let down by the Spartans, who had not lived up to their promise to make their stand at Thermopylai, thereby protecting Attica from invasion. When they learned that Thermopylai had fallen and the road to central Greece lay open to the Persians, the Greek fleet retreated from Artemision, and the question was what the Athenians would do now. They couldn't hope to defend Attica now that the Spartans had stayed in the Peloponnesos, and there seemed to be only three options open to them: to surrender to the Persians; to take all their people and movable goods on board their triremes and flee to found a new city somewhere in the west; or to make a last stand at the borders of Attica and go down fighting. They did none of the three: they decided to stand by their alliance with the Spartans, to evacuate their people from Attica to the offshore islands of Salamis and Aigina and to the Peloponnesos—abandoning their empty homeland to Persian occupation—and to fight on beside the Spartans from their ships. In this way they protected the Peloponnesos from sea-borne invasion by the Persians, though the Spartans had failed to protect Attica from land invasion as they had promised to do.

It's likely that the deep impression made by the heroic and suicidal stand of Leonidas and his 300 helped decide the Athenians to this course. Led by Themistokles, the Athenians manned their 200 triremes and, with the 180 or so ships of the rest of the Greeks, confronted the Persian fleet in the narrow waters between Salamis island and the coast of Attica. Xerxes and his army, who had occupied and sacked the deserted Attica and Athens, watched the battle from the shore and saw the triumph of the new Athenian fleet. Because the Greek fleet, spearheaded by the Athenians and the Aiginetans, inflicted a decisive defeat on the Persians and thereby saved the Peloponnesos.

Reflecting on these events a generation later, Herodotos insisted that, though he knew that in his day this view would be unpopular, he nevertheless had to conclude that it was above all the

Athenians who saved Greece, and not the Spartans. Because if the Athenian fleet had not existed, or if the Athenians had refused to fight on after Thermopylai, the Spartan strategy of making a stand at the Isthmos would have been hopeless: Persian forces landed by ship inside the Peloponnesos would have turned the Spartan position; and though no one doubted the Spartans would have fought nobly to the end, he did not see how they could have won under those circumstances. His judgment makes sense. The Athenians were crucial to the Greek success.

After the defeat at Salamis, Xerxes returned to Asia with part of the army leaving Mardonios with the larger part to "finish off" the conquest of Greece. Mardonios retreated to winter quarters in Thessaly and sent envoys to Athens inviting the Athenians to change sides, promising them very favorable treatment if they did so. Alarmed, the Spartans also sent envoys urging the Athenians to stand by their alliance, promising that they really would leave the Peloponnesos and fight together with the Athenians in central Greece, if only the Athenians would stand firm. The Athenians did so. But in the spring, when Mardonios marched south, no Spartan army marched through the Isthmos, and once again the Athenians had to evacuate their land and see it occupied and laid waste by the Persians. They sent an embassy to Sparta to remonstrate with the Spartans, threatening that if the Spartans would not live up to their promise to fight outside the Peloponnesos, then for their part the Athenians would abandon the fight and sail to Siris in southern Italy, to found a new city for themselves there.

This threat finally galvanized the Spartans into action: they knew that their position was hopeless without the Athenians, and so finally they sent their main army—5,000 Spartiates, 5,000 *perioikoi*, and about 15,000 allies from the rest of the Peloponnesos—through the Isthmos and into southern Boiotia, where they joined up with an army of 8,000 Athenian hoplites at Plataia. The final battle of the Persian invasion was fought there, with the Spartiate Pausanias, nephew of Leonidas and regent for Leonidas's infant son, in command. Plataia was the Spartans' battle. Though Pausanias seems to have made a mess of the tactics, to judge from Herodotos's account, when push came to shove the Spartan phalanx charged into the elite force of Persians commanded by Mardonios himself and pushed them from the field of battle and into defeat and flight. Mardonios died in the fighting, the Persian camp was captured, and the Greek victory was complete. The Persians never again mounted a credible threat to Greek freedom, and because it was the Spartan hoplites who won the final battle, it was the Spartans who got the credit, unfairly on the whole, for saving Greek liberty.

This defeat of the mighty Persian Empire gave the Greeks an enormous boost of optimism; especially, of course, the Athenians. The victory was so unexpected and yet so complete that, in its aftermath, it seemed for a couple of generations that anything was possible, if one just tried. To stay with military history first, the Athenians immediately led a Greek counterattack against the Persians. In principle this counterattack was the Spartans' to lead, but they quickly showed they had no appetite for it: it would require extensive operations on the eastern side of the Aegean.

Already in 479, at the time of the campaign of Plataia, a Greek fleet of mostly Athenian ships but commanded by the Spartan king Leotychidas had crossed the Aegean in pursuit of the defeated Persian fleet. They found the remnant of the Persian fleet at Cape Mykale on the coast of Asia Minor, near Samos, and inflicted another crushing defeat on it. Leotychidas then decided that enough was enough and returned to the Greek mainland; but the Athenian ships, commanded by Xanthippos, sailed to the Hellespont to ensure the destruction of Xerxes' bridge. Finding the bridge no longer there, they besieged the city of Sestos on the European side and captured it, killing the Persian garrison and taking the papyrus cables from the former bridge as booty. This was the first step in a decades long Athenian offensive against the remains of Persian power in the Aegean. The stated goal was to free all Greeks from Persian control, and to punish the Persians for the "wrongs done to the Greeks"; but more than anything it involved the creation of an Aegean-wide alliance system that made the Athenians a great power in Greek affairs to rival the Spartans and their "Peloponnesian League."

The Athenian alliance system that emerged from the Persian invasion is generally known as the "Delian League" since it was, for a time, headquartered on the sacred islet of Delos in the Cyclades. The Athenians were from the beginning the acknowledged leaders of the alliance: they provided the commanders for all allied military actions, they provided the treasurers for the alliance's funds, it was the Athenian statesman Aristides the Just who set the proper contributions of the initial allies to joint undertakings, and the Athenian state set the alliance's policies.

The allies were effectively divided into two groups: a small group of powerful allies who maintained considerable independence and contributed military and naval forces to joint actions; and a much larger group of small allies who made annual contributions of money to fund the alliance's activities, on the understanding that the Athenians would use the funds so contributed to pay for ships and men to fight the alliance's battles. In this way, in effect, Athens' allies funded an enormous expansion of the Athenian armed forces, especially their fleet which grew to over 400 sea-worthy vessels. From very early on the Athenians began to treat the smaller allies as subordinates, and eventually Athens came to be seen as a "tyrant city." But, led above all by Kimon the son of Miltiades, the Athenians really did use their power and allies to drive Persian power out of the Aegean region. First the north Aegean region and Hellespont were cleared of Persian garrisons; all of the Ionian cities were freed and brought into the alliance; and a great Persian counter attack to—at a minimum—recover control of Ionia was defeated in a great double engagement, at sea and on land, at the mouth of the river Eurymedon in Pamphylia around 468.

Athenian support for an Egyptian rebellion against the Persians in the 450s ended in disaster when the Persian commander Megabyxos reconquered Egypt and destroyed an Athenian force

A bust of the great Athenian statesman Perikles. This bust, which is currently in the Altes Museum in Berlin, was created in the first century C.E., after the original Greek sculpture of 429 B.C.E.

aiding the Egyptians. But another attempt by the Persians to stage a come back in the Aegean was soundly defeated by the Athenians in a great double victory, at sea and on land, at Cypriot Salamis a little before 450. The Persians recognized that they had not the right kind of forces to engage the Greeks at sea or on land with success, while the Athenians, embroiled since 460 in hostilities with the Spartans and their allies, were ready to come to terms. Negotiations carried out on the Athenian side by a wealthy political leader named Kallias—an associate of Athens' leading statesman of this time, Perikles—led to a peace agreement between the Athenians and the Persians, the so-called "Peace of Kallias" of around 447, named after the Athenian negotiator.

By this peace the Athenians agreed not to molest the Persians any further or aid Persian subjects to rebel, and the Persians for their part agreed to stay out of the Aegean Sea entirely, and not to approach within a day's horse ride of the west coast of Anatolia—by implication ceding control of the Ionian cities. At the same time, in 446, after nearly fifteen years of hostilities, the Athenians and

247

Spartans agreed to a peace, the "30 Years Peace" so called from its expected duration, whereby the Spartans—in return for peace—essentially accepted the Athenian alliance system and acknowledged the Athenians as their equals. Militarily, the next fifteen years represented the high water mark of Athenian power and prestige, and these years—which are particularly associated with the leadership of the great statesman Perikles—represented the height of Athenian material prosperity and cultural achievement too.

The democracy founded by Kleisthenes and the Athenians of his time and defended so effectively in battle against the Thebans and Chalkidians, and on the field of Marathon, had thrived. Filled with confidence from those successes, and the great successes of Salamis and the Eurymedon too, the Athenians believed completely in their right and ability to govern themselves by collective decision making and action, and they extended that idea in a set of reforms passed in the late 460s, on the proposal of a leader named Ephialtes. These reforms stripped the upper class Areopagos Council of most of its remaining powers, most notably the powers of examining candidates for public office as to their eligibility and suitability (*dokimasia*), and reviewing the conduct and accounts of all magistrates and office holders after their year in office to check for any wrong doing (*euthynai*). These responsibilities were passed directly to the people, operating through public law courts staffed by juries of 200 to 500 citizens drawn from an annual panel of 6,000 citizens willing and eligible for service. And a law passed by Perikles a few years later in the 450s granted a daily pay of three obols (enough to feed himself and his family) to each man who served on a jury, encouraging even the poorest Athenian citizens to make themselves eligible for jury service.

Further, the archons were stripped of any remaining power to act as judges. Instead they were to see to the preliminaries of all judicial cases—receiving accusations, meeting with the plaintiff and defendant to make sure there was a case to answer and determine how to proceed, and such—while hearing and deciding the cases was made the responsibility of the public law courts, that is, of juries of ordinary citizens, with the archons merely presiding.

The port of Athens, the Peiraieus, had become the most important harbor in the Greek world, with much of the trade of the Aegean and eastern Mediterranean passing through it. Athenian writers, such as Aristophanes, liked to boast of the immense variety of goods that came to the Peiraieus, meaning that all the products of "the world" were available to the Athenians. The Athenian economy boomed as a result, and thousands of Greeks from all over the Greek world came to Athens to participate in this economic boom, registering themselves as permanent resident aliens (*metoikoi*) and paying a monthly tax for the privilege of living at Athens and setting up a business there. These metics, as they are generally called, were artisans and business men: since they were not permitted to own land or houses in Attica, they operated trading enterprises, artisan workshops, and manufactories.

At the height of Athenian prosperity there were upwards of 10,000 metics living in Attica, paying taxes to the Athenian state, renting their housing from Athenian citizens, and boosting the economy of Athens by their productive activities. Since all goods passing in and out of the Peiraieus were subject to import and export duties; since every vessel using the port paid harbor dues; since every item bought or sold and every market stall holder in the market place *(agora)* paid a market tax, all of this economic activity brought enormous revenues to the Athenian state. These were in addition to the revenues from the silver mines at Laureion in southern Attica, and to the annual contributions from the allies, which amounted to over 360 talents per year (a vast sum).

Prosperous, powerful, and democratic, a place where freedom of thought and speech were a way of life, Athens was a mecca for intellectuals, artists, and writers of all sorts, who flocked there from all over the Greek world to exchange ideas and seek opportunities. One source of opportunity was the famous building program Perikles persuaded the Athenians to undertake. As the most powerful and progressive state in Greece, Athens should have public buildings and monuments suited to its status, he argued; and over the course of the 440s and subsequent decades, a series of great building projects were undertaken that employed architects, sculptors, artists, stonemasons, and workers of all sorts. The prize piece of this building program, and one of the world's most famous buildings ever since, was the Parthenon, the temple of Athena the Maiden (*Parthenos*). The architects of this building were Iktinos and Kallikrates, and they applied to its design the latest refinements of engineering and optical science, incorporating a wide range of precise refinements in the delicate curvature of the building's base, columns, and pediment, all of which aimed to produce a building of visual perfection. Iktinos wrote a book describing the design refinements that produced this effect of visual perfection, of which we know through its use by the Roman architectural writer Vitruvius.

Thanks to Vitruvius's work, and the impression of the building itself, the Parthenon has been one of the most lauded works of architecture in western history. Many other impressive buildings were created in this period, however: the Erechtheion and Propylaia (entrance hall) on the Akropolis; the great Theatre of Dionysos on the Akropolis's southern slope; the Odeion ("concert hall") of Perikles; the fortification walls of Athens and of the Peiraieus; and in some ways most impressive of all, the three great "long walls" that connected Athens to the Peiraieus and Phaleron, turning the city and its port into a kind of fortified island. These long walls, built so wide that the tops carried roadways on which carriages could pass each other, meant that a besieging army could never starve the Athenians into surrender so long as the Athenian fleet controlled the sea and enabled imports to flow into the Peiraieus.

Perhaps the most important and characteristic cultural product of Athens in this era was the invention of drama. Tragic and comic drama, whose roots went back to the choral song and dance of the sixth century, were inextricably intertwined with the Athenian democracy. The Homeric epics were composed for aristocratic

An ancient Greek theatre at which tragedies and comedies were performed: the Theatre of Ephesos.

audiences, to entertain the guests at aristocratic feasts. The songs of archaic Greece were composed for and sung at parties of various sorts: mostly private parties given and attended by the well-to-do, but also more "public" parties such as those for weddings and athletic victories. Choral song was an important part of public festivals in honor of the gods, where the participants forming the audience were more numerous, and these choral songs could hence be regarded as more "popular" in aim. But drama was the first truly "popular" cultural entertainment.

Drama came into being in the context of the festivals in honor of the god Dionysos at Athens, and from the first the performances in which actors took on the roles of characters in the stories being told drew wide audiences of citizens, who sat in specially designed *theatra* (literally "viewing spaces"; theaters, as we call them now). The plays of the great tragic dramatists of fifth century Athens—Aischylos, Sophokles, Euripides—are still read and performed as classics of the dramatic genre; and the comedies of the fifth century Aristophanes and the fourth century Menandros are similarly widely prized. These playwrights were regarded as national teachers by the

Athenian people, commenting on and making the citizens think about the ideas and policies, concerns and foibles of the political, social, cultural, religious, and military life of the city.

Another invention of this period was analytical historiography. The first historian to analyze events rationally and produce an elaborate historical narrative that was not just a bare recital of events but looked into the social and cultural backgrounds that made people who they were and infused their decision making, and tried to understand not just *what* happened, but *why*, was of course Herodotos. He came from the city of Halikarnassos on the west coast of Asia Minor, but spent many years at Athens working on his history, and eventually joined a colony the Athenians sent out to Thourioi in southern Italy, where he died and was buried. Herodotos's inspiration and aim was to tell of and explain the great conflict between the Persians and the Greeks, and especially of course how, against all odds, the Greeks came to win and preserve their freedom. A generation after Herodotos, the Athenian Thucydides followed his example in writing about the great war between the Athenians and Spartans and their respective allies: the so-called Peloponnesian War. Thucydides was even more carefully rationalist in his method than Herodotos had been, and his concern especially to illustrate timeless lessons about the nature of politics and warfare has rendered him the "father of political science," just as Herodotos is seen as the "father of history."

Philosophy is another discipline in which the contributions of fifth and fourth century classical Greeks were foundational. The early Ionian rationalists such as Thales and Anaximandros had begun rational inquiry by analyzing the physical world, and thinkers such as Xenophanes and Herakleitos had turned rational analysis to areas more directly of human concern; e.g. religion, ontology, and epistemology. Both tracks of rational inquiry continued in the fifth century. Scientific enquirers like Anaxagoras of Klazomenai, a close friend of the Athenian statesman Perikles, and Demokritos of Abdera, who established the atomist theory, made enormous progress in the understanding of physical reality. More important, though, the so-called sophistic movement, concentrating on issues such as epistemology, communication and meaning, ethics, and politics, began a fundamental reappraisal of the nature of human understanding and human sociability. Accepting the rationalist approach of the early Ionians and the relativism of Herakleitos, philosophers such as Protagoras, Gorgias, Prodikos, and Sokrates disputed received ideas about knowledge, language, virtue, morality, justice, and piety. Although conservative contemporaries, such as Aristophanes, in his play, *The Clouds*, criticized them for undermining traditional values without offering anything but skepticism and self-interest in their place, in fact the sophists cleared the way for the great philosophers of the fourth century— Plato and Aristotle—by showing the flaws in standard ideas of morality, knowledge, and virtue, and establishing how to go about the work of creating philosophically sound theories in such areas. And their impact on wider Greek culture in their day—on such figures as the historian Thucydides, the tragedian Euripides, or the orator Isokrates—was profound. Essentially, Plato's entire philosophical career was an extended response to, a critical engagement with,

*A bust of Sokrates,
the fifth century
Athenian philosopher.*

the sophistic movement, of which his teacher Sokrates had been a key figure—though Plato pretended he was not.

Through Gorgias, whose interest in meaning and communication had led him to develop the first rules of effective argument and persuasive arrangement of ideas that led to the art of rhetoric, the great Attic orators of the fourth century—Isokrates, Lysias, Isaios, Aischines, Hypereides, Lykourgos, Demades, and above all Demosthenes—owed a direct debt to the sophistic movement. And these Attic orators, and especially Isokrates through his school of rhetoric that set the standard for subsequent Greek higher education, had an enormous impact on subsequent Greco-Roman and, after the Renaissance, Western European literary theory and principles of style. Underlying all this was an idea of perfectibility that infused the sophistic critique of traditional values and ideas.

That same idea of perfectibility became important to Greek art, as sculptors such as the Athenians Myron and Pheidias, but above all also Polykleitos, Praxiteles, and Lysippos, sought to express in the round the ideal of the human form. Polykleitos's *kanon*, his set of rules and spatial relationships that established a rational theory for the perfect male form, was embodied in his statue the *doryphoros* (spear-bearer) of which numerous Roman copies survive. Praxiteles attempted a depiction of the ideal female form in his Aphrodite of Knidos, which became famous throughout the ancient world. And of course the pursuit of visual perfection in architecture that Iktinos and Kallikrates attempted with the Parthenon, and explained and justified rationally in Iktinos's book, has been discussed above.

Reading through all of this rather positive presentation of Greek and Athenian history and culture of the fifth century and later, the reader may be wondering what all this has to do with the Battle of Marathon, and why the darker side of Greek society and culture is neglected. For there certainly was a darker side: slavery, oppression of women, infant exposure, naked imperialism, and so on. The point of this book, though, is to show what would have been lost if the Athenians had been defeated and conquered at

Marathon: hence the emphasis on the positive achievements of the Athenians and other Greeks after Marathon. And that these things would have been lost, that a different outcome at Marathon really would have fundamentally changed classical Greek culture, can be demonstrated—I believe—beyond reasonable doubt. As a rule historians are reluctant to speculate about "what might have happened" if only some action or event had had a different outcome or not taken place, and with good reason: as a rule, we just cannot be sure at all what would have resulted from alternative outcomes. In the case of Marathon, however, we do happen to know with virtual certainty what the Persians would have done with and to the Athenians had they (the Persians) won; and we do know that what the Persians planned would have changed everything.

IF THE PERSIANS HAD WON

When the Persians captured and sacked the city of Miletos in 494, they rounded up those Milesians who survived the sack and transported them to Susa to be judged by King Darius. The king chose to be merciful: the Milesian survivors were resettled peaceably near the Persian Gulf. Of course, the descendants of these Milesians played no further role in Greek history and culture. The city of Miletos itself was soon resettled with a new population, but it was never more than a shadow of its former self, and its inhabitants made no such great contributions to Greek culture as had the Milesians of the sixth century.

In about 510 or so the city of Barka in the Cyrenaica (modern Libya) was captured and, as a punishment, its people were likewise deported to be judged by Darius. Most important, the aim of the expedition of 490 was not just to establish a base in central Greece from which to subject the rest the Greeks, it was specifically to punish the Eretrians and Athenians. When Eretria had been captured and sacked, the surviving population of the city was embarked on ships and, eventually, brought to Susa to face Darius's judgment: their fate was, like that of the Milesians, resettlement in Iran. And again, there the descendants of the Eretrians were lost to Greek history and culture; and the resettled Eretria of classical times and later was just a shadow of its former self.

Had the Persians won at Marathon and captured Athens, there can really be no doubt what the fate of the Athenians would have been: they would have been rounded up—the survivors that is—and transported to Susa along with the surviving Eretrians, and would have disappeared into new settlements near the Persian Gulf.

It may be objected that the Persians brought Hippias with them to Attica and planned to reinstate him as tyrant of Athens. Though I don't believe we can be sure of it, as this claim may have been invented by Hippias's descendents, they may indeed have done that had they won. But what we can be sure of is that, if Hippias had been installed again as tyrant of Athens under the Persians, it would have been a sadly diminished Athens over which he ruled, an Athens populated by a remnant, the poorest and the country folk of Attica, and by other new settlers. The fate of the Athenians proper was clearly to be the same as that of the Eretrians and Milesians. And the effects of the destruction of Athens and deportation of its people would have been huge.

For a start, Athenian democracy would have disappeared, only fifteen years after its invention, and would be known to history, if at all, only as a brief and failed experiment. What that would have meant for the later history of democratic theory and democratic governing systems can only be guessed at; but it is obvious that without its most successful model, the story of democracy in ancient Greece would have very different and likely much poorer; and the concept of democracy as a viable governing system, indeed the whole vocabulary of democratic politics, would have been radically different. It can be seriously doubted whether Europeans and Americans would live under governing systems called democracies today.

A captured Athens under Persian control would have had a major impact on the rest of Greece. Since the communities of central and northern Greece, north of Attica, had mostly offered earth and water, the tokens of submission, to Darius in 491; and since those same regions submitted to Persian control without a fight in 480, we can confidently say that a Persian victory at Marathon would have secured Persian control of all of Greece down to the Isthmos of Corinth. Only the Peloponnesos under Spartan leadership would have remained free.

Would the Spartans have been able to hold out against the Persians under those circumstances? Herodotos thought not, and with good reason. The Spartan strategy was to fortify the narrows of the Isthmos of Corinth and hold the Persian army there. And they could certainly have succeeded at that, so far as it went. But the Peloponnesian states had no substantial fleet: the Athenian fleet of 200 triremes that fought at Salamis would never have come into existence. Only the Corinthians had any substantial number of triremes, and even they could not have mobilized as many as a hundred. The rest of the Peloponnesians could hardly have gotten together as many as a hundred ships all together. That is to say, the Peloponnesians had no fleet large enough to prevent the Persians from landing troops wherever they chose to do so within the Peloponnesos; and in Sparta's bitter rival Argos there was a safe landing area for the Persians. Persian forces could, thus, have attacked the Spartans and their allies at the Isthmos from both sides, and it's very hard to see how the outcome would have been anything but a victory for the Persians. In other words, the almost certain outcome of a Persian victory at Marathon would have been a complete Persian conquest and subjection of Greece; and a fifth century Greece that was a Persian province, without the great city-state of Athens, would have produced a very different fifth century Greek culture.

Can we even imagine a classical Greek culture under Persian rule? We must bear in mind that none of those seminal Athenian figures who played such a significant role in fifth and fourth century intellectual and cultural life would have been there. Aischylos, for example, would likely have died fighting in a lost Battle of

Marathon; or if he survived, would have been captured and deported to Susa with the other Athenians. None of his great plays would ever have been written. Sophokles would have lived his life in obscurity near the Persian Gulf, as would have Euripides, if indeed he had been born at all. Athenian tragedy, that is, would have been cut short in its infancy, like the democracy: only a few plays by Phrynichos (none of which survive today) would have borne witness to what Athenian tragedy might have been. Would other Greeks, perhaps in Sicilian Syracuse for example, have developed tragic drama? We cannot say. But we can say that if tragedy had developed at all, it would have been radically different than the tragedy we know. Most likely, there would simply never have been Greek tragic drama.

As it would have played out for the great tragedians, the comic dramatists of Athens also would never have come to write their plays. The plays of the pioneers Kratinos and Eupolis, and the plays of the great Aristophanes which still survive (eleven of them), couldn't have been written, because their authors would have been living, if at all, in obscurity somewhere in Iran. And without the great pioneers of Attic comedy, we can hardly imagine the new comedy of Menandros in the late fourth century either. With the loss of Attic drama, modern culture would be enormously impoverished, and not just by not having those plays. Marlowe, Shakespeare, Ben Jonson, Racine, Corneille, Molière, Goethe, Ionesco, Miller, Williams, O'Neill: the list of great Western writers whose works and genres were inspired by, indeed dependent on Athenian drama is very long. In fact, every time one goes to see a movie, or sits down to watch a TV drama, or a sitcom, or the comedy of the likes of *Monty Python* or *Saturday Night Live*, one owes for one's entertainment a direct debt to the Athenian dramatists of old who were the source and inspiration for the dramatic tradition in western culture. Would our lives be different if those Athenian dramatists had never written anything? Incalculably so!

For historians, a particularly poignant loss would be the work of Thucydides. There would have been no Peloponnesian War for him to write about, and, in any case, he would have spent his life, assuming he ever lived at all, in Iran along with the rest of the former Athenians. Of course it could be suggested that at least Herodotos, who was not an Athenian, wouldn't have been affected: we'd still have his history, and the idea of analytical history writing would have been there. But would it? Herodotos's inspiration was to tell and explain the history of how the Greeks, few and poor as they were relatively speaking, managed to stand up to and defeat the mighty Persian Empire. Would he have been inspired to write if the Greeks had been tamely conquered by the Persians, the likely outcome of a Persian victory at Marathon? It seems very unlikely. Some sort of history writing might have come about all the same; but again, it would have been very different than what we have, lacking the great histories of Herodotos and Thucydides as inspiration.

As to philosophy, we would have to try to imagine the history of philosophy without Sokrates and Plato. Indeed, our loss wouldn't stop with those two Athenians: what sort of philosophy, if any, would Aristotle have produced with no Athens to go to, no academy to study at, no Plato to teach him and stimulate his mind? It has sometimes been said that all of philosophy is but an extended response to and critique of Plato and Aristotle: with no Plato and Aristotle to provide the categories and methods and inspiration, would there be western philosophy at all? At any rate western philosophy would be radically different than what it is. It's perhaps worth noting, since I referred above to the darker side of Greek history, that Plato was the first great intellectual leader in the human record to advocate equal treatment for women, socially and politically. No one took this idea seriously for centuries; but when feminism did arise in late eighteenth century Europe, the authority of Plato, so much admired by "Enlightenment" thinkers, couldn't be dismissed lightly by feminism's opponents.

The theories of communication and rhetoric—the art of effective communication—were developed originally by non-Athenians such as Protagoras of Abdera, Prodikos of Keos, and Gorgias of Leontinoi. It's worth noting, however, that they all traveled to Athens and spent a great deal of time at Athens, discussing and debating with each other and with Sokrates, and honing their ideas through that free-wheeling debate Athens made possible. Still, even without Athens it is clearly possible that they would have developed their ideas even so, though perhaps somewhat differently. But their writings don't survive, because the great teachers and exponents of rhetoric turned out to be men of succeeding generations, and men who were Athenians: Isokrates above all, whose school of rhetoric established the basic higher education system and curriculum for all of antiquity, and the great orators Lysias and Demosthenes. The ideas and principles of literary style and composition these men worked out and embodied in their writings have had an enormous impact down through Western literature. To take just one notable example, we can hardly imagine the works of the great Roman orator and writer Cicero without the works of Isokrates and Demosthenes on which he modeled himself.

In art and architecture finally, there would have been no Parthenon, no Iktinos, no Pheidias and Myron, the great Athenian sculptors of the fifth century: the history of Western art would have been hugely different too.

In short, we can see that, beyond any reasonable doubt, the impact of an Athenian defeat at Marathon, not just on Athenian history, not even just on classical Greek history, but on the history and culture of all of Western civilization would have been huge: everything would have been different. Of course it might be argued that even without classical Athens and the contributions of the great Athenians, the Greeks might have somehow managed to keep the Persians at bay under Spartan leadership, and some form of classical Greek culture might have arisen under the leadership and inspiration of other Greeks. Perhaps the Greeks of the west, of Sicily and Italy, would have played a bigger role. Perhaps the Syracusans or Tarentines would have pioneered political and intellectual development, drama and historiography, philosophy and art. Perhaps they might have. Or perhaps not: Greek culture might just as well have gone into a decline and faded away under the depressing impact of Persian predominance.

Whatever might have come about, it undoubtedly would have been radically different than what did happen, without the seminal contributions of Athenians such as Themistokles and Perikles, Aischylos, Sophokles, and Euripides, Aristophanes and Menandros, Thucydides and Sokrates, Plato and Aristotle, Isokrates and Demosthenes, Iktinos and Pheidias, and all the rest. As unfashionable as it is to say it, the Battle of Marathon really was a decisive turning point in Western civilization; the 10,000 Athenians who made their stand that day really did, in a very meaningful sense, "save Western civilization."

CHRONOLOGY OF KEY EVENTS IN ANCIENT GREECE AND THE PERSIAN EMPIRE

All dates are B.C.E.; dates before 500 are often only approximate.

776 (trad. date) first Olympic festival

ca. 740-720   Homer composes his epic poems

ca. 730-710   Spartans invade and conquer Messenia

ca. 720-700   Median leader Daiukku/Deiokes in conflict with Assyrians

ca. 700   Hesiod composes his epics

ca. 680-660   Archilochos of Paros composes songs

ca. 670   Pheidon of Argos first archaic tyrant

ca. 660-640   Median ruler Khshathrita unifies Media and fights Assyrians

ca. 650-630   Messenian revolt against Spartans leads to creation of Spartan *agoge*

ca. 632   Kylon attempts to become tyrant at Athens

ca. 630   Median king Frawartish/Phraortes

ca. 625-585   Huwakhshatra/Kyaxares rules the Medes and founds the Median Empire

ca. 621   Drakon legislates at Athens

612   sack of Nineveh by Medes under Kyaxares and Babylonians under Nabopolassar

594   legislation of Solon at Athens

585   Thales of Miletos, the first Greek philosopher, predicts an eclipse of the sun

585-550   Astyages king of Median Empire

ca. 570   strife at Athens between *Pedieis, Paralioi, and Hyperakrioi*

ca. 570   marriage of Megakles the Alkmaionid to Agariste daughter of Kleisthenes of Sikyon, leading to birth of Kleisthenes the Alkmaioinid

560   Cyrus the Great becomes king of Persian Anshan

ca. 558   Peisistratos tyrant of Athens during brief alliance with Megakles

ca. 556   Peisistratos forced to flee from Athens

550   Cyrus of Persia rebels against Astyages of Media, founding the Achaemenid Persian Empire

ca. 548/7   Peisistratos and his sons return to Athens and found the Peisistratid tyranny

ca. 546   Croesus of Lydia attacks Cyrus of Persia, leading to Persian conquest of Lydia and Ionia

ca. 539/8   Persian conquest of Babylonia under Cyrus

ca. 530s-522	Polykrates is tyrant of Samos
530	Cyrus the Great dies in battle
530-522	Kambyses rules Persian Empire
ca. 528	Peisistratos dies and is succeeded as tyrant of Athens by his son Hippias
ca. 526-524	Kambyses conquers Egypt
522	death of Kambyses, Smerdis becomes king of Persia
522	Darius and six confederates kill Smerdis, Darius becomes king
522-521	Darius successfully combats numerous insurrections throughout the Persian Empire, and confirms his kingship
ca. 520	Kleomenes becomes king of Sparta in Agiad line of succession
514	at Athens, Hipparchos brother of the tyrant Hippias is slain
ca. 512	Darius crosses Hellespont and conquers Thrace; attack on Skythians fails
ca. 510	Kleomenes of Sparta forces Hippias and his family to leave Athens
ca. 508	Kleisthenes' reforms at Athens begin world's first known democracy
ca. 506	Kleomenes fails to end Athenian reforms; Athenian democracy defends itself from attacks by Thebans and Chalkidians
500	Persian attack on Naxos, led by Megabates and Aristagoras of Miletos, fails
499	Aristagoras of Miletos abdicates tyranny at Miletos, and Ionian Revolt against Persia begins
498	Ionian Greeks, aided by Athenians and Eretrians, sack Sardis
494	Kleomenes and Spartans defeat Argives at battle of Sepeia
494	Ionians defeated at Battle of Lade; sack of Miletos; failure of Ionian Revolt
493/2	Themistokles is archon at Athens and begins development of harbor at Peiraieus
492	Mardonios attempts to invade Greece by land and sea from north, but fails
491	Darius demands earth and water from Greek states; most except for Sparta and allies and Athens comply; Kleomenes deposes co-king Demaratos at Sparta in dispute over Aigina
ca. 490	Kleomenes forced to flee from Sparta
490	Darius sends Datis the Mede and Artaphernes in command of amphibious attack on Cyclades islands, Eretria, and Athens; sack of Naxos and Eretria; in August, Battle of Marathon ends in Persian defeat as Miltiades' strategy and tactics save Athens
ca. 489	death of Kleomenes at Sparta
489	Miltiades defeated at Paros, fined by Athenians, dies of gangrene
487	Athenians end election of archons, ostracise Hippias son of Charmos
486	death of Darius, Xerxes become king of Persians; revolt in Egypt against Persian rule

484	ostracism of Aristides leaves Themistokles as dominant leader in Athens
484-481	Xerxes orders preparation for invasion of Greece, including canal at Mt. Athos and bridge across Hellespont
483-481	profits from Laureion silver mines enable Athenians to build 200 new triremes (warships)
480	Persian invasion of Greece led by Xerxes; death of Spartan king Leonidas and his 298 Spartiates at Thermopylai; invasion and destruction of abandoned Athens; at Battle of Salamis Athenian and Greek fleet defeats Persian fleet
479	Persian army under Mardonios defeated by Greek army led by Spartans at Plataia; Greek force destroys remnant of Persian fleet at Cape Mykale
477	foundation of Athenian-led Delian League
470s	Kimon leads Athenian counter-attack against Persians, driving them from the Aegean region and confirming Athenian leadership
472	ostracism of Themistokles
ca. 470	Athenian dramatist Aischylos at the height of his success
469	birth of Sokrates
ca. 468	led by Kimon, Athenians defeat Persians on sea and land at the Eurymedon
465	Xerxes killed; Artaxerxes becomes king of the Persians
464	great earthquake at Sparta, followed by great Helot revolt
462/1	Kimon leads Athenian force to aid Spartans; when the Spartans dismiss the Athenian aid, Kimon is ostracised from Athens, and Ephialtes passes radical democratic reforms
460-446	first "Peloponnesian War" between Spartans and Athenians
ca. 455-429	Perikles becomes dominant leader of Athenian democracy
ca. 454	Egyptian revolt defeated by Persians; Athenian allied force in Egypt destroyed
ca. 452	Kimon recalled, wins double victory over Persians by land and sea at Cypriot Salamis
ca. 447	Peace of Kallias between Persians and Athenians
446/5	Thirty Years Peace between Athenians and Spartans
440s-420s	Periklean building program at Athens leads to construction of Parthenon, Erechtheion, Propylaia, Theatre of Dionysos, Odeion of Perikles, and other buildings
ca. 440s-405	Sophokles and Euripides leading tragedians at Athens
ca. 440s-399	the Sophistic movement centered at Athens, with philosophers Protagoras, Gorgias, and Sokrates
ca. 440s-420s	Herodotos compiles his *Histories*
432	so-called "Peloponnesian War" begins between Spartans and Athenians, lasting until 404

429	death of Perikles
425/4	Persian king Artaxerxes dies; Darius II succeeds to Persian throne
420s-390s	Aristophanes writes comedies for Athenian stage
421-416	Peace of Nikias fails to end Peloponnesian War
414	Alkibiades persuades Athenians to launch Sicilian expedition
413	Alkibiades exiled, takes refuge in Sparta
412	destruction of Sicilian expedition; alliance between Spartans and Persians against Athens
410	Athenians recall Alkibiades and begin revival of military fortunes
407	second exile of Alkibiades begins final decline of Athenian power
405	deaths of Sophokles and Euripides; battle of Aigospotamoi ends Athenian naval power
405/4	Persian king Darius II dies; Artaxerxes II succeeds as king
404	final surrender of Athens; reign of "Thirty Tyrants" at Athens; Sparta is the leading power in Greece
403	restoration of Athenian democracy; beginning of Athenian recovery
403-401	Cyrus the Younger attempts to gain Persian throne with 10,000 Greek mercenaries, but dies at Battle of Kunaxa
ca. 400	death of Thucydides, leaving his history of the Peloponnesian War incomplete
399	death of Sokrates
380s-340s	Plato founds and leads philosophical school at the Academy in Athens
380s-340s	Isokrates founds and leads school of rhetoric at Athens
371	Thebans, led by Epaminondas, defeat Spartans at Battle of Leuktra
369/8	Epaminondas frees Messenia from Spartan control and ends Spartan domination of the Peloponnesos
359	Philip II becomes king of Macedonia and begins building Macedonia into a great power
359	Artaxerxes II dies and is succeeded as Persian king by Artaxerxes III
350s-340s	Aristotle studies at Plato's Academy in Athens
356	birth of Alexander the Great
ca. 343-340	Aristotle tutors Alexander the Great
338	Battle of Chaironeia leaves Philip II in control of Greece
336	Philip II assassinated; Alexander becomes king of Macedonia; Aristotle founds philosophical school at the Lyceum in Athens; Artaxerxes III of Persia dies, succeeded by Darius III
334-323	Alexander invades and conquers the Persian Empire; he dies in Babylon aged thirty-three
322	failed Athenian rebellion against Macedonian power leads to end of the Athenian democracy

GLOSSARY OF TERMS

abattis lines of untrimmed trees with their branches towards the enemy forming an anti-cavalry obstacle on each flank

Achaeans the main name Homer used for the Greeks

agoge the training system of the Spartiate boy that instilled hardiness, a rigid discipline, physical fitness and endurance, and familiarity with the weapons, armor, and tactics of the hoplite warrior and phalanx

agon competition; the root of the English word "agony," and the "agonistic" (competitive) spirit that at all times infused Greek culture

agora central town square or marketplace in a Greek city

Alkmaionidai influential Athenian aristocratic family that opposed a potential Athenian tyrant but was placed under a religious curse by the Oracle of Apollo at Delphi; Megakles and Kleisthenes were of this family

archons chief magistrates of Athens, the executive officers and chief judges of the community

Areopagos Council after a year in office, archons became life members of this state council, which acted as a kind of "supreme court" on major political and social issues and trials

aretê excellence, later understood as virtue

aristeia a term which literally means "bestness"—from the Greek word *aristos* meaning best; it is often translated as "courage" or "excellence"

Boule a state council, especially the Athenian Council of the 500, so-named because it had 500 members, carefully designed to form a representative sample of the Athenian people

demarchoi   magistrates responsible to the assembly of each deme at Athens

demes   local villages and regions of Attica; the basis for Athenian citizenship

demokrateia   rule by the people

demos   people

diaulos   a double pipe or recorder used in Greek music, especially as the musical accompaniment for some kinds of lyric, sung poetry

dokimasia   the examination of candidates for public office as to their eligibility and suitability, a power originally held at Athens by the Areopagos Council

doryphoros   spear-bearer; Polykleitos's statue that embodies his *kanon*, the set of rules and spatial relationships that established a rational theory for the perfect male form

Ephoroi   ephors, or "overseers," the five chief magistrates of the Spartan state, effectively overseers and judges of Spartan society, including the two kings

eris   strife; in Hesiod a good kind and a bad kind. The bad kind was the strife that could tear a community apart by unhealthy and violent striving for power and position. The good kind was the desire to better one's neighbors.

Eupatridai   well-born ones, the hereditary aristocracy of Athens

euthyne   formal review of the conduct and accounts of all magistrates and office holders after their year in office to check for any wrong doing, originally at Athens a power of the upper class Areopagos Council

genos   clan, such as the *Bakkhiadai* of Corinth or the *Penthilidai* of Mitylene

gerousia   elders, the members of the Spartan state council, selected from aristocratic families; so called because the minimum age for membership was 60

hektemoroi   "one-sixth share men," farmers at Athens who worked land claimed by aristocratic families, and paid one sixth of their produce which the aristocratic would-be owners regarded as "rent"

Helots   the country people of Lakedaimon and Messenia that were reduced by the Spartans to a slave-like condition similar to that of medieval serfs. They maintained a normal family life and lived in their own small communities, but belonged to the Spartan masters who owned the land they farmed, and were obliged to pay half of their produce to their Spartan masters, as well as performing other chores for them

hippeis   wealthy Athenians who could afford to own horses and serve as cavalry

hoplite   the fully armed Greek heavy infantryman who fought in a phalanx formation and carried some 60 pounds or more of equipment about his person

Hyperakrioi   one of the three factions in the society of Attica; the men of eastern Attica (from the perspective of Athens, from "beyond the hills" – the Pentele range – which is what *hyperakrioi* means), led by Peisistratos

hypomeion   lesser; a boy deemed to have failed the *agoge* and not permitted full Spartiate citizenship on reaching adulthood

isegoria   equality of meeting in and addressing the assembly; the right of all citizens to meet in decision making assemblies, and to discuss, debate, and decide public policy freely and with essential equality in those assemblies

isonomia   equality before or under the law; the fundamental political equality of all citizens under Athenian democracy

kanon   created by Polykleitos, a set of rules and spatial relationships that established a rational theory for the perfect male form; it was embodied in his statue the *doryphoros* (spear-bearer) of which numerous Roman copies survive

krypteia   literally, the secret band; an elite unit at Sparta that recruited the boys who had withstood the *agoge* the best. Its task was to move quietly around the Messenian countryside, staying under cover and observing and terrorizing the Helots

Marathonomachoi   the men who fought at Marathon who, for Aristophanes, were the supreme expression of what Athenian citizens could be

metoikoi   permanent resident aliens that paid a monthly tax for the privilege of living at Athens and setting up a business there

Myceneans   the great Bronze Age civilization of Greece

oikoi   families, estates

ostrakismos   the origin of the English word ostracism; process held at annual assembly meeting in Athens to determine whether there was some prominent leader in Athens who seemed a threat to the democracy and who should be exiled for 10 years

paian   the simple hymn in honor of Apollo as protector and bringer of victory, sung by Greek armies as they advanced into battle. Every Greek state had its particular version; its effect was to foster among the men, as they advanced into the fearful act of battle, a sense of cohesion and common purpose, to still the fears and settle the nerves

Panathenaia   the festival of Athena held every year at Athens, but with special splendor, and as an international festival, every fourth year

pandemei   in full force

panoply   coat of arms, especially the full equipment of the hoplite warrior

Paralioi   one of three factions in the society of Attica; the men of the coastal region of southern Attica (called the *paralia*), led by the head of the Almaionid family, Megakles (grandson of the first Megakles)

patrios politeia   ancestral constitution, especially of the Athenians

Pedieis   one of three factions in the society of Attica; the men who lived in the Athenian plain (*to pedion*) around the city of Athens itself, led by a Eupatrid named Lykourgos

pentekonters   fifty-oared galleys, an early form of Greek war ship

perioikoi   "those living round about"—meaning round about Sparta itself; free but politically subservient Lakedaimonians

phratries   notionally kinship groups, but in reality religio-social organ-

270

izations through which communal, religious, and military participation, as well as whatever limited political activity was open to
"commoners," was organized, especially at Athens

phylai   usually, if misleadingly, translated as "tribes"; ten subdivisions
of the Athenian people under Athenian democracy

poleis   towns or cities, especially city-states; the singular is *polis*

polemarchos   war *archon*; the Athenian commander in chief whose
council was formed by the ten annual *strategoi* from each tribe

polis   see above under *poleis*

pyrtany   established by Kleisthenes, a political "month" of thirty-six
days making up a political year of 10 units, each of which was associated with one of the ten Athenian tribes, or *phylai*

salpinktes   trumpeter

seisachtheia   "throwing off a burden"; chief magistrate Solon's reform program that transformed the agricultural lands of Attica
into small farms owned and worked by independent and moderately well-to-do farmers rather than estates owned by the aristocracy and farmed by tenants

Soros   a great funeral mound at Marathon, still visible today, where
the Athenian dead had been buried collectively; this mound was
monumentalized by the setting up of stone columns on the top
with the names of those who had died in the battle and been
buried there

stade   a measurement of distance, about one-eighth of one mile

stoa poikile   literally "painted porch"; a public building in the central square of Athens in which was a mural painting of the battle of Marathon; several gods and the hero Theseus were depicted
fighting for the Athenians, and the *polemarch* Kallimachos and
general Miltiades were prominently shown fighting in the front
ranks

strategos   general; each Athenian tribe annually elected a *strategos* to
organize and command the tribe's *taxis* of the phalanx and to
serve on the military council of the Athenian commander in chief,
the *polemarchos* (war archon)

symposion   literally "drinking together; convivial evening of drinking wine and entertainment

syssition or *phidition*   a military dining group of which every Spartiate was required, in order to hold full citizenship, to be a member

taxeis   regiments, ten of which made up the Athenian hoplite phalanx; each *phyle*, or tribe, provided a *taxis*

theatra   literally "viewing spaces," origin of the English word "theatre"

triremes   ancient Greek and Phoenician warships; they were galleys with three banks of oars, one above the other, providing space for about 170 rowers; on top was a deck on which stood the captain, pilot, and a band of marines who fought the marines on other warships that came close

trittyes   thirds; each *phyle*, or tribe, in the Athenian democratic system was divided into thirds, and each third came from one of the three regions of Attica (*Pedieis, Paralioi,* and *Hyperakrioi*)

tyrannos   a non-Greek word in origin (possibly adapted from a Phoenician term for ruler), referring to an autocratic usurper who did not hold power according to traditional rules and norms, as opposed to a traditional *basileus* (king), who did so and was thus limited by the traditional rules and customs of his society

PERSIAN WORDS

Apadana   an audience hall, such as that of the Persian emperor Darius at Persepolis

Magoi (or Magi)   a priestly tribe or caste in Iranian religion who were perhaps specifically Median in origin but seem to have enjoyed special prestige throughout the Iranian lands

satrap (khshathrapan)   a military and political governor who ruled one of the well defined provinces of the Persian empire, each paying a defined tribute to the imperial treasury

FURTHER READING AND BIBLIOGRAPHY

FURTHER READING

As an aid to the non-expert reader, I offer here some pointers to key, focused readings regarding our source materials for the history recounted in this book and also for the individual chapters and various topics. I have not necessarily listed the most recent works available in each case but those that, in my view, are the most useful/readable/accessible. For those wishing to pursue this history further, and for the more expert reader, a fuller listing of available scholarship is given in the bibliography at the end, though this is still selective, as the literature is vast. In particular, I focus mainly on English language scholarship, though I do note a few books and articles in other languages when they have made particularly important contributions. My further reading suggestions for each chapter are fairly general; only for the core chapter 5, the reconstruction of the actual Battle of Marathon, do I go into more detail.

SOURCES

For the main chapters of this book, that is, chapters 1 through 5, the source upon whom we are overwhelmingly dependent for what we know is Herodotos. His *Histories*, written between about 445 and 425 B.C.E.—a generation after the Persian Wars—give us the word "history," which has named the subject of research into and narration/analysis of the past ever since. In the original Greek, Herodotos's term *historiai* meant something like "researches" or "inquiries," and he tells us he spent years traveling around the eastern Mediterranean and near eastern world, viewing the sites of the events he reports, interviewing people about their communities' customs and histories, and especially, of course, interviewing surviving participants or the sons of participants in the Greco-Persian Wars. Many of the stories he tells are fantastic, but he shows a clear awareness of this, telling us he saw his job as reporting what he was told, whether or not he believed it. He made efforts to get as accurate a picture of events as he could; he not infrequently reports variant versions of events on which different reports were current, and he occasionally reveals his own disbelief of a given story or version and preference for one of several versions of an event. That is to say, his determination to report the stories he was told, even when incredible, does not mean he was an uncritical or unsophisticated researcher. In fact, in his recognition that variant versions of an event may each contain a part of the truth, as seen from the vantage points of different participants, he shows sound historical sense.

Thus far Herodotos's own account of his practice. From early times, he has come under criticism, at times amounting to radical disbelief in his methods and claims: in modern times, the most radical form of disbelief was expressed by Fehling 1989; but Fehling's over the top criticism has been answered by various scholars—notably Pritchett's rather rambling and at times over vehement response in 1993—and most modern scholars are inclined to believe Herodotos on the whole and with certain reservations. A major reason for this positive appraisal of Herodotos is the advance in our knowledge made through archaeological discoveries, which have frequently tended to corroborate Herodotos's information. A famous example of this was the discovery of King Darius's "autobiographical" inscription at Bisutun, discussed in chapter 2, which confirmed Herodotos's account of Darius's coup. The literature on Herodotos is vast. He should be read, by the English reading non-specialist, in the translation by Robin Waterfield in the Oxford World Classics series (1998), though the Penguin Classics translation by A. de Selincourt, revised by J. Marincola (1996) is also very good. An excellent general introduction to Herodotos and the various issues raised by his life and work is Dewald and Marincola 2006. See further Gould 1989; Hartog 1988; Thomas 2000; Munson 2001; Marincola 2001. The study by the great Arnaldo Momigliano (1966) is also still well worth reading. Further, a number of collected studies on Herodotos have been published in recent years: I recommend Bakker et al. 2002; Derow and Parker 2003; Karagheorgis and Taifacos 2004.

Besides Herodotos, there are various "Lives" of ancient Greek leaders by Plutarch, notably those of Lykourgos, Solon, Aristides, and Themistokles, which are all accessible through the Loeb Classics series, as is Plutarch's essay "On the Malignity of Herodotos" for which see now Bowen 1992. Pausanias's *Guide to Greece* is another valuable source and can be easily read in English in Peter Levi's translation in the Penguin Classics series (1971); and on Pausanias as a writer and historical source one may read with great profit Habicht 1985. A good selection of documentary and fragmentary source materials, finally, have been collected and translated into English by Crawford and Whitehead 1983.

INTRODUCTION

For the grand painting of the Battle of Marathon on the wall of the *stoa poikile* and other commemorations see Harrison 1972, Wycherly 1972, Massaro 1978, Perry 2001. Aischylos's epitaph was quoted by Athenaios *Deipnosophistai* 14.627d. The passages cited from fifth and fourth century Athenian authors concerning Marathon are: Aristophanes *Acharnians* 172, *Knights* 133-34 and 781-85, *Wasps* 696, *Lysistrata* 281, and the fragment of the lost play *Holkades* is quoted by Athenaios 3.111a; the Kritias fragment also comes from Athenaios: 1.28; Isokrates *Panegyrikos* 71, *Peri to zeugous* 27, *On the Peace* 38, *Panathenaikos* 195, *Plataiikos* 57 and 62, *To Philip* 129; Aischines *On the Embassy* 75, *Against Ktesiphon* 181, 186, 259; Demosthenes *On the False Embassy* 311-12, *Against Aristokrates* 196, *Funeral Oration* 11; and the passages from Herakleides Pontikos and Douris of Samos are both quoted by Athenaios, at 12.512 and 6.253 respectively. On the Athenian funeral oration tradition and its (mis)representation of Athenian history, see Loraux 1986, Walters 1981. For the representation of Marathon on the frieze of the Nike temple: Harrison 1972 and Palagia 2005. The legend of the Marathon run was told by Plutarch "On the Glory of the Athenians" at *Moralia* 347C and Lucian *A Slip in Greeting* 3.

On the history of George Grote, see Momigliano 1952, Calder 1996, Demetriou 1999; and for the liberal milieu to which he belonged, and his relationship to John Stuart Mill and his circle, see now the excellent biography of Mill by Reeves 2007. For some updatings/revisions of Creasy's list of decisive battles, illustrating his influence, see e.g. Fuller 1954-56, Pratt 1956, Mitchell 1964, Frankland and Dowling 1976, Davis 1999, Hanson 2001. For the historiography of the modern Olympic movement see now Buchanan & Mallon 2006; also Young 1996, Findling & Pelle 2004. For the invention of the modern Marathon run in particular, the historical introduction in Jones 2003 is a good resource. Anyone interested in the movie *The Giant of Marathon* can view it on the internet at http://www.archive.org /details/CCO_TheGiantofMarathon.

CHAPTER 1: THE ANCIENT GREEKS

To get a further acquaintance with the ancient Greeks, there are numerous good, general histories available. Besides George Grote's great multivolume history, cited in the introduction, and the relevant volumes of the *Cambridge Ancient History*, that is, especially volumes III.3 and IV, which should be read in the revised edition prepared in the 1980s, I recommend Hammond 1959 which should now be read in the 3rd edition of 1989; Sealey 1976; Freeman 1999; Osborne 1996; Boardman, Griffin, and Murray 1986; Orrieux and Schmitt Pantel 1999; Cartledge 2001b; Morris and Powell 2006; Pomeroy, Burstein, Donlan, and Roberts 2007; and there are many others. Austin and Vidal-Naquet 1977 combines excellent social and economic history with translated primary sources. For early Greece especially, the particular topic of this chapter, Murray 1983 is an excellent read, and Snodgrass 1980 is valuable for its familiarity especially with the archaeological evidence.

Excellent up to date resources for Homer are the commentaries edited by Kirk on the *Iliad* 1985-93 and by Heubeck, West, Hainsworth et al. on the *Odyssey* 1998-93. For the use of Homer as a historical resource, Finley 1976 is crucial, and see also I. Morris 1986. On Homeric values, and archaic Greek value systems generally, Nagy 1979, Adkins 1972, Fisher 1992.

On Greek colonization, Graham 1964 is fundamental, and for a brief and updated version of his views see his chapter in the *Cambridge Ancient History* vol. III.3 1982 chap. 38; see further Boardman 1999; Ridgway 1992; Malkin 1987 and 1998. On the Greek tyrants, Andrewes 1956, Berve 1967, Pleket 1969, and McGlew 1993. On Greek warfare see Hanson 1998 and 1999, van Wees 1992 and 2004. For Greek economic growth, and especially trade, see Austin and Vidal-Naquet 1977, Bresson 2000, and Cartledge, Cohen and Foxhall 2002. For the Chalkidian role in developing carbonized steel technology in early Greece, Bakhuizen 1976. The key text for the development of the Greek alphabet is still Jeffery 1990 (2nd ed. with additions by Johnston); see also Powell 1991. An excellent selection of lyric poetry in translation is Lattimore 1960; fuller collections can be found in the

Loeb Classical Library series in the 5 volumes of *Greek Lyric Poetry* by D.A. Campbell (1982-1993), and the two volumes *Greek Iambic Poetry* and *Greek Elegiac Poetry* by D.E. Gerber (both 1999). Bowra 1936, though dated, is still one of the best evocations of the cultural atmosphere of the Greek lyric poets in my view; see further now Campbell 1982, M. West 1993. On the importance of the symposion for Greek culture, see e.g. the collection of papers edited by Murray 1990. For the Ionian rationalists, the best resource for English readers is Kirk, Raven, Schofield 1983; see further Vlastos 1995, Barnes 1982, Guthrie 1991, A.A. Long 1999; and Nietzsche's book *Philosophy in the Tragic Age of the Greeks* (written in 1873 but published posthumously) is, like everything written by this great philosopher, full of unique insights. For Sparta, finally, the works of Cartledge are excellent (2001a, 2003), and see also Forrest 1968, Fitzhardinge 1980, Hooker 1980, and Figueira 2004.

CHAPTER 2: THE PERSIAN EMPIRE
For the history of the Persian Empire, Herodotos, though an outsider, is our best source; but his information is supplemented, and at times corrected, by a variety of Persian and other near eastern documentary sources, a good selection of which can be found in Kent 1954.

In this chapter I have relied mainly on Cook 1983, an excellent and readable account of the Persian Empire. Though in many respects out of date, Olmstead 1948 can still be read with profit; Frye 1963 and 1984 are excellent, as are Gershevitz 1985, Dandamaev 1989, and Curtis 2000; but above all now those interested in a detailed account of the Persian Achaemenid Empire should consult Briant 2002. Allen 2005 also deserves special mention here; further works can be found in the bibliography.

On Persepolis see Herzfeld 1968, Cameron 1948, Lewis 1994, Brosius 2000 and 2003. On Pasargadai, Stronach 1978. Susa has not been well published, though a good basic account with some illustrations is offered in Olmstead 1948. On Persian art and archaeology generally see Root 1979, Boardman 1999 and 2000, Loukonine and Ivanov 2003, and also Curtis and Tallis 2005.

On Persian warfare, Sekunda and Chew 1992; on Zoroastrianism see the three-volume work of Boyce 1975/1982/1991; on the Medes particularly see Cuyler Young 1988; and for the general near eastern context the two-volume work of A. Kuhrt 1995 is outstanding, and the

Cambridge Ancient History (vols. I-IV, to be read in the newest edition published in the 1980s) is always an excellent resource.

CHAPTER 3: THE ATHENIANS

Herodotos's account of Kleisthenes' reforms can be found at 5.62-73; other references to and stories about early Athens can be found via the index in Waterfield's translation. Plutarch's *Life of Solon* is an important source for Solon's reforms. The most important source on the political structures and developments of early Athens, however, is the *Athenaion Politeia* ("Constitution of the Athenians") attributed by most scholars (rightly in my view) to Aristotle. This text can be consulted by English readers in Moore 1975, with a useful commentary. Book 1 of Pausanias's *Guide to Greece* is also useful.

Scholarship on ancient Athens is abundant, and only a handful of key works will be pointed to here. An excellent general history of Athens is Roberts 1984. For Athenian political development a good starting point is Hignett 1952, to be supplemented and updated by Ostwald 1986, Sealey 1987, McDowell 1978, Manville 1990, Wood 1988. An outstanding recent analysis of Athens'development in the 6th century, and especially of the purpose and context of Kleisthenes' reforms, is Anderson 2003, though I feel he somewhat underplays Kleisthenes' invention of democracy. For the development of Athenian democracy see further Morris and Raaflaub 1998, and Raaflaub, Ober, and Wallace 2007. On issues of the Athenian population and demography Hansen 1986 offers a sophisticated analysis, and see also Hansen 2006.

On the English "Enclosure Acts" see e.g. Neeson 1993 and Shaw-Taylor 2001; the American "Homestead Act" is discussed in e.g. Lause 2005. So far as I am aware, no previous historian has seen Solon's land reform as responding to an attempted "land grab" similar to these modern examples.

CHAPTER 4: PERSIA AND THE GREEKS

Once again, our source is basically Herodotos. Still fundamental is A.R. Burn's 1962 book, now available in a revised ed. 1984; and see for a good recent treatment de Souza 2003. An extremely interesting approach, trying to see the wars from the Persian perspective, is Cawkwell 2004. For the Ionian Revolt specifically, Evans 1976, Murray 1988, and Georges 2000. On Datis see Lewis 1980.

CHAPTER 5: THE BATTLE OF MARATHON

Our knowledge of the great battle itself comes overwhelmingly from Herodotos, who offers not only the earliest account, based on the reports of eyewitnesses or their sons, but also by far the fullest. The account of the battle is found in bk. 6 sections 102 to 120. Herodotos's account can be supplemented by a few details found elsewhere, but by and large it is on Herodotos that we must depend. Other sources are: Plutarch *Life of Aristides* 5 (giving us the detail that Aristides and Themistokles participated in the battle); Pausanias 1.32, and also 4.22 & 10.20; Cornelius Nepos *Miltiades*; and Justin 2.9. On the matter of troop strengths at Marathon, Herodotos does not give specific numbers, but Cornelius Nepos *Miltiades* 5, Plutarch *Moralia* 305B, and Pausanias 10.20 all state that 9,000 Athenians and 1,000 Plataians fought, giving 10,000 in all; obviously these numbers are rounded. Justin 2.9 perhaps confuses the total for the number of Athenians when he speaks of 10,000 Athenians and 1,000 Plataians. Important is that these numbers are consistent with the number of Athenians and Plataians Herodotos says fought at the battle of Plataia ten years later, in 479: about 8,000 Athenians and 600 Plataians (Herodotos 9.28). It seems unlikely that more Plataians fought at Marathon than in front of their own city, so the 1,000 Plataians is probably rounded up and 600 a more plausible number; as to the Athenians, one should recall that in 479 they also had men serving on their ships in the Mykale campaign (Herodotos 9.90-106), so a total of 9,000 or more for their hoplite phalanx in 490 is perfectly plausible. Nepos, Plutarch and the rest probably reflect a strong tradition that about 10,000 Greeks fought at Marathon, 90 percent or more of them Athenians, and that tradition makes sense. As to the Persian forces, there is a great variance in our sources, though in all cases the numbers mentioned are huge beyond belief: Nepos *Miltiades* 4 says 200,000 infantry and 10,000 cavalry; Plutarch *Moralia* 305B and Pausanias 4.22 speak of 300,000 Persians; Justin 2.9 says 600,000 Persians fought. Such numbers are not late: already in the fifth and fourth centuries authors such as Simonides, Lysias (*Funeral Oration* 21), and Plato (*Menexenos* 240A) mentioned 200,000 or half a million Persians. None of these numbers is credible, as I have pointed out in my text.

Modern reconstructions or accounts of the battle are numerous, going all the way back to the works of George Grote and Edward Creasy cited in the introduction, and beyond. Helpful modern treatments of the battle are to be found, for example, in: G.B. Grundy 1901; A.R. Burn 1962; J.F. Lazenby 1993; P. Green 1996; P. Davis 1999; P. de Souza 2003; A. Lloyd 2004; and T. Holland 2006. Besides these general accounts of the Persian wars and the individual campaigns and battles, including especially the Battle of Marathon of course, there are numerous special studies of individual topics.

In the first place, crucial work on the topography of the Marathon plain and the battle site, begun by Grundy in his visits to Greece in the 1890s, was done by W.K. Pritchett 1960; and see further the results of various excavations in and around the burial mound and the plain in P.G. Themelis 1974 and J.A.G. Van der Veer 1982; also A.R. Burn 1977. Another important issue is that of the battle's exact date: it has generally been thought, following August Boeckh 1855, to have been fought in early September, but A.R Burn 1962 esp. pp. 240-241 n. 10 and p. 257 argued very convincingly for August as preferable, and see now D.W. Olson 2004 astronomically establishing the likelihood of the August date by confirmation of the first new moon of the year 490/489.

In terms of the battle itself, any reconstruction in detail must be more or less hypothetical as Whatley 1964 reminds us. Nevertheless, the reconstruction I have offered is based on the premise that Herodotos, since he was able to interview participants in the battle and their sons, cannot have gotten the outlines of the battle seriously wrong. Granted that premise, which enables us to use Herodotos's narrative as our basic outline for the battle, there are five key issues that must be decided: why did the Athenians decide to come down and fight when they did, rather than awaiting the reinforcements from Sparta? When, how, and why did Persian ships sail around Attica to the Bay of Phaleron? Why did cavalry not play a major part in the battle on the Persian side? How far did the Athenians actually run to go into battle, and why? When and why did the Athenians run (or speed march, rather) back to Athens?

Key to answering all these questions, I believe, is a basic observation about the Persian voyage around Attica: if the Persians only set out after the battle, they could not have reached Phaleron the same day, as a simple calculation of distance and plausible ship speed demonstrates: see J.T. Hodge 1975a and 1975b, pointing out that the distance is a good seventy miles or so and that ancient ships, even triremes rowing at their best speed, could not have covered that distance in an afternoon. Hodge argued that the ancient tradition (Plutarch *Aristides* 5.5) of a same day voyage must be wrong; but we know that ancient triremes could make about five knots (roughly six mph) when necessary, and that would enable them to row from Marathon to Phaleron if they set out at dawn, not after the battle in early afternoon, as usually thought. For the ancient trireme and its construction and abilities, see Coates, Morrison, Rankov 2007. If the Persians set out to round Attica at dawn, and the Athenian leaders knew this, that would at once explain their decision to come down and fight. A passage in a Byzantine encyclopedia called the *Suda* suggests just this and also explains the near absence of cavalry in the battle: for under the heading *choris hippeis* ("without cavalry"), it states that Ionian informants warned the Athenians at Marathon that "the cavalry were away; and Miltiades understanding their departure, attacked and so achieved victory": see Burn 1962 p. 247 giving the original Greek text in n. 23. With the cavalry gone, the Greeks could fight the Persians on more even terms; with a Persian squadron headed for Phaleron and due to arrive there in about twelve hours from dawn, the Athenians had to fight or withdraw.

Thus, the simple assumption that the Persian ships with the cavalry and other troops set out for Phaleron at dawn, rather than after the battle, explains the absence of the cavalry and the decision of the Athenians to come down and fight, and it also explains the forced march back to Athens after the battle: the victorious Athenians had to reach Athens before the Persian ships could get there at about six or seven o'clock in the evening. Herodotos 6.116 is emphatic that the Athenian march was a matter of great haste and urgency because of the need to beat the Persian ships. J.P. Holoka 1997 argues that the Athenians did not and could not have marched the same day as the battle, something he regards as a superhuman feat; instead the march must have taken place several days (perhaps six days) later. But modern armchair historians used to motorized transport should not be deciding what was or was not doable for ancient Greek warriors used to walking everywhere throughout their lives. Hammond 1959 p. 216 n. 2 states that he personally walked from Athens to Marathon in six hours, and back the same day in seven hours, which tells us that a speed march in seven hours or so is definitely possible and leads me to accept the clear implication of Herodotos. A very similar reconstruction of the battle has been proposed by Holland 2006, which I only saw after I had reached my own reconstruction.

It remains to discuss the Athenian run to battle. Donlan and

Thompson 1976 and 1979 argued for a run of only about 200 meters, because to run a full mile in armor would have been impractical, if not impossible, and unnecessary given the range of Persian archery. Despite arguments by some scholars that ancient bows could fire arrows much greater distances than 200 meters—as much as 500 meters being apparently attested, see e.g. W. McLeod 1970—I believe Donlan and Thompson are correct. The issue is not how far a highly trained archer could fire an arrow with a top quality bow. Persian military archery was a matter of thousands of archers firing as quickly as they could: the aim was to attain a very high volume of fire; the ability of individuals to fire arrows (inevitably slowly) at extreme ranges was not of use in confronting large enemy formations. And thousands of archers concentrating on firing an arrow every few seconds in unison into a large moving mass of men, will not have been effective over distances greater than those estimated by Donlan and Thompson, if even so far: I suggest 150 meters as the greatest distance the Athenians will have needed to run, and thus will have run. One hundred meters or so may be even more likely.

For some Persian cavalry playing a role at Marathon, according to the Nike temple frieze, see Palagia 2005; further on the Marathon "run" see Frost 1979 and Kertesz 1991; for a variant reading of the *Suda* fragment, which seems to me to do violence to its text, see Shrimpton 1980; other reconstructions of the battle or various details can be found in J.A.S. Evans 1984 and 1993, N.A. Doenges 1998; J.H. Schreiner 1970 and 2004.

CHAPTER 6: AFTERMATH AND IMPORTANCE
For the history of the Persian Wars after Marathon, see the works cited under chapter 4 above. For Athens, and Athenian power, after the Persian Wars, Meiggs 1972 and de Ste. Croix 1972 are still extremely valuable. See now also A. Powell 1988, J.K. Davies 1993, and the general histories listed under chapter 1 above. For classical Greek culture see e.g. Cartledge 2001b; the writings of the key cultural figures I have emphasized—Aischylos, Sophokles, Euripides, Aristophanes, Herodotos, Thucydides, Plato, Aristotle, Isokrates, Lysias, Demosthenes, and the rest—are widely available in the Penguin Classics series and the Loeb Classical Library. For the Sophistic movement see especially Kerferd 1981 and de Romilly 1998, and the collection of texts by Dillon 2003.

BIBLIOGRAPHY

A.W.H. Adkins, 1972: *Moral Values and Political Behaviour in Ancient Greece From Homer to the End of the Fifth Century* W.W. Norton & Co.

L. Allen, 2005: *The Persian Empire. A History* British Museum Press

G. Anderson, 2003: *The Athenian Experiment. Building an Imagined Political Community inAncient Attica, 508-490 BC* University of Michigan Press

A.A. Andrewes, 1956: *The Greek Tyrants* Hutchinson & Co.

M.M. Austin, P. Vidal-Naquet, 1977: *Economic and Social History of Ancient Greece. An Introduction* University of California Press

M.M. Austin, 1990: "Greek tyrants and the Persians, 546-479 BCE" *Classical Quarterly* n.s. 40, pp. 289-306

S.C. Bakhuizen, R. Kreulen, 1976: *Chalcis-in-Euboea, Iron, and Chalcidians Abroad* Brill

E.J. Bakker, I.J. de Jong, H. van Wees (eds.), 2002: *Brill's Companion to Herodotus* Brill

J.M. Balcer, 1989: "The Persian Wars against Greece: a reassessment" *Historia* 38, pp. 127-43

J.M. Balcer, 1993: *A Prosopographical Study of the Ancient Persians Royal and Noble c. 550- 450 BC* Lewiston

J.M. Balcer, 1995: *The Persian Conquest of the Greeks 545-450 BC* Universitaets Verlag Konstanz

J. Barnes, 1982: *The Presocratic Philosophers* Routledge

H. Berve, 1967: *Die Tyrannis bei den Griechen* Beck

J. Boardman, J. Griffin, O. Murray, 1986: *Greece and the Hellenistic World* Oxford U P

J. Boardman, 1999: *The Greeks Overseas* 4th ed. Thames & Hudson

J. Boardman, 2000: *Persia and the West. An Archaeological Investigation of the Genesis of Achaemenid Art* Thames & Hudson

A. Boeckh, 1855: *Zur Geschichte der Mondcyclen der Hellenen* Teubner

D. Boedeker, 1987: "Herodotus and the invention of history" *Arethusa* 20, pp. 5-8

D. Boedeker, 1998: "The New Simonides and heroization at Plataea" in N. Fisher & H. van Wees (eds.) *Archaic Greece: New Approaches and New Evidence* Duckworth pp. 231-49

D. Boedeker, D. Sider, 2001: *The New Simonides: Contexts of Praise and Desire* Oxford U P

A.J. Bowen (ed.), 1992: *Plutarch: The Malice of Herodotus* Aris & Philips

C.M Bowra, 1936: *Greek Lyric Poetry from Alcman to Simonides* Oxford U P

M. Boyce, 1975, 1982, 1991: *A History of Zoroastrianism* 3 vols. Brill

A. Bresson, 2000: *La cite marchande* de Boccard

283

P. Briant, 1989: "History and Ideology: the Greeks and Persian 'decadence'" now best read in T. Harrison (ed.) 2002

P. Briant, 1999: "The Achaemenid Empire" in K. Raaflaub & N. Rosenstein (eds.) *War and Society in the Ancient and Medieval Worlds. Asia, the Mediterranean, Europe, and Mesoamerica* Center for Hellenic Studies pp. 105-28

P. Briant, 2002: *From Cyrus to Alexander. A History of the Persian Empire* Eisenbrauns (trans. of 1996 French language original)

M. Brosius, 2000: *The Persian Empire from Cyrus II to Aratxerxes I* LACTOR 16

M. Brosius, 2003: "Reconstructing an archive: account and journal texts from Persepolis" in Brosius (ed.) *Ancient Archives and Archival Traditions. Concepts of Record-Keeping in the Ancient World* Oxford U P pp. 264-83

I. Buchanan, W. Mallon, 2006: *A Historical Dictionary of the Olympic Movement* Scarecrow Press

A.R. Burn, 1960: *The Lyric Age of Greece* Arnold

A.R. Burn, 1977: "Thermopylai revisited and some topographical notes on Marathon and Plataiai" in K.H. Kinzl (ed.) *Greece and the Ancient Mediterranean in Ancient History and Prehistory. Studies Presented to Fritz Schachermeyr on his Eightieth Birthday* de Gruyter pp. 89-105

A.R. Burn, 1962/1984: *Persia and the Greeks. The Defence of the West 546-478 BC* 2nd ed. Duckworth (1st ed. Arnold)

W. Calder, S. Trzaskoma (eds.), 1996: *George Grote Reconsidered: a 200th Birthday Celebration* Weidmann

G.G. Cameron, 1948: *Persepolis Treasury Tablets* Oriental Institute Chicago

D.A. Campbell, 1982-93: *Greek Lyric Poetry* 5 vols, Loeb Classical Library

D.A. Campbell, 1982: *Greek Lyric Poetry: A Selection of Early Greek Lyric, Elegiac, and Iambic Poetry* Duckworth

P.A. Cartledge, 2001a: *Sparta and Lakonia. A Regional History 1300-362 BC* 2nd ed. Routledge

P.A. Cartledge, 2001b: *The Greeks. Crucible of Civilization* BBC Books

P.A. Cartledge, E. Cohen, L. Foxhall, 2002: *Money, Labour and Land: Approaches to the Economies of Ancient Greece* Routledge

P.A. Cartledge, 2003: *The Spartans. An Epic History* 2nd ed. Pan Macmillan

P.A. Cartledge, 2006: *Thermopylae. The Battle that Changed the World* The Overlook Press

G.L. Cawkwell, 2004: *The Greek Wars. The Failure of Persia* Oxford U P

K. Christ (ed.), 1986: *Sparta* Wissenschaftliches Buchgesellschaft Darmstadt

J. Coates, J. Morrison, N.B. Rankov, 2007: *The Athenian Trireme. The History and Reconstruction of an Ancient Warship* 2nd ed. Cambridge U P

J.E. Coleman, C.E. Walz (eds.), 1997: *Greeks and Barbarians. Essays on the*

Interactions between Greeks and Non-Greeks in Antiquity and the Consequences for Euro-Centrism Occasional Publications of the Dept. of Near Eastern Studies and the Program of Jewish Studies, Cornell U

J.M. Cook, 1983: *The Persian Empire* Dent

M. Crawford, D. Whitehead, 1983: *Archaic and Classical Greece* Cambridge U P

E. Creasy, 1851: *The Fifteen Decisive Battles of the World: From Marathon to Waterloo* R. Bentley

J. Curtis, 2000: *Ancient Persia* 2nd ed. British Museum Press

J. Curtis, N. Tallis (eds.), 2005: *Forgotten Empire: The World of Ancient Persia* British Museum Press

T. Cuyler Young, 1988: "The early history of the Medes and the Persians and the Achaemenid Empire to the death of Cambyses" in *Cambridge Ancient History* vol. IV, 2nd ed., pp. 1-52

M.A. Dandamaev, 1989: *A Political History of the Achaemenid Empire* Brill

A. Davies, 1981: "Lyric and Other Poetry" in M.I. Finley (ed.) *The Legacy of Greece: A New Appraisal* Oxford U P pp. 93-119

J.K. Davies, 1993: *Democracy and Classical Greece* 2nd ed. Harvard U P

M. Davies, 2004: "Simonides and the 'Grateful Dead'" *Prometheus* 30.3 pp. 275-81

P. Davis, 1999: *100 Decisive Battles.* Oxford University Press

K. Demetriou, 1999: *George Grote on Plato and Athenian Democracy. A Study in Classical Reception* Peter Lang

P. Derow, R. Parker (eds.), 2003: *Herodotus and his World* Oxford U P

C. Dewald, J. Marincola, 2006: *The Cambridge Companion to Herodotus* Cambridge U P

J. Dillon, 2003: *The Greek Sophists* Penguin Classics

N.A. Doenges, 1998: "The campaign and battle of Marathon" *Historia* 47 pp. 1-17

W. Donlan, J. Thompson, 1976: "The charge at Marathon, Herod. 6.112" *CJ* 71 pp. 339-43

W. Donlan, J. Thompson, 1979: "The charge at Marathon again" *CW* 72 pp. 419-20

R. Drews, 1973: *The Greek Accounts of Eastern History* Center for Hellenic Studies

P. Ellinger, 2002: "Artemis, Pan, et Marathon. Mythe, polytheisme et evenement historique" in S. des Bouvrie (ed.) *Myth and Symbol I. Symbolic Phenomena in Ancient Greek Culture* Norwegian Institute at Athens pp. 313-32

J.A.S. Evans, 1976: "Herodotus and the Ionian revolt" *Historia* 25 pp. 31-37

J.A.S. Evans, 1984: "Herodotus and Marathon" *Florilegium* 6 pp. 1-27

J.A.S. Evans, 1993: "Herodotus and the Battle of Marathon" *Historia* 42 pp. 279-307

D. Fehling, 1989: *Herodotus and his 'Sources'. Citation, Invention and Narrative Art* tr. J.G. Howie, Leeds Latin Seminar (from German original 1971)

T.J. Figueira (ed.), 2004: *Spartan Society* Classical Press of Wales

J.E. Findling, K.D. Pelle, 2004: *Encyclopedia of the Modern Olympic Movement* Greenwood Press

N.R.E. Fisher, 1992: *Hybris. A Study in the Values of Honour and Shame* Aris & Phillips

L.F. Fitzhardinge, 1980: *The Spartans* Thames & Hudson

W.G. Forrest, 1968: *A History of Sparta 950-192 BC* Hutchinson

W.G. Forrest, 1979: "Motivation in Herodotus: the case of the Ionian Revolt" *International History Review* 1 pp. 311-22

S. Forsdyke, 2001: "Athenian democratic ideology and Herodotus' Histories" *AJP* 122 pp. 333-62

H. Frankfort, 1970: "The art of Ancient Persia" in *The Art and Architecture of the Ancient Orient* 4th ed. Penguin chap. 12

N. Frankland, C. Dowling, 1976: *Decisive Battles of the 20th Century* Sidgwick & Jackson

C. Freeman, 1999: *The Greek Achievement* Oxford U P

F.J. Frost, 1979: "The dubious origins of the 'marathon'" *AJAH* 4 pp. 159-63

R.N. Frye, 1963: *The Heritage of Persia* World Publishing Co.

R.N. Frye, 1984: *History of Ancient Iran* Beck

J.F.C. Fuller, 1954-56: *The Decisive Battles of the Western World and their Influence upon History* Eyre & Spottiswoode

P. Georges, 1994: *Barbarian Asia and the Greek Experience. From the Archaic Period to the Age of Xenophon* Johns Hopkins U Press

P. Georges, 2000: "Persian Ionia under Darius: the Revolt reconsidered" *Historia* 49 pp. 1-39

D.E. Gerber, 1999: *Greek Elegiac Poetry* Loeb Classical Library

D.E. Gerber, 1999: *Greek Iambic Poetry* Loeb Classical Library

I. Gershevitch (ed.), 1985 *The Cambridge History of Iran: The Median and Achaemenid Periods* Cambridge U P

J. Gould, 1989: *Herodotus* Weidenfeld & Nicolson

D.F. Graf, 1994: "The Persian Royal Road system" *Achaemenid History* 8 pp. 167-89

P. Green, 1996: *The Greco-Persian Wars* 2nd ed. University of California Press

P. Green, 2006: *Diodorus Siculus, Book 11-12.37.1 Greek History, 480-431 BC – the Alternative Version* University of Texas Press

G. Grote, 1846-56: *History of Greece* 12 vols. John Murray

G.B. Grundy, 1901: *The Great Persian War and Its Preliminaries: a Study of the Evidence, Literary and Topographical* Scribner's

W.K.C. Guthrie, 1991: *A History of Greek Philosophy I: The Earlier Presocratics and the Pythagoreans* Cambridge U P

C. Habicht, 1986: *Pausanias' Guide to Ancient Greece* University of California Press

E. Hall, 1989: *Inventing the Barbarian. Greek Self-definition through Tragedy* Oxford U P

J.M. Hall, 2002: *Hellenicity: Between Ethnicity and Culture* University of Chicago Press

R.T. Hallock, 1969: *Persepolis Fortification Tablets* University of Chicago Press

R.T. Hallock, 1972: *The Evidence of the Persepolis Tablets* Camridge U P

N.G.L. Hammond, 1959/1984: *A History of Greece* Clarendon Press

M.H. Hansen, 1986: *Demography and Democracy. The Number of Athenian Citizens in the 4th Century BC* Forlaget Systime

M.H. Hansen, 2006: *The Shotgun Method. The Demography of the Ancient Greek City-State Culture* University of Missouri Press

V.D. Hanson, 1998: *The Western Way of War. Infantry Battle in Classical Greece* 2nd ed. University of California Press

V.D. Hanson, 1999: *The Wars of the Ancient Greeks and their Invention of Western Military Culture* Cassell

V.D. Hanson, 2001: *Carnage and Culture. Landmark Battles in the Rise of Western Power* Doubleday

E.B. Harrison, 1972: "The south frieze of the Nike Temple and the Marathon painting in the Painted Stoa" *AJA* 76 pp. 353-378

T. Harrison (ed.), 2002: *Greeks and Barbarians* Edinburgh U P

F. Hartog, 1988: *The Mirror of Herodotus. An Essay in the Interpretation of the Other* University of California Press (trans. of 1980 French original)

E. Herzfeld, 1968: *The Persian Empire. Studies in Geography and Ethnography of the Ancient Near East* Franz Steiner

A. Heubeck, S. West, J.B Hainsworth, et al., 1988-93: *A Commentary on Homer's Odyssey* 3 vols. Oxford U P

C. Hignett, 1970: *A History of the Athenian Constitution to the End of the 5th Century BC* Clarendon Press

A.T. Hodge, 1975a: "Marathon. The Persians' Voyage" *TAPhA* 105 pp. 155-73

A.T. Hodge, 1975b: "Marathon to Phalerum" *JHS* 95 pp. 169-71

K.-J. Hoelkeskamp, 2001: "Marathon – vom Monument zum Mythos" in D. Papenfuss, V.M. Strocka (eds.) *Gab es das Grichiescher Wunder? Griechenland zwischen dem Ende des 6. und der mitte des 5. Jahrhunderts v. Chr.* Philipp von Zabern pp. 329-53

T. Holland, 2006: *Persian Fire: the First World Empire and the Battle for the West* Abacus

J.P. Holoka, 1997: "Marathon and the myth of the same day march" *GRBS* 38 pp. 329-53

J.T. Hooker, 1980: *The Ancient Spartans* Dent

S. Hornblower, 2001: "Greeks and Persians. West against East" in A.V. Hartmann, B. Heuser (eds.) *War, Peace, and World Orders in European History* Routledge pp. 48-61

P. Hunt, 1998: *Slaves, Warfare and Ideology in the Greek Historians* Cambridge U P

L.H. Jeffery, 1990: *The Local Scripts of Archaic Greece. A Study of the origin of the Greek Alphabet and its Development from the Eighth to the Fifth Centuries BC* 2nd ed. revised by A.W. Johnston, Oxford U P

H. Jones, 2003: *The Expert's Guide to Marathon Training* Carlton Books

V. Karageorghis, I. Taifacos (eds.), 2004: *The World of Herodotus* A.G. Leventis Foundation

R.G. Kent, 1954: *Old Persian: Grammar, Texts, Lexicon* American Oriental Society

G.B. Kerferd, 1981: *The Sophistic Movement* Cambridge U P

I. Kertesz, 1991: "Schlacht und 'Lauf' bei Marathon: Legende und Wirklichkeit" *Nikephoros* 4 pp. 155-60

G.S. Kirk, J.E. Raven, M. Schofield, 1983: *The Presocratic Philosophers: A Critical History with a Selection of Texts* 2nd ed., Cambridge U P

G.S. Kirk (ed.), 1985-93: *The Iliad. A Commentary* 6 vols. Cambridge U P

D. Konstan, 1987: "Persians, Greeks and Empire" *Arethusa* 20 pp. 59-73

A. Kuhrt, 1988: "Earth and Water" *Achaemenid History* 3 pp. 87-99

A. Kuhrt, 1995: *The Ancient Near East, c. 3000-330 BC* 2 vols. Routledge

D. Lateiner, 1989: *The Historical Method of Herodotus* University of Toronto Press

R. Lattimore, 1960: *Greek Lyrics* University of Chicago Press

M.A. Lause, 2005: *Young America: Land, Labor, and the Republican Community* University of Illinois Press

J.F. Lazenby, 1985: *The Spartan Army* Aris & Phillips

J.F. Lazenby, 1993: *The Defence of Greece 490–479 BC.* Aris & Phillips Ltd.

D.M. Lewis, 1977: *Sparta and Persia* Brill

D.M. Lewis, 1980: "Datis the Mede" *JHS* 100 pp. 194-95

D.M. Lewis, 1994: "The Persepolis Tablets: speech, seal and script" in A.K. Bowman, G. Woolf (eds.) *Literacy and Power in the Ancient World* Cambridge U P pp. 17-32

A. Lloyd, 2004: *Marathon: the Crucial Battle that created Western Democracy* Souvenir Press

A.A. Long, 1999: *The Cambridge Companion to Early Greek Philosophy* Cambridge U P

A.H.M. Jones, 1967: *Sparta* Blackwell

N. Loraux, 1986: *The Invention of Athens. The Funeral Oration in the Classical City* (tr. A. Sheridan) Harvard U P

V. Loukonine, A. Ivanov, 2003: *Persian Art* Sirocco

N. Louraghi (ed.), 2001: *The Historian's Craft in the Age of Herodotos* Oxford U P

D.M. MacDowell, 1978: *The Law in Classical Athens* Cornell U P

I. Malkin (ed.), 2001: *Ancient Perceptions of Greek Ethnicity* Harvard U P

I. Malkin, 2004: "Postcolonial concepts and ancient Greek colonization" *Modern Language Quarterly* 65.3 pp. 341-64

P.B. Manville, 1990: *The Origins of Citizenship in Ancient Athens* Princeton U P

J. Marincola, 2001: "Herodotus" in *Greek Historians* (*Greece & Rome* New Surveys in the Classics 31) pp. 19-60

V. Massaro, 1978: "Herodotos' account of the battle of Marathon and the picture in the Stoa Poikile" *AC* 47 pp. 458-75

W. McLeod, 1970: "The bowshot and Marathon" *JHS* 90 pp. 197-98

R. Meiggs, 1972: *The Athenian Empire* Clarendon Press

J.D. Mikalson, 2003: *Herodotus and Religion in the Persian Wars* University of North Carolina Press

M.C. Miller, 1997: *Athens and Persia in the Fifth Century BC. A Study in Receptivity* Cambridge U P

J.B. Mitchell, 1964: *Twenty Decisive Battles of the World* Macmillan

J.H. Molyneux, 1992: *Simonides. A Historical Study* Bolchazy-Carducci

A.D. Momigliano, 1952: *George Grote and the Study of Greek History* H.K. Lewis

A.D. Momigliano, 1966: "The place of Herodotus in the history of historiography" in *Studies in Historiography* Weidenfeld & Nicolson pp. 127-42

A.D. Momigliano, 1975: *Alien Wisdom. The Limits of Hellenization* Cambridge U P

J.M. Moore, 1975: *Aristotle and Xenophon on Democracy and Oligarchy* University of California Press

I. Morris, K. Raaflaub (eds.), 1998: *Democracy 2500? Questions and Challenges* Kendal Hunt Publishing Co.

I. Morris, B.B. Powell, 2006: *The Greeks: History, Culture, and Society* Prentice Hall

R.V. Munson, 2001: *Telling Wonders. Ethnographic and Political Discourse in the Work of Herodotus* University of Michigan Press

O. Murray, 1980: *Early Greece* Fontana

O. Murray, 1987: "Herodotus and oral history" in Luraghi (ed.) 2001 pp. 314-25

O. Murray, 1988: "The Ionian Revolt" in *Cambridge Ancient History* vol. IV, 2nd ed., pp. 461-90

O. Murray, 1990: *Sympotica. A Symposium on the Symposion* Clarendon Press

G. Nagy, 1979: *The Best of the Achaeans. Concepts of the Hero in Archaic Greek Poetry* Johns Hopkins U P

J.M. Neeson, 1993: *Commoners: Common Right, Enclosure and Social Change in England, 1700-1820* Cambridge U P

F. Nietzsche, 1873: *Philosophy in the Tragic Age of the Greeks* tr. Marianne Cowan, Gateway Editions, 1996

C. Nylander, 1970: *Ionians in Pasargadae. Studies in Old Persian Architecture* Acta Universitatis Upsaliensis

F. Ollier, 1933/1943: *Le mirage spartiate. Etude sur l'idealisation de Sparte dans l'antiquite grecque* 2 vols. de Boccard

A.T. Olmstead, 1948: *History of the Persian Empire* University of Chicago Press

D.W. Olson *et al.,* 2004: "The Moon and Marathon" *Sky & Telescope* 108.3, pp. 34-41

C. Orrieux, P. Schmitt Pantel, 1999: *A History of Ancient Greece* Blackwell's

R.G. Osborne, 1996: *Greece in the Making 1200-479 BCE* Methuen

M. Ostwald, 1986: *From Popular Sovereignty to the Sovereignty of the Law* University of California Press

O. Palagia, 2005: "Interpretations of Two Athenian Friezes: the Temple on the Ilissos and the Temple of Athena Nike" in J.M. Barringer, J.M. Hurwit (eds.) *Periklean Athens and Its Legacy* pp. 177-92

E.E. Perry, 2001: "Iconography and the dynamics of patronage" *Hesperia* 70 pp. 461-92

S. Pomeroy, S. Burstein, W. Donlan, J. Roberts, 2007: *Ancient Greece. A Political, Social, and Cultural History* 2nd ed., Oxford U P

A. Powell, 1988: *Athens and Sparta. Constructing Greek Political and Social History from 478 BC* Routledge

A. Powell (ed.), 1989: *Classical Sparta: Techniques Behind Her Success* Routledge

A. Powell, S. Hodkinson (eds.), 2002: *Sparta. Beyond the Mirage* Classical Press of Wales

B.B. Powell, 1991: *Homer and the Origin of the Greek Alphabet* Cambridge U P

F. Pratt, 1956: *The Battles that Changed History* Doubleday & Co.

W.K. Pritchett, 1960: "Marathon" *University of California Studies in Classical Antiquity* 4.2 pp. 137-75

W.K. Pritchett, 1971-1991: *The Greek State at War* 5 vols. University of California Press

W.K. Pritchett, 1993: *The Liar School of Herodotus* Gieben

K.A. Raaflaub, 1987: "Herodotus, political thought, and the meaning of history" *Arethusa* 20 pp. 221-48

K.A. Raaflaub, J. Ober, R. Wallace (eds.), 2007: *Origins of Democracy in Ancient Greece* University of California Press

E. Rawson, 1969: *The Spartan Tradition in European Thought* Oxford U P

J.M. Redfield, 1985: "Herodotus the tourist" *Classical Philology* 80 pp. 97-118

R. Reeves, 2007: *John Stuart Mill: Victorian Firebrand* The Overlook Press

J.W. Roberts, 1984: *City of Sokrates: An Introduction to Classical Athens* Routledge

A. Robinson, 1995: *The Story of Writing* Thames & Hudson

J. de Romilly, 1998: *The Great Sophists in Periclean Athens* (tr. Janet Lloyd) Clarendon Press

J.S. Romm, 1998: *Herodotus* Yale U P

J.S. Romm (ed.), 2003: *Herodotus on the War for Greek Freedom. Selections from the Histories* Hackett

M.C. Root, 1979: *The King and Kingship in Achaemenid Art. Essays on the Creation of an Iconography of Empire* Brill

G.E.M. De Ste. Croix, 1972: *The Origins of the Peloponnesian War* Cornell University Press

G.E.M. De Ste. Croix, 1981: *The Class Struggle in the Ancient World* Cornell University Press

G.E.M. De Ste. Croix, 2004: "Herodotus and king Cleomenes of Sparta" in *Athenian Democratic Origins and Other Essays* (ed. by D. Harvey, R. Parker) Oxford U P pp. 421-40

H. Sancisi-Weerdenburg, A. Kuhrt (eds.), 1987-91: *Achaemenid History* 6 vols. Brill

J.H. Schreiner, 1970: "The battles of 490 BC" *PCPhS* 196 pp. 97-112

J.H. Schreiner, 2004: *Two Battles and Two Bills. Marathon and the Athenian Fleet* The Norwegian Institute at Athens Monographs no. 3

R. Sealey, 1976a: *A History of the Greek City-States 700-338 BC* University of California Press

R. Sealey, 1976b: "The pit and the well: the Persian heralds of 491 BC" *Classical Journal* 72 pp. 13-20

R. Sealey, 1987: *The Athenian Republic: Democracy or the Rule of Law?* Pennsylvania State University Press

N. Sekunda, S. Chew, 1992: *The Persian Army 560-330 BC* Osprey

N. Sekunda, R. Hook, 1998: *The Spartan Army* Osprey

L. Shaw-Taylor, 2001: "Parliamentary Enclosure and the Emergence of an

English Rural Proletariat" *Journal of Economic History* 61 pp. 640-62

G. Shrimpton, 1980: "The Persian cavalry at Marathon" *Phoenix* 34 pp. 20-37

P. de Souza, 2003: *The Greek and Persian Wars, 499-386 BC* Osprey

C.G. Starr, 1979: "Why did the Greeks defeat the Persians?" in *Essays on Ancient History* (ed. by A. Ferrill, T. Kelly) Brill pp. 193-204

M.W. Stolper, 1985: *Entrepreneurs and Empire. The Murashu Archive, the Murashu Firm, and Persian Rule in Babylonia* Netherlands Historical-Archaeological Institute Istanbul

B.S. Strauss, 2004: *Salamis. The Greatest Naval Battle of the Ancient World* Simon &   Schuster

D. Stronach, 1978: *Pasargadae* Oxford U P

J. Stronk, 1990/91: "Sparta and Persia" *Talanta* 22/3 pp. 117-36

R. Talbert (ed.), 2005: *Plutarch on Sparta* Penguin

P.G. Themelis, 1974: "Marathon. The recent finds in relation to the battle" *AD* 29 pp. 226-44

R. Thomas, 2000: *Herodotus in Context. Ethnography, Science, and the Art of Persuasion* Cambridge U P

J.A.G. van der Veer, 1982: "The Battle of Marathon: a topographical survey" *Mnemosyne* 35 pp. 290-321

H. van Wees, 1992: *Status Warriors. War, Violence, and Society in Homer and History* J.C. Gieben

H. van Wees, 1994: "The Homeric way of war: the Iliad and the hoplite phalanx (I) and (II)" *Greece & Rome* 41 pp. 1-18 & 131-55

H. van Wees, 2004: *Greek Warfare. Myths and Realities* Duckworth

G. Vlastos, 1995: *Studies in Greek Philosophy:the Presocratics* Princeton University Press

G. Walser, 1984: *Hellas und Iran: Studien zu den griechisch-persischen Beziehungen vor Alexander* Wissenschaftliches Buchgesellschaft Darmstadt

K.R. Walters, 1981: "We fought alone at Marathon. Historical falsification in the Attic funeral oration" *RhM* 124 pp. 204-11

K.H. Waters, 1971: *Herodotus on Tyrants and Despots: a Study in Objectivity* Steiner

M.L. West, 1993: *Greek Lyric Poetry* Oxford U P

M.L. West, 1997: *The East Face of Helicon* Oxford U P

N. Whatley, 1964: "On the possibility of reconstructing Marathon and other ancient battles" *JHS* 84 pp. 119-39

M. Whitby (ed.), 2001: *Sparta* Edinburgh U P

E.M. Wood, 1988: *Peasant-Citizen & Slave: the Foundations of Athenian Democracy* Verso

R.E. Wycherly, 1972: "Marathon in the Poikile" *PCPhS* 18 p. 78

D.C. Young, 1996: *The Modern Olympics: a Struggle for Revival* Johns Hopkins U P

ACKNOWLEDGMENTS

ONE OF THE PLEASANTER DUTIES OF THE AUTHOR IS TO acknowledge the aid and assistance of those who have contributed to making his work the best it can be. I should like to start by thanking Paul Cartledge particularly for reading the original manuscript of this book: his numerous comments and criticisms were a great help, giving me much food for thought leading to a number of improvements, and saving me from several errors. Further, I thank Roberta Stewart and Jeremy Rutter of Dartmouth College for inviting me to lecture there on the subject of this book, and for their thoughtful comments both at the lecture and during conversations afterwards. The idea to write this book originated with Peter Mayer: I thank him for the opportunity to express long held views on the Persian-Greek conflicts and the role of the Battle of Marathon in those conflicts. Thanks are also due to Juliet Grames, who proposed that I should write this book and saw the project through its early stages, and to Tracy Carns for her sterling work in shepherding the manuscript through the final publication process. Finally, many thanks to the staff and freelancers of The Overlook Press more generally for all their efforts in bringing this work to completion, and particularly to Jack Lamplough in publicity, Bernard Schleifer for his layout and design, including the family trees, and to Miranda Ottewell for undertaking the very necessary but inevitably tedious task of compiling the index.

INDEX